EVERYWHERE ALL THE TIME:
A NEW DESCHOOLING READER

EVERYWHERE ALL THE TIME: A NEW DESCHOOLING READER

Edited by Matt Hern

AK Press

Everywhere All the Time: A New Deschooling Reader
edited by Matt Hern

ISBN 978 1 904859 83 3
Library of Congress Number: 2008927318

©2008 Matt Hern

This edition ©2008 AK Press

Cover Design: Chris Wright
Layout: C. Weigl
Linocuts by Dan Bushnell

AK Press
370 Ryan Avenue #100
Chico, CA 95973
www.akpress.org
akpress@akpress.org
510.208.1700

AK Press U.K.
33 Tower St.
Edinburgh EH6 7BN
Scotland
www.akuk.com
ak@akedin.demon.co.uk
0131.555.5165

Printed in the United States.

TABLE OF CONTENTS

IV

Preface: Why This Collection Now?

M any years ago, back in the early 1990s, when I was young and our first daughter was born, I first started getting excited by alternative school and deschooling writing. I looked for a collection or a reader, something that brought together a lot of writing in one place, so I could begin to get a grasp of the landscape: something that would help me develop a broader view of radical thinking around schools and alternatives to them. But I couldn't find one. I read pretty much everything I could find, and the closest to what I was after was Joel Spring's *A Primer of Libertarian Education*.

That was, and remains, a great book, but for a lot of reasons it didn't quite answer what I was looking for. So, with little help, and after running into a small publishing grant, I put together a one-off magazine called *A Deschooling Reader: Alternatives, Analysis, and Ideas for Doing Things Better*. It was twenty-eight pages, with eight essays from people like John Gatto, Grace Llewellyn, and David Guterson, who kindly responded to an unsolicited call from a kid in a corner of the continent. I printed fifteen thousand copies of the thing and distributed them all over the world using some decidedly low-tech methods. I had no idea if it was reaching anyone until I started getting a flood of (pre-email) letters and phone calls from all kinds of people from all over the world with all kinds of reactions.

Soon after that, I received an offer from New Society to publish it in book form, so I made some more calls and assembled a larger collection of writing that was called *Deschooling Our Lives*. It was pretty good, but frankly, in my youthful ignorance I missed a lot and included some pieces (mostly my own somewhat frothing-at-the-mouth writing) that would really have been better left out. But apparently it found a certain audience.

Nine years down the road, the book sold out after apparently making it to almost every part of the world and getting translated into Korean and Turkish. Other parts of the book have been translated and published in eight other languages. Now, AK Press has agreed to republish it: which is what you have in your hands. This new version includes lots of the old book, with a few revisions, and a whole whack of new essays that I think really fill it out and add nuance and breadth.

The stream of interest in the book has stayed pretty steady through the years, and it appears to me that popular (and radical) engagement in homeschooling, unschooling, deschooling, and alternative schools is careening forward with an increasing momentum. Maybe its just me, but I think these writings are more relevant than ever, and that more and more people all over the globe are looking for alternatives to compulsory state schooling.

This book brings together the best writing I know of about deschooling and resisting monopoly schooling and compulsory education. It covers a pretty wide range of thinking and highlights some of the most compelling projects I know of around the world. The book is still pretty North American-centric, because that's what I know the most about, but it includes a lot more pieces this time from other parts of the world: India, Turkey, Israel, Mali, Thailand, Mexico, and more. As well, I have included some youth voices, writing from kids that I know, to offer their perspectives on their experiences doing something other than exclusive traditional schooling.

I like to think that this new collection will be useful to anyone who is considering these ideas, whether they are kids, have kids, are thinking about having some, are researchers, or are just trying to get a grip on the incredible phenomenon that is compulsory schooling. I hope you like it, and I hope you find it useful. And please do let me know what you think.

Peace. M.

Foreword

Ivan Illich

(written in 1995 for the original version of this book)

Leafing through the pages of *Deschooling Our Lives* transports me back to the year 1970 when, together with Everett Reimer at the Center for Intercultural Documentation (CIDOC) in Cuernavaca, I gathered together some of the more thoughtful critics of education (Paulo Freire, John Holt, Paul Goodman, Jonathan Kozol, Joel Spring, George Dennison, and others) to address the futility of schooling—not only in Latin America, which was already obvious, but also in the so-called developed, industrialized world.

On Wednesday mornings during the spring and summer of that year, I distributed drafts of essays that eventually became chapters of my book, *Deschooling Society*. Looking back over a quarter century, many of the views and criticisms that seemed so radical back in 1970 today seem rather naive. While my criticisms of schooling in that book may have helped some people reflect on the unwanted social side effects of that institution—and perhaps pursue meaningful alternatives to it—I now realize that I was largely barking up the wrong tree. To understand why I feel this way and to get a glimpse of where I am today, I invite readers to accompany me on the journey I took after *Deschooling Society*.

My travelogue begins twenty-five years ago, when *Deschooling Society* was about to appear. During the nine months the manuscript was at the publishers, I grew more and more dissatisfied with the text, which, by the way, did not argue for the elimination of schools. This misapprehension I owe to Cass Canfield Sr., Harper's president, who named the book and in so doing misrepresented my thoughts. The book advocates the disestablishment of schools, in the sense in which the Church has been disestablished in the United States. By disestablishment, I meant, first, not paying public monies and, second, not granting any special social privileges to either church- or school-goers. (I even suggested that instead of financing schools, we should go further than we went with religion and have schools pay taxes, so that schooling would become a luxury object and be recognized as such.)

I called for the disestablishment of schools for the sake of improving education and here, I noticed, lay my mistake. Much more important than the disestablishment of schools, I began to see, was the reversal of those trends that make of education a pressing need rather than a gift of gratuitous leisure. I began to fear that the disestablishment of the educational church would lead to a fanatical revival of many forms of degraded, all-encompassing education, making the world into a universal classroom, a global schoolhouse. The more important question became, "Why do so many people—even ardent critics of schooling—become addicted to education, as to a drug?"

Norman Cousins published my own recantation in the Saturday Review during the very week *Deschooling Society* came out. In it I argued that the alternative to schooling was not some other type of educational agency, or the design of educational opportunities in every aspect of life, but a society which fosters a different attitude of people toward tools.

I expanded and generalized this argument in my next book, *Tools for Conviviality*.

Largely through the help of my friend and colleague Wolfgang Sachs, I came to see that the educational function was already emigrating from the schools and that, increasingly, other forms of compulsory learning would be instituted in modern society. It would become compulsory not by law, but by other tricks, such as making people believe that they are learning something from TV, or compelling people to attend in-service training, or getting people to pay huge amounts of money in order to be taught how to have better sex, how to be more sensitive, how to know more about the vitamins they need, how to play games, and so on. This talk of "lifelong learning" and "learning needs" has thoroughly polluted society, and not just schools, with the stench of education.

Then came the third stage, in the late seventies and early eighties, when my curiosity and reflections focused on the historical circumstances under which the very idea of educational needs can arise. When I wrote *Deschooling Society*, the social effects, and not the historical substance of education, were still at the core of my interest. I had questioned schooling as a desirable means, but I had not questioned education as a desirable end. I still accepted that, fundamentally, educational needs of some kind were an historical given of human nature. I no longer accept this today.

As I refocused my attention from schooling to education, from the process toward its orientation, I came to understand education as learning when it takes place under the assumption of scarcity in the means which produce it. The "need" for education from this perspective appears as a result of societal beliefs and arrangements which make the means for so-called socialization scarce. And, from this same perspective, I began to notice that educational rituals reflected, reinforced, and actually created belief in the value of learning pursued under conditions of scarcity. Such beliefs, arrangements, and rituals, I came to see, could easily survive and thrive under the rubrics of deschooling, free schooling, or homeschooling (which, for the most part, are limited to the commendable rejection of authoritarian methods).

What does scarcity have to do with education? If the means for learning (in general) are abundant, rather than scarce, then education never arises—one does not need to make special arrangements for "learning." If, on the other hand, the means for learning are in scarce supply, or are assumed to be scarce, then educational arrangements crop up to "ensure" that certain, important knowledge, ideas, skills, attitudes, etc., are "transmitted." Education then becomes an economic commodity, which one consumes, or, to use common language, which one "gets." Scarcity emerges both from our perceptions, which are massaged by education professionals who are in the business of imputing educational needs, and from actual societal arrangements that make access to tools and to skilled, knowledgeable people hard to come by—that is, scarce.

If there were one thing I could wish for the readers (and some of the writers) of *Deschooling Our Lives*, it would be this: If people are seriously to think about deschooling their lives, and not just escape from the corrosive effects of compulsory schooling, they could do no better than to develop the habit of setting a mental question mark beside all discourse on young people's "educational needs" or "learning needs," or about their need for a "preparation for life." I would like them to reflect on the historicity of these very ideas. Such reflection would take the new crop of deschoolers a step further from where the younger and somewhat naive Ivan was situated, back when talk of "deschooling" was born.

Bremen, Germany Summer 1995

SECTION I

From On Education

Leo Tolstoy

Leo Tolstoy was born into Russian aristocracy, joined the army and fought in the Crimean War, then founded a school at his estate. He wrote prolifically: plays, novels, novellas, treatises, and letters, including Anna Karenina, War and Peace, The Death of Ivan Illyich, *and* Resurrection. *His writings on education, nonviolence, anarchism, asceticism, and spirituality found a worldwide audience, deeply influencing Gandhi and Martin Luther King among millions of others.*

This article is a conglomeration of excerpts from various essays Tolstoy wrote in the 1860s in the periodical he published called Yasnaya Polyana, *named after, and based on his experiences at, the school on his estate. Tolstoy's thinking is unrelentingly honest, as he rigorously applies his Christian, anarchist, nonviolent, and communitarian ideals to his daily relations with the children. Although more than a century old, his writing still sheds much light on current educational theory and clearly anticipates much of the work of A. S. Neill and the free school movement.*

School justly presents itself to the child's mind as an establishment where he is taught that which nobody understands; where he is generally compelled to speak not his native patois, *Mundart,* but a foreign language; where the teacher for the greater part sees in his pupils his natural enemies, who, out of their own malice and that of their parents, do not wish to learn that which he has learned; and where the pupils, on their side, look upon their teacher as their enemy, who only out of personal spite compels them to learn such difficult things. In such a situation they are obliged to pass six years and about six hours every day. What the results must be, we again see from what they really are, not according to the reports, but from actual facts.

In Germany, nine-tenths of the school population take away from school a mechanical knowledge of reading and writing, and such a strong loathing for the paths of science traversed by them that they never again take a book into their hands.

It is enough to look at one and the same child at home, in the street, or at school: now you see a vivacious, curious child, with a smile in his eyes and on his lips, seeking instruction in everything, as he would seek pleasure, clearly, and frequently strongly expressing his thoughts in his own words; now again you see a worn out, retiring being, with an expression of fatigue, terror, and ennui, repeating with the lips only strange words in a strange language—a being whose soul has, like a snail, retreated into its house. It is enough to look at these two conditions in order to decide which of the two is more advantageous for the child's development.

That strange psychological condition which I will call the scholastic condition of the soul, and which all of us, unfortunately, know too well, consists in that all the higher faculties, imagination, creativeness, inventiveness, give way to other, semi-animal faculties, which consist in pronouncing sounds independently from any concept, in counting numbers in succession, 1, 2, 3, 4, 5, in perceiving words, without allowing imagination to substitute images for these sounds, in short, in developing a faculty for crushing all higher faculties, so that only those might be evolved which coincide with the scholastic condition of fear, and of straining memory and attention.

Every pupil is so long an anomaly at school as he has not fallen into the rut of this semi-animal condition. The moment a child has reached that state and has lost all his independence and originality, the moment there appears in him various symptoms of disease—hypocrisy, aimless lying, dullness, and so forth—he no longer is an anomaly: he has fallen into the rut, and the teacher begins to be satisfied with him. Then there happens those by no means accidental and frequently repeated phenomena, that the dullest boy becomes the best pupil, and the most intelligent the worst. It seems to me that this fact is sufficiently significant to make people think and try to explain it. It seems to me that one such fact serves as a palpable proof of the fallacy of the principle of compulsory education.

More than that. Besides this negative injury, which consists in removing the children from the unconscious education which they receive at home, at work, in the street, the schools are physically injurious—for the body, which at this early age is inseparable from the soul. This injury is especially important on account of the monotony of the scholastic education, even if it were good. For the agriculturist it is impossible to substitute anything for those conditions of labor, life in the field, conversation of elders, and so forth, which surround him; even so it is with the artisan and, in general, with the inhabitant of the city.

Not by accident, but designedly, has Nature surrounded the agriculturist with rustic conditions, and the city dweller with urban conditions. These conditions are most highly instructive, and only in them can each develop. And yet, school lays down as the first condition of education the alienation from these conditions.

More than that. School is not satisfied with tearing the child away from life for six hours a day, during the best years of the child—it wants to tear three-year-old children away from the influence of their mothers. They have invented institutions (*Kleinkinderbewahranstalt*, infant schools, *salles d'asile*) of which we shall have occasion to speak more in detail. All that is lacking now is the invention of a steam engine to take the place of wet nurses.

The School at Yasnaya Polyana

... In the village, people rise with the fires. From the school the fires have long been observed in the windows, and half an hour after the ringing of the bell there appear, in the mist, in the rain, or in the oblique rays of the autumnal sun, dark figures, by twos, by threes, or singly, on the mounds (the village is separated from the school by a ravine). The herding feeling has long disappeared in the pupils. A pupil no longer has the need of waiting and shouting: "O boys, let's to school! She has begun." He knows by this time that "school" is neuter, and he knows a few other things, and, strange to say, for that very reason has no longer any need of a crowd. When the time comes to go, he goes. It seems to me that the personalities are becoming more independent, their characters more sharply defined, with every day. I have never noticed the pupils playing on their way, unless it be a very young child, or a new pupil, who had begun his instruction in some other school. The children bring nothing with them, neither books, nor copybooks. No lessons are given for home.

Not only do they carry nothing in their hands, but they have nothing to carry even in their heads. They are not obliged to remember any lesson—nothing that they were doing the day before. They are not vexed by the thought of the impending lesson. They bring with them nothing but their impressionable natures and their convictions that today it will be as jolly in school as it was yesterday. They do not think of their classes until they have begun.

All the pupils meet together for the class of religion, which is the only regular class we have, because the teacher lives two versts away and comes only twice a week; they also meet together for the drawing class. Before those classes, there is animation, fighting, shouting, and the most pronounced external disorder: some drag the benches from one room into another; some fight; some of the children of the manorial servants run home for some bread, which they roast in the stove; one is taking something away from a boy; another is doing some gymnastics, and, just as in the disorder of the morning, it is much easier to allow them to quiet themselves and resume their natural order than forcibly to settle them. With the present spirit of the school, it would be physically impossible to stop them. The louder the teacher calls—this has actually happened—the louder they shout: his loud voice only excites them. If you stop them, or if you can not do that, if you carry them away into another direction, this small sea begins to billow less and less until it finally grows calm. In the majority of cases, there is no need to say anything. The drawing class, everybody's favorite class, is at noon when, after three hours' work, the children are beginning to be hungry, and the benches and tables have to be taken from one room to another, and there is a terrible hubbub; and yet, in spite of it, the moment the teacher is ready, the pupils are, too, and if one of them should keep them back from starting, he gets his punishment meted out to him by the children themselves.

I must explain myself. In presenting a description of the Yasnaya Polyana school, I do not mean to offer a model of what is needed and is good for a school, but simply to furnish an actual description of the school. I presume that such descriptions may have their use. If I shall succeed in the following numbers in presenting a clear account of the evolution of the school, it will become intelligible to the reader what it is that has led to the formation of the present character of the school, why I regard such an order as good, and why it would be absolutely impossible for me to change it, even if I wanted.

The school has evolved freely from the principles introduced into it by teacher and pupils. In spite of the preponderating influence of the teacher, the pupil has always the right not to come to school, or, having come, not to listen to the teacher. The teacher has had the right not to admit a pupil, and has had the possibility of bringing to bear all the force of his influence on the majority of pupils, on the society, always composed of the school children.

I am convinced that the school ought not to interfere in that part of the education which belongs to the family; that the school has no right and ought not to reward and punish; that the best police and administration of a school consist in giving full liberty to the pupils to study and settle their disputes as they know best. I am convinced of it, and yet, in spite of it, the old habits of the educational schools are so strong in us that we frequently depart from that rule in the Yasnaya Polyana school...

Education and Culture

... Culture in general is to be understood as the consequence of all those influences which life exerts on man ... Education is the action of one man upon another for the purpose of making the person under education acquire certain moral habits...

Instruction is the transmission of one man's information to another (one may instruct in the game of chess, in history, in the shoemaker's art). Teaching, a shade of instruction, is the action of one man upon another for the purpose of making the pupil acquire certain physical habits (one teaches how to sing, do carpentry, dance, row, declaim). Instruction and teaching are the means of culture, when they are free, and means of education, when the teaching is forced upon the pupil, and when the instruction is exclusive, that is, when only those subjects are taught which the educator regards as necessary. The truth presents itself clearly and instinctively to everybody. However much we may try to weld what is disconnected, and to subdivide what is inseparable, and to subordinate thought to the existing order of things—truth is apparent.

Education is a compulsory, forcible action of one person upon another for the purpose of forming a man such as will appear to us to be good; but culture is the free relation of people, having for its basis the need of one man to acquire knowledge, and of the other to impart that which he has acquired. Instruction, *Unterricht*, is a means of both culture and education. The difference between education and culture lies only in the compulsion, which education deems itself in the right to exert. Education is culture under restraint. Culture is free.

I spoke in my first article on the right of compulsion in matters of education and have endeavored to prove that, firstly, compulsion is impossible; secondly, that it brings no results or only sad results; thirdly, that compulsion can have no other basis but arbitrary will ... Education as a subject of science does not exist. Education is the tendency toward moral despotism raised to a principle. Education is, I shall not say an expression of the bad side of human nature, but a phenomenon which proves the undeveloped condition of human thought, and therefore, it cannot be put at the base of intelligent human activity—of science.

Education is the tendency of one man to make another just like himself. (The tendency of a poor man to take the wealth away from the rich man, the feeling of envy in an old man at the sight of fresh and vigorous youth—the feeling of envy, raised to a principle and theory). I am convinced that the educator undertakes with such zeal the education of the child, because at the base of this tendency lies his envy of the child's purity, and his desire to make him like himself, that is, to spoil him.

From The Intimate and the Ultimate

Vinoba Bhave

Vinoba Bhave was born in the Indian state of Maharashtra in 1895 to Brahman parents. In 1932, he was sent to jail for his resistance to British colonial rule. In 1940, Gandhi named him the first Satyagrahi *(an individual standing up for Truth) against the British rule. Bhave founded the Bhoodan Yajna or land-gift movement in 1951, and walked to all corners of India, collecting gifts of five million acres of land, which he distributed to the poor. Gandhi identified Bhave as his spiritual successor.*

Many people would agree about the importance of self-reliance in education. Self-reliance has a very profound meaning. There must be economic self-reliance through manual labor. Everyone must learn to use his hands. If the whole population were to take up some kind of handicraft, it would bring all sorts of benefits; class divisions would be overcome, production would rise, prosperity and health would improve. So that, at the very least, this measure of self-sufficiency must form part of our educational program.

Education must be of such a quality that it will train students in intellectual self-reliance and make them independent thinkers. If this were to become the chief aim of learning, the whole process of learning would be transformed. The present school syllabus contains a multiplicity of languages and subjects, and the student feels that in every one of these he needs the teacher's help for years together. But a student should be so taught that he is capable of going forward and acquiring knowledge for himself. There is an infinite sum of knowledge in the world, and each one needs some finite portion of it for the conduct of his affairs. But it is a mistake to think that this life-knowledge can only be had in any school. Life-knowledge can only be had from life. The task of the school is to awaken in its pupils the wish to learn from life.

Most parents are anxious for their children to complete the school course so that they can get a salaried job and lead an easy life. This is the wrong way to look at education. Learning has value in its own right. The purpose of learning is freedom. Freedom implies not only independence of other people but also independence of one's own moods and impulses. The man who is a slave to his senses and cannot keep his impulses under control is neither free nor self-sufficient.

The goal of education must be freedom from fear. In the *Upanishads*, when the guru is teaching his disciples he says to them: "O my students, whatever good conduct you find in me, that follow; whatever you do not find good, that do not follow." That is to say, the guru gives students freedom. He tells them to use their own judgment in deciding what is right and what is wrong. They are not to think that whatever their guru says is wholly right. It is certainly true that the guru is endeavoring to live by the truth, otherwise he would not be a guru; but he nevertheless cannot claim that his every action will be in harmony with truth. And so he tells his students to be alert, to use their intelligence and examine his conduct, and to disregard whatever seems to them wrong. And by this means he enables his students to grow into fearlessness.

Fearlessness means that we should neither fear anything, nor inflict fear on others. Both those things are parts of fearlessness. A tiger cannot be called fearless; it may not be afraid of any other animal, but it is afraid of a gun, and it also inspires fear in other creatures. True fearlessness neither enslaves another, nor does it slavishly submit to another.

The only sufficient basis for such fearlessness is the knowledge of the self. This self-knowledge is the foundation of education. But the education which children get today is the direct opposite of this. If a child commits some fault we slap it, and it begins to obey us because it is afraid. But we have taught it nothing of truth by our action. Until education is really based on fearlessness there is no hope of any change in society. We ought to teach children never to submit to those who bear and strike them.

No Knowledge Without Action

The separation of learning from labor results also in social injustice. Some people do nothing but study and others nothing but hard labor, and as a result society is split in two. Those who earn their bread by manual labor form one social class and those who do only intellectual work form another. In India, manual laborers are paid one rupee a day, intellectual workers are paid twenty-five or thirty rupees. A very great injustice has been done by rating the value of manual and intellectual labor so differently. And it is the abolition of such injustice that must be the goal of our education.

Human lives are like trees, which cannot live if they are cut off from the soil, but at the same time the business of agriculture must be done so efficiently that the smallest possible number of people are tied entirely to the land. These two principles may seem to be mutually contradictory, but they are both parts of Basic Education. It is a basic need of humanity to be in touch with the earth, and any nation or civilization which is cut off from it slowly but surely loses its vigor and degenerates.

If a man's house is full of medicine bottles, we infer that the man is probably ill. But if his house is full of books, we conclude that he is intelligent. Surely that is not right? The first rule of health is to take medicine only when it is absolutely necessary. By the same token, the first rule of intelligence ought to be to avoid, so far as possible, burying one's eyes in books. We consider medicine bottles to be a sign of a sick body; we ought to consider books, whether secular or religious, as the sign of a sick mind!

Student Teacher Comradeship

An interesting light is cast on the Indian attitude to education by the fact that in all fourteen languages of India there is no root word corresponding to English "teach." We can learn, we can help others to learn, but we cannot "teach." The use of two distinct words, "teach" and "learn," suggests that these two processes may be thought of as independent of one another. But that is merely the professional vanity of the "teacher," and we shall not understand the nature of education unless we rid ourselves of that vanity.

Our first task is to realize that an "uneducated" human being is nowhere to be found. But today, all too often, an ordinary schoolboy treats a first-class carpenter as if he were an ignorant boor. The carpenter may be a man of maturity and experience, a wise and skilled workman, who is of real service to his community. But simply because he cannot read or write, the "educated" boy treats him as an inferior.

Wherever two people live together in this kind of comradeship, giving and receiving mutual help, there real education is in progress. The place of books is, therefore, secondary This idea troubles many people, who think that if the place assigned to books is reduced the students will be deprived of the most valuable tools of knowledge. Books do have a place as tools of knowledge, but it is a very minor place. The major need is for teacher and student to become work-partners, and this can happen only when the distinction between the teacher "teaching" and the student "learning" can be overcome.

In matters of knowledge, no orders can be given. Education does not "discipline" students, it gives them complete freedom. Whether or not society free from governments is ever built in the larger world, such a society must be found in the world of students. If there is one thing of supreme importance for students, it is this freedom.

Only Teaching

A young man said that he wished to do some good work for society.

"Tell me," I said, "what kind of work do you feel you could do well?"

"Only teaching, I think," replied the young man. "I can't do anything else, I can only teach, but I am interested in it and I feel sure that I shall be able to do it well."

"Yes, yes, I do not doubt that, but what are you going to teach? Spinning? Carding? Weaving? Could you teach any of these?"

"No, I can't teach those."

"Then tailoring, or dyeing, or carpentry?"

"No, I know nothing about them."

"Perhaps you could teach cooking, grinding, and other household skills?"

"No, I have never done any work like that. I can only teach..."

"My dear friend, you answer 'No' to every question, and yet you keep saying you can only teach. What do you mean? Can you teach gardening?"

The would-be teacher said, rather angrily, "Why do you ask all this? I told you at the beginning, I can do nothing else. I can teach literature."

"Good! Good! I am beginning to understand now. You mean you can teach people to write books like Tagore and Shakespeare?" This made the young man so angry that he began to splutter.

"Take it easy," I laughed. "Can you teach patience?"

That was too much.

"I know what you mean," I said. "You can teach reading, writing, history, and geography. Well, they are not entirely useless, there are times in life when they are needed. But they are not basic to life. Would you be willing to learn weaving?"

"I don't want to learn anything new now. Besides I couldn't learn to weave, I have never before done any kind of handwork."

"In that case, it might, of course, take you longer to learn, but why should you be unable to learn it?"

"I don't think I could ever learn it. But even supposing I could, it would mean a lot of hard work and a great deal of trouble. So please understand that I could not undertake it."

This conversation is quite enough to enable us to understand the psychology and characteristics of far too many of our "teachers." To be "only a teacher" means to be: completely ignorant of any kind of practical skill which might be useful in real life; incapable of learning anything new and indifferent towards any kind of craftsmanship; conceited; and buried in books. "Only teaching" means being a corpse cut off from life.

Government Control of Education Is Dangerous

Throughout the world education is under the control of governments. This is extremely dangerous. Governments ought to have no authority over education. The work of education should be in the hands of men of wisdom, but governments have got it in their grasp; every student in the country has to study whatever book is prescribed by the education department. If the government is fascist, students will be taught fascism; if it is communist, it will preach communism; if it is capitalist, it will proclaim the greatness of capitalism; if it believes in planning, the students will be taught all about planning.

We in India used to hold to the principle that education should be completely free from state control. Kings exercised no authority over the gurus. The king had absolutely no power to control education. The consequence was that Sanskrit literature achieved a degree of freedom of thought such as can be seen nowhere else, so much so that no less than six mutually incompatible philosophies have arisen within the Hindu philosophy. This vigor is due to the freedom of education from state control.

The status of teachers has sunk so low that they feel themselves to have no authority at all. They must follow whatever path the government directs. They are under orders, the servants of authority. They may perhaps modify the government schemes by a comma here or a semi-colon there, but they cannot do more than that. Today there is an attempt to expand education, and the number of schools and of teachers is being increased, but the spirit of the true guru is not there. A good teacher means one who is a good servant; a bad teacher means a bad servant; good or bad, he remains a servant.

All this results from the fact that the education department is a government department, it is not independent. The judges of the high court are also appointed by the government, and they are bound by the laws which the government makes. Nevertheless, they are much more independent. They have power, within the bounds of law, to give a verdict against the government. The teacher ought to have a much greater freedom than the judge, yet today the education department is less independent than the department of justice.

The universities should demonstrate how every student, by his own labor, can gain food through knowledge and knowledge through food, nourishing his stomach with his two hands and his mind with his two eyes. They should show how the breach between knowledge and work can be closed. The students should have no fees to pay, there should be no hostel expenses and no salaries for the teachers. The workshop, the library, and the laboratory should be provided by the government. There should be no need for holiday periods, for no one will feel any sense of confinement there.

The universities of today are not fitted for the poor, even though a few poor students may be admitted without fees as an act of grace. But the universities we envisage should be open to all. If the children of the rich cannot adjust themselves to such hard work, we may have to excuse them for an hour or two of labor as an act of grace.

From Deschooling Society

Ivan Illich

Ivan Illich was born in 1926 in Vienna, Austria. After pursuing studies in the natural sciences, he obtained degrees in history, philosophy, and theology, and lived and taught throughout the world. From 1962–76 he directed research seminars at the Center for Intercultural Documentation (CIDOC) in Cuernavaca. His many books include Tools for Conviviality, Celebration of Awareness, Gender, Shadow Work, Limits to Medicine, Energy and Equity, *and* Toward a History of Needs.

Why We Must Disestablish School

Many students, especially those who are poor, intuitively know what the schools do for them. They school them to confuse process and substance. Once these become blurred, a new logic is assumed: the more treatment there is, the better are the results; or, escalation leads to success.

The pupil is thereby "schooled" to confuse teaching with learning, grade advancement with education, a diploma with competence, and fluency with the ability to say something new. His imagination is "schooled" to accept service in place of value. Medical treatment is mistaken for health care, social work for the improvement of community life, police protection for safety, military poise for national security, the rat race for productive work. Health, learning, dignity, independence, and creative endeavor are defined as little more than the performance of the institutions which claim to serve these ends, and their improvement is made to depend on allocating more resources to the management of hospitals, schools, and other agencies in question.

I will show that the institutionalization of values leads inevitably to physical pollution, social polarization, and psychological impotence: three dimensions in a process of global degradation and modernized misery. I will explain how this process of degradation is accelerated when non-material needs are transformed into demands for commodities; when health, education, personal mobility, welfare, or psychological healing are defined as the result of services or "treatments." I do this because I believe that most of the research now going on about the future tends to advocate further increases in the institutionalization of values and that we must define conditions which would permit precisely the contrary to happen. We need research on the possible use of technology to create institutions which serve personal, creative, and autonomous interaction and emergence of values which cannot be substantially controlled by technocrats. We need counterfoil research to current futurology.

I want to raise the general question of the mutual definitions of man's nature and the nature of modern institutions which characterize our world view and language. To do so, I have chosen the school as my paradigm, and I therefore deal only indirectly with other bureaucratic agencies of the corporate state: the consumer-family, the party, the army, the church, the media. My analysis of the hidden curriculum of school should make it evident that public education would profit from the deschooling of society, just as family life, politics, security, faith, and communications would profit from an analogous process.

Not only education but social reality itself has become schooled. It costs roughly the same to school both rich and poor in the same dependency. The yearly expenditure per pupil in the slums and in the rich suburbs of any one of twenty U.S. cities lies in the same range—and sometimes is favorable to the poor. Rich and poor alike depend on schools and hospitals which guide their lives, form their world view, and define for them what is legitimate and what is not. Both view doctoring oneself as irresponsible, learning on one's own as unreliable, and community organization, when not paid for by those in authority, as a form of aggression or subversion. For both groups the reliance on institutional treatment renders independent accomplishment suspect. The progressive underdevelopment of self- and community-reliance is even more typical in Westchester than it is in the northeast of Brazil. Everywhere, not only education, but society as a whole needs "deschooling."

Equal educational opportunity is, indeed, both a desirable and a feasible goal, but to equate this with obligatory schooling is to confuse salvation with the Church. School has become the world religion of a modernized proletariat, and makes futile promises of salvation to the poor of the technological age. The nation-state has adopted it, drafting all citizens into a graded curriculum leading to sequential diplomas not unlike the initiation rituals and hieratic promotions of former times. The modern state has assumed the duty of enforcing the judgment of its educators through well-meant truant officers and job requirements, much as did the Spanish kings who enforced the judgments of their theologians through the conquistadors and the Inquisition.

Two centuries ago, the United States led the world in a movement to disestablish the monopoly of a single church. Now we need the constitutional disestablishment of the monopoly of the school, and thereby of a system which legally combines prejudice and discrimination...

Schools as False Public Utilities

Like highways, schools, at first glance, give the impression of being equally open to all corners. They are, in fact, open only to those who consistently renew their credentials. Just as highways create the impression that their present level of cost per year is necessary if people are to move, so schools are presumed essential for attaining the competence required by a society which uses modern technology. We have exposed speedways as spurious public utilities by noting their dependence on private automobiles. Schools are based upon the equally spurious hypothesis that learning is the result of curricular teaching.

Highways result from a perversion of the desire and need for mobility into the demand for a private car. Schools themselves pervert the natural inclination to grow and learn into the demand for instruction. Demand for manufactured maturity is a far greater abnegation of self-initiated activity than the demand for manufactured goods. Schools are not only to the right of highways and cars; they belong near the extreme of the institutional spectrum occupied by total asylums. Even the producers of body counts kill only bodies. By making men abdicate the responsibility for their own growth, school leads many to a kind of spiritual suicide.

Highways are paid for in part by those who use them, since tolls and gasoline taxes are extracted only from drivers. School, on the other hand, is a perfect system of regressive taxation, where the privileged graduates ride on the back of the entire paying public. School puts a head tax on promotion. The underconsumption of highway mileage is not nearly so costly as the underconsumption of schooling. The man who does not own a car in Los Angeles may be almost immobilized, but if he can somehow manage to reach a work place, he can get and hold a job. The school dropout has no alternative route. The suburbanite with his new Lincoln and his country cousin who drives a beat-up jalopy get essentially the same use out of the highway, even though one man's car costs thirty times more than the other's. The value of a man's schooling is a function of the number of years he has completed and of the costliness of the schools he has attended. The law compels no one to drive, whereas it obliges everyone to go to school.

From Instead of Education

John Holt

John Holt (1923–1985) was a writer, educator, lecturer, and amateur musician who wrote ten books, including How Children Fail, How Children Learn, Never Too Late, Teach Your Own, *and* Freedom and Beyond. *His work has been translated into fourteen languages and* How Children Fail *has sold over a million copies in its many editions. The magazine he founded,* Growing Without Schooling, *and the associated organization, Holt Associates keep his vision and legacy alive.*

This is a book in favor of *doing*—self-directed, purposeful, meaningful life and work, and *against* "education"—learning cut off from active life and done under pressure of bribe or threat, greed and fear.

It is a book about people doing things, and doing them better; about the conditions under which we may be able to do things better; about some of the ways in which, *given those conditions*, other people may be able to help us (or we them) to do things better; and about the reasons why these conditions do not exist and *cannot be made to exist* within compulsory, coercive, competitive schools.

Not all persons will give the word "education" the meaning I give it here. Some may think of it, as I once described it, as "something a person gets for himself, not that which someone else gives or does to him." But I choose to define it here as most people do, something that some people do to others for their own good, molding and shaping them, and trying to make them learn what they think they ought to know. Today, everywhere in the world, that is what "education" has become, and I am wholly against it. People still spend a great deal of time—as for years I did myself—talking about how to make "education" more effective and efficient, or how to do it or give it to more people, or how to reform or humanize it. But to make it more effective and efficient will only be to make it worse, and to help it do even more harm. It cannot be reformed, cannot be carried out wisely or humanely, because its purpose is neither wise nor humane.

Next to the right to life itself, the most fundamental of all human rights is the right to control our own minds and thoughts. That means the right to decide for ourselves how we will explore the world around us, think about our own and other persons' experiences, and find and make the meaning of our own lives. Whoever takes that right away from us, as the educators do, attacks the very center of our being and does us a most profound and lasting injury. He tells us, in effect, that we cannot be trusted even to think, that for all our lives we must depend on others to tell us the meaning of our world and our lives, and that any meaning we may make for ourselves, out of our own experience, has no value.

Education, with its supporting system of compulsory and competitive schooling, all its carrots and sticks, its grades, diplomas, and credentials, now seems to me perhaps the most authoritarian and dangerous of all the social inventions of mankind. It is the deepest foundation of the modern and world-wide slave state, in which most people feel themselves to be nothing but producers, consumers, spectators, and "fans," driven more and more, in all parts of their lives, by greed, envy, and fear. My concern is not to improve "education" but to do away with it, to end the ugly and antihuman business of people-shaping and let people shape themselves.

By "doing" I do not mean only things done with the body, the muscles, with hands and tools, rather than with the mind alone. I am not trying to separate or put in opposition what many might call the "physical" and the "intellectual." Such distinctions are unreal and harmful. Only in words can the mind and body be separated. In reality they are one; they act together. So, by "doing" I include such actions as talking, listening, writing, reading, thinking, even dreaming.

The point is that it is the do-er, not someone else, who has decided what he will say, hear, read, write, or think or dream about. He is at the center of his own actions. He plans, directs, controls, and judges them. He does them for his own purposes—which may, of course, include a common purpose with others. His actions are not ordered and controlled from outside. They belong to him and are a part of him.

This is not a book about such a doing society, or what it might be like. Enough to say that it would be a society whose tools and institutions would be much smaller in scale, serving human beings rather then being served by them; a society modest and sparing in its use of energy and materials, and reverent and loving in its attitude towards nature and the natural world. This is a book about how we might make the societies we have slightly more useful and livable for do-ers, about the resources that might help some people, at least, to lead more active and interesting lives— and, perhaps, to make some of the beginnings, or very small models, of such a society. It is not a book about how to solve or deal with such urgent problems as poverty, idleness, discrimination, exploitation, waste, and suffering. These are not education problems or school problems. They have not been and cannot and will not be solved by things done in compulsory schools, and they will not be solved by changing these schools (or even by doing away with them altogether). The most that may happen is that, once freed of the delusion that schools can solve these problems, we might begin to confront them directly, realistically, and intelligently.

The trouble with talk about "learning experiences" is that it implies that all experiences can be divided into two kinds, those from which we learn something, and those from which we learn nothing. But there are no experiences from which we learn nothing. We learn something from everything we do, and everything that happens to us or is done to us. What we learn may make us more informed or more ignorant, wiser or stupider, stronger or weaker, but we always learn something. What it is depends on the experience, and above all, on how we feel about it.

A central point of this book is that we are very unlikely to learn anything good from experiences which do not seem to us closely connected with what is interesting and important in the rest of our lives. Curiosity is never idle; it grows out of real concerns and real needs. Even more important, we are even less likely to learn anything good from coerced experiences, things that others have bribed, threatened, bullied, wheedled, or tricked us into doing. From such we learn mostly anger, resentment, and above all self-contempt and self-hatred for having allowed ourselves to be pushed around or used by others, for not having been smart enough or strong enough to resist and refuse. Some would claim that most people in their daily lives do a great many things—dull, repetitious, and meaningless work, driving a car for hours in traffic, watching television—from which they learn nothing. But of course they learn something. The people doing moronic work learn to hate that work, and themselves for having to do it—and, in time, all those who do not have to do it. The people driving cars in traffic learn to think of all the other people they see, driving or walking, as nuisances, obstructions, even as enemies, preventing them from getting where they want to go. And people watching television learn over and over again that the people they see on the screen, "real" or imaginary, are in every way better than they are—younger, handsomer, sexier, smarter, stronger, faster, braver, richer, happier, more successful and respected. When the time finally comes to come back from Dreamland to reality, and get up wearily and turn off the set, the thought is even more strongly in their minds, "Why couldn't I have been more like them?"

Doing Is Learning

Another common and mistaken idea hidden in the word "learning" is that learning and doing are different kinds of acts. Thus, not many years ago I began to play the cello. I love the instrument, spend many hours a day playing it, work hard at it, and mean someday to play it well. Most people would say that what I am doing is "learning to play the cello." Our language gives us no other words to say it. But these words carry into our minds the strange idea that there exists two different processes: (1) learning to play the cello; and (2) playing the cello. They imply that I will do the first until I have completed it, at which point I will stop the first process and begin the second; in short, that I will go on "learning to play" until I "have learned to play," and that then I will begin "to play."

Of course, this is nonsense. There are not two processes, but one. We learn to do something by doing it. There is no other way. When we first do something, we probably will not do it well. But if we keep on doing it, have good models to follow and helpful advice if and when we feel we need it, and always do it as well as we can, we will do it better. In time, we may do it very well. This process never ends. The finest musicians, dancers, athletes, surgeons, pilots, or whatever they may be, must constantly practice their art or craft. Every day the musicians do their scales, the dancers exercise at the barre, and so on. A surgeon I knew would from time to time, when not otherwise busy, tie knots in fine surgical gut with one hand, without looking, just to keep in practice. In that sense, people never stop "learning to do" what they know how to do, no matter how well they do it. They must "learn" every day to do it as well as they can, or they will soon do it less well. The principal flutist of the Boston Symphony under Koussevitsky used to say, "If I miss a day's practice, I hear the difference; if I miss two days', the conductor hears the difference; if I miss three days', the audience hears the difference."

Unschooled Kids'
Comments I:

As I was putting this new edition together, I wanted to add some youth voices—kids who have deschooled themselves; who have spent some or all of their childhoods not going to school; have attended alternative schools and/or are attending democratic schools—kids who are doing something different.

I put a quick call out and got a bunch of good responses back pretty quickly. I asked each kid ten questions, requesting that they answer honestly and straight up, not trying to do a sales-job for deschooling, but fairly describing and assessing their experiences.

So following, divided up into four separate chapters are their answers. You will note that all of the kids are from Vancouver and all are friends of mine and our family, so the responses have a certain kind of perspective. The kids range in age from nine to twenty-three and their backgrounds, approaches, and experiences are fairly diverse. All have attended Windsor House for at least some of their childhood, some have only gone part-time, some only to alternative schools, some have had a wide range of schooling encounters.

I have taken their answers and edited them down somewhat. I have not included all their full answers to every question, just a representative and insightful few for each question. I think their stories and opinions add a lot of contour and colour to the collection.

1. Describe what you have done through your school years. How you have spent your time, whether you have been in school or not, how much, and what you anticipate doing in the future. When you weren't in school, what did you do instead?

Gen Robertson: *Genevieve Robertson was born in Vancouver and went to Windsor House until she was fifteen. After that, she attended an alternative high school, where she graduated in 2002. She is now living in Halifax, pursuing her BFA.*

After a traumatic Grade One in a regular elementary school, my mum pulled my brother and I out and put us in Windsor House. I stayed there for seven years, until I transferred into an outdoor program called Trek. The program consisted of half a year of outdoor adventure, and half a year of condensed Grade Ten curriculum work. After the first term, I dropped out and came back to Windsor House to finish my year there. Because a lot of my peers were in regular school and did not understand the concept of deschooling or even alternative education, I felt pressure to get my Grade Twelve. So after dropping out of Trek, I spent the end of my year frantically preparing to leave again. I graduated from City School (a small "enrichment" program) two years later. Now it's been five years since I graduated. I spent my first two years working, traveling, and generally bumming around. After that, I began the Capilano College Studio Art program. I just spent another year working, doing art, and traveling, and am about to move to Halifax to finish my art degree.

Maya Motoi: Maya grew up in Japan where she has lived in the city and the countryside. She has attended public school, an alternative boarding school, unschooled and raised ducks at home, and traveled around Canada with her mother. When she was thirteen, she moved to Canada by herself and now attends Windsor House while staying with a family.

For Grade One I went to a Japanese public school (in Japan, where I am from) that only had twenty students. Then for Grade Two I went to a larger Japanese public school because the small one got closed down and was joined with a few other small schools to make a big one. For most of my third year I traveled around Canada with my mom. In fourth grade, I decided not to go to school, so I was unschooled. The most memorable and big thing I did that year was raise ducks with my mom and dad. In my fifth grade I decided to go to an alternative boarding school in Japan called Katsuyama Children's Village. I went to this school for all my Grade Five year and until Christmas in Grade Six, when I quit. Then, for some months, I didn't really know what I wanted to do. Then we thought of the idea of me coming to Windsor House. Me and my mom visited in April and I decided to go there in September, so that's where I am now.

I'm doing all the academic stuff and am trying to finish Grade Nine by the end of January so I can do the Grade Ten provincials at the end of this school year, so I can go to high school in Japan, which starts in the middle of Grade Ten here. But they need to see a junior high graduation first and completion of Grade Ten over here would be the equivalent of that. I really want to get into this sort-of-hard-to-get-into high school because they have a really cool visual design program that I think takes up 40% of the curriculum.

I have no idea if I will do any post-secondary studies, because I recently discovered that the many things which I thought were my passions were really just my interests. I thought these things were what I wanted to do forever, but now none of them are going to be the only thing I will ever do. This discovery has developed so much more of my understanding of myself, but in the end it might not change that much, but I am closer to myself now.

David Gagnon: David Gagnon is currently working as stage carpenter. His long-time love of theatre has led him to this great "day job." In his spare time, David produces LEGO events/displays and works on various community projects. He is currently the coordinator for the 16th International Democratic Education Conference which will come to Canada for the first time in August 2008 in Vancouver.

I began my formal learning in kindergarten at a "normal" or "traditional" public school. I didn't enjoy the experience: by Grade Three I was ready to curl up and die. My parents, without any knowledge of options, called me in sick. Weeks went by and, before long, I was sick all the time. My mom was home with my two-year-old sister, so the opportunity for me not to go to school existed. We identified at some point that we were "homeschooling" and about eight months passed in this way. Besides watching TV, fighting with my sister, and building with my Lego, I wasn't outwardly doing anything. I was, however, inwardly reorganizing myself. I started to enjoy language, building my vocabulary simply for the sake of being able to use it (this was in part an "I'm not dumb cause I don't go to school" response); I became vegetarian when I started thinking about animal rights; and, most importantly, I started feeling stronger about who I was.

After eight months in relative isolation, I was ready to be surrounded by kids again. My parents discovered a private alternative school, and I fit right in. The small-school environment and wonderful teachers were perfect. I stayed a year and a half, till for various reasons I had to leave. After nine more months of homeschooling, I visited Windsor House and found a bunch of kids in the back, digging a large hole, which they hoped would soon become a pool. I grabbed a shovel and discovered my new home.

As to the future, there are many things I would like to study on a post-secondary level. I have yet to find the time to do so, but I will. For now work and travel consume my time and I have yet to encounter a situation where I need some level of formal training to do what I want to do.

Fyona DeBalasi Brown: Fiona is sixteen years old, attends Templeton Secondary School part-time, and keeps busy with many community-oriented activities. She is involved in the theatre program at her school, the VECC's Youth Program, and the spoken word and slam poetry community in Vancouver.

From birth to age ten I was unschooled, and was part of a large homeschooling community in Vancouver. During those years, I spent a lot of time with my older brother and my parents, went on many a play date, and attended events such as singing day (a day in which many families congregated in one home and usually the parents played music and the kids played with friends) and theme day (a day in which a theme was picked ahead of time and parents and children did research presentations around the topic). Tea was usually a key part of these events also.

When I was ten, my brother started going to an alternative school called Windsor House.

At the time a lot of my friends were starting to go to school or simply getting busy with other parts of their lives, and I found myself getting pretty bored. The next year I decided to join him there.

After four years at Windsor House, I started to feel frustrated with the way the school was being run. At a time in my life when I craved a large social group, the numbers at my school were dropping; not only that, but I no longer felt like I had a say in the way things were done there. Ironically, though craving democracy, I decided it was time to try attending a regular high school.

Mari Piggott: My name is Mari Piggott and I am thirteen years old. Since kindergarten, I have attended Windsor House School, an alternative, non-coercive, and democratically run school. In September 2007, I attended the International Democratic Education Conference in Sao Paulo Brazil.

I go to Windsor House school part-time and I do a lot of Cirkids School of Circus Arts. I also do lots of home learning: lots of music (my parents are both professional musicians), reading, writing, math with my parents, drawing, etc.

Nigel Boeur: Nigel Boeur is a multi-talented fifteen year old who has a passion for photography, music, girls, bikes, and the outdoors (skiing, surfing, boarding, hiking etc). He has been unschooling for most of his life, and has all the time in the world to hone his skills.

I started going to school part-time at Windsor House, when I was around ten years old. When I wasn't at school, I spent most of my time playing music, fixing bikes, doing woodworking, photography, all sorts of outdoor activities (mainly skiing, biking, board sports, hiking and camping), and hanging out with my family and friends. In the fairly near future, I anticipate doing lots of the outdoor stuff I love, playing gigs with my band, traveling, and going tree planting.

Daisy Couture: Daisy Couture is ten years old and enjoys reading, writing, listening to audio books, and hanging out with friends. She attends a circus school where she learns how to juggle, ride a unicycle, do tricks on the trampoline, tumble, do stuff on the trapeze, and lots more. She goes to Windsor House and has an older sister named Sadie.

I have gone to Windsor House for pretty much my whole life. I have never gone full-time. When I was like five, I went one or two days a week, then I went more often as I got older. Last year, I went three days a week and stayed home one day a week with my mother and one day with my dad. Now I go to school (which is not really a school) four days a week and, on Tuesdays, I stay home with Matt and do geography, math, and writing in the mornings, then in the afternoon we go hiking or swimming with Maizy and Sky.

At Windsor House, you don't have to take classes if you don't want to so for most of my time there I have just played with my friends. Now I take classes maybe half the time I am there and play the rest of the day. I'm not planning to go to high school, but probably university because I want to be a librarian. Maybe a writer. That's all my career plan.

When I am not at school, whether it's a weekend or weekday I read a lot, play with my cats, play with friends, go to circus training, go outside, go to the beach, visit people, go to the library ... whatever. Mostly read.

Russ Gendron: Russell kept it real by saying "no" to the public school system and instead became active in an alternative school. Since then, he has taken the solid and valuable skills he acquired into several of life's experiences such as travel, academics, working with youth, cycling tours, and human encounters to name only a few. He is twenty-one years old and thrives on life in the city of Vancouver.

I began "regular" school at the age of five and transferred to alternative schooling at the beginning of my Grade Three year. Four years later, I enrolled in the regular system again and completed high school at the ripe age of eighteen. I have completed one year of college and am now twenty-one. Throughout most of my life, I have tried to pay attention to what I want to do with my days, whether I was in school or not. In both public and alternative schooling, I experienced times where I was not doing what I wanted—both institutions brought their respective deadlines and responsibilities in different forms. Travel, sports, friends, music, and reading have been some major interests of mine, which I explored inside and outside of school.

Sadie Couture: Sadie is fifteen years old and lives in East Vancouver. She likes reading, drinking tea, playing with her cats, talking trash, and looking for / causing trouble.
For almost my entire life, I have been involved with some sort of an alternative school. When I was about a year old, my parents started the Eastside Learning Centre, an alternative school in East Vancouver and I was the baby of the school. When that fell apart, we merged with a school called Windsor House and I attended from Kindergarten until Grade Seven. Mostly play, not a whole lot of work. At the end of Grade Seven, I was ready to move on. I didn't like Windsor House much any more and I wanted to try something new. My parents didn't want me to go to a regular school and there weren't many options for Grade Eight, so I went back to Windsor House. I was really frustrated, and when the opportunity to go to Templeton Mini School (an "enriched" program within a large traditional high school) appeared, I leapt on it. I changed schools halfway through Grade Eight in January 2006 and I have just finished Grade Nine.

2. Please talk briefly about your feelings about not being in a regular school. How did you feel then, how do you feel now? Do you feel grateful, resentful, like you missed out, like you would have missed out on stuff if you had been in school?

Nigel Boeur: I've felt great about my choices throughout my whole life, and I don't think I missed out whatsoever. I'm grateful that my parents chose to educate me at home, and I think I would have missed out on a ton of awesome experiences had I been enrolled full-time in school

Sadie Couture: When I was at Windsor House up until about Grade Seven, I didn't do much traditional school work. I took a class on Ancient History or made a magazine, but that was about it. Then I realized I was old enough to take a class called *What Have I Missed*. This was really exciting for me and I was quite keen. I got a binder and school supplies and showed up for every class. I think I was probably just curious about what almost everyone else my age did all day. Looking back, I feel glad that I haven't had a traditional schooling background and glad that my childhood was so carefree. I feel that if I had gone to elementary school I would have spent my time working hard instead of playing hard.

Walker Banerd: Walker spent the first years of his schooling at home, driven by the belief that life is a constant source of learning and going to school only serves to extinguish the innate desire to learn. After a few years of unschooling, Walker and his family found Windsor House, a public school that reflected their values, where he remained through Grade Twelve. Upon graduating, Walker was accepted into the University Transfer program at Capilano College.

As I near graduation, I've been thinking about my schooling as a whole. I recently asked myself "Was it worth it?" I thought, I've been in school for close to ten years, and my high school diploma will probably only affect my life for two or three years at the most.

But then I realized that in asking I was missing the point, that I was forgetting the reason that I stayed at my alternative program and never went to a "normal" high school. I realized that every day in and of itself has been its own reward, and its own worth. Only when I steer myself towards a more traditional model of formal classes and standardized tests do I begin to lose this feeling. Only then do I look forward to the end of the week, or to the end of the year. But as I occasionally steer myself into this rut, I can steer out of it too.

No one has ever told me how I should go about my schooling, or even if I should at all. I believe this freedom to think critically is the most important thing of all. I found the educational path that I believe was best for me, and I re-evaluated at every step knowing that I had options. I have known people who needed to have a mainstream education to thrive, and I have known people who did not need school at all. But I have also known people who were not in a system that suited them, that didn't even know there were options. I don't feel that I have missed out on anything in my education, because I have had what I feel to be the most important thing: choice.

Mari Piggott: I don't feel like I have missed out on a lot except that Windsor House is pretty small and I haven't got to do lots of group activities, things like sports and large choirs. I think there's so many more pros than cons for me about going to an alternative school that in the long run it's way worth it.

David Gagnon: I am glad my parents had the courage to pull me out of school. As a small, non-violent, dyslexic child, I didn't have a chance. My home life was strong enough that I would have survived the full twelve grades, but given that it took me several years of deschooling to recover from three years of schooling, I would perhaps only now (at age twenty-three) be ready to explore who I am.

I've known a lot of people who have never been to a normal school and while I envy the time they saved themselves, I do appreciate the perspective that it gave me. I know that I am committed to being a part of the deschooling movement for the rest of my life and I may very well not have that level of conviction if I had not started with a negative school experience. Having said that, it's all relative. My sister has been in a normal public school her whole life and wouldn't trade it for anything. I wouldn't trade any part of my schooling away either. It's all played a role in my life and I'm happy with the result.

Russ Gendron: Being involved in an alternative school made me feel more aware of the kind of person I was becoming. This type of school was designed to allow me to create my days independent of outside influence or force, whereas, in public school, I was robbed of this responsibility and, instead, told what to do. I was happy with this alternative set up and I still believe that it contributed greatly to the kind of person I am today. Although regular high school has done the same, I believe the impact of the alternative style stuck with me and has always reminded me that there are always options in life. I am definitely grateful for the alternative system, the teachers, and the freedom I was given. I changed back to the regular program because I wanted to try something new, which caused me to miss out on a lot of cool shit but, I may have felt just the same if I had stayed.

Maizy Thorvaldson: Maizy is twelve years old and attends Windsor House. She lives with her parents and younger sister Gloria. She likes singing, dancing, drama, putting on plays, horses, and hanging out with her friends.

I feel very lucky to be part of this system. I feel grateful that I can tell my kids that this was there.

Maya Motoi: It has always been part of me to do what I want to do, which has basically been something different every year. I feel the need to seek something new out as soon as what I am doing gets familiar. So I can't even imagine how suffocated I would feel if I had gone to a mainstream school for the traditional twelve years.

I can almost say that I don't feel that I am missing out on anything, but I have to admit that I am not feeling so great about my ability to read and write Japanese. It would have been much better if I had stayed in a Japanese public school.

Gen Robertson: At this point in my life, I feel very grateful to have gone to a democratic school. As a young kid, it was an exciting place to be: running around, forts, art, plays, big kids to follow around. It was not until my last few years there that I did not always feel satisfied. I think I left because I found it so difficult to create what I wanted there. It was easy to envision a challenging, stimulating learning environment, but I found it difficult to realize. I would start taking classes and my interest would slowly die off or I would lose my enthusiasm after other peers slowly stopped showing up and I found myself alone.

I think I put a lot of pressure on myself to be self-directed enough to succeed in the task of inventing my own education. In the end, my desire to be challenged grew, and I didn't know how to satisfy it. I think I also had an unconscious need to compare myself to the "regular school kids." Looking back on my later years, I realize that I was being challenged indeed; it was a personal challenge that outdid any academic challenge I experienced later. To be comfortable with my own decisions about how I wanted to live my life and how I wanted to spend my energy was a huge challenge that was pretty difficult to figure out at that point.

Looking back on it, leaving and getting my Grade Twelve was the easy way out. Although the school I graduated from was in no way regular, it offered curriculum-based courses, so the academic challenge that I sought earlier was satisfied there. However, in almost every other way, those two years are missing from my life. I think I was very stressed out by leaving the Windsor House community and my friends. I became withdrawn socially and pretty unhappy and isolated.

I think my way of escaping that was to pour every drop of energy into schoolwork, whether I cared about it or not. I felt so much pressure to do well. I really don't know where it came from, not from my family or community, that's for sure. I lost all sense of my own interests and desires, and basically became numb, completing menial time-filler tasks from morning till night. OK. I think I'm being a bit dramatic. I was interested in some of it and the years weren't total hell, but in general, it wasn't a great time. There was this chair in my room that I would sit and do my math and Spanish homework in. I still want to wriggle when I think of that chair. I think I could have used my time a lot better during those years, but at the time I didn't know how.

The Parrot's Tale

Rabindranath Tagore

Rabindranath (1861–1941) was a Bengali poet, philosopher, artist, playwright, novelist, musician, painter, and composer. Throughout his life and work, he was a non-conformist, unconventional innovator, and amazingly prolific. His writing was voluminous: novels, short-stories, collections of songs, travelogues, dance-drama, political and personal essays. He was also a political activist, protesting against the British Raj and supporting the Indian Independence Movement, and founded the Visva-Bharati University.

As both a writer and cultural reformer, Tagore was a polymath who modernized Bengali art, created new syntheses of writing styles, published magazines, set up the Institute for Rural Reconstruction, and traveled widely. Two songs from his rabindrasangeet canon are now the national anthems of Bangladesh and India: the Amar Shonar Bangla *and the* Jana Gana Mana. *He became Asia's first Nobel laureate when he won the 1913 Nobel Prize in Literature.*

Once upon a time, there was a bird. It was ignorant. It sang all right, but never recited scriptures. It hopped pretty frequently, but lacked manners.

Said the Raja to himself: "Ignorance is costly in the long run. For fools consume as much food as their betters, and yet give nothing in return."

He called his nephews to his presence and told them that the bird must have a sound schooling. The pundits were summoned, and at once went to the root of the matter. They decided that the ignorance of birds was due to their natural habit of living in poor nests. Therefore, according to the pundits, the first thing necessary for this bird's education was a suitable cage.

The pundits had their rewards and went home happy.

A golden cage was built with gorgeous decorations. Crowds came to see it from all parts of the world. "Culture, captured and caged!" exclaimed some, in a rapture of ecstasy, and burst into tears. Others remarked: "Even if culture is missed, the cage will remain, to the end, a substantial fact. How fortunate for the bird!"

The goldsmith filled his bag with money and lost no time in sailing homewards. The pundit sat down to educate the bird. With proper deliberation he took his pinch of snuff: as he said: "Textbooks can never be too many for our purpose!"

The nephews brought together an enormous crowd of scribes. They copied from books, and copied from copies, till the manuscripts were piled up to an unreachable height. Men murmured in amazement. "Oh, the tower of culture, egregiously high! The end of it lost in the clouds!"

The scribes, with light hearts, hurried home, their pockets heavily laden.

The nephews were furiously busy keeping the cage in proper trim. As their constant scrubbing and polishing went on, the people said with satisfaction: "This is progress indeed!"

Men were employed in large numbers and supervisors were still more numerous. These, with their cousins of all different degrees of distance, built a palace for themselves and lived there happily ever after.

Whatever may be its other deficiencies, the world is never in want of faultfinders; and they went about saying that every creature remotely connected with the cage flourished beyond words, excepting only the bird.

When this remark reached the Raja's ears, he summoned his nephews before him and said: "My dear nephews, what is this that we hear?"

The nephews said in answer: "Sire, let the testimony of the goldsmiths and the pundits, the scribes and the supervisors be taken, if the truth is to be known. Food is scarce with the fault-finders, and that is why their tongues have gained in sharpness."

The explanation was so luminously satisfactory that the Raja decorated each one of his nephews with his own rare jewels.

The Raja, at length, being desirous of seeing with his own eyes how his Education Department busied itself with the little bird, made his appearance one day at the great Hall of Learning. From the gate rose the sounds of conch-shells and gongs, horns, bugles and trumpets, cymbals, drums and kettledrums, tomtoms, tambourines, flutes, fifes, barrel-organs and bagpipes. The pundits began chanting mantras with their topmost voices, while the goldsmiths, scribes, supervisors, and their numberless cousins of all different degrees of distance, loudly raised a round of cheers.

The nephews smiled and said: "Sire, what do you think of it all?"

The Raja said: "It does seem so fearfully like a sound principle of Education!"

Mightily pleased, the Raja was about to remount his elephant, when the fault-finder, from behind some bush, cried out: "Maharaja, have you seen the bird?"

"Indeed, I have not!" exclaimed the Raja. "I completely forgot about the bird."

Turning back, he asked the pundits about the method they followed in instructing the bird. It was shown to him. He was immensely impressed. The method was so stupendous that the bird looked ridiculously unimportant in comparison. The Raja was satisfied that there was no flaw in the arrangements. As for any complaint from the bird itself, that simply could not be expected. Its throat was so completely choked with the leaves from the books that it could neither whistle nor whisper. It sent a thrill through one's body to watch the process.

This time, while remounting his elephant, the Raja ordered his State ear-puller to give a thorough good pull at both the ears of the fault-finder.

The bird thus crawled on, duly and properly, to the safest verge of inanity. In fact, its progress was satisfactory in the extreme.

Nevertheless, Nature occasionally triumphed over training, and when the morning light peeped into the bird's cage it sometimes fluttered its wings in a reprehensible manner. And, though it is hard to believe, it pitifully pecked at its bars with its feeble beak.

"What impertinence!" growled the kotwal.

The blacksmith, with his forge and hammer, took his place in the Raja's Department of Education. Oh, what resounding blows! The iron chain was soon completed, and the bird's wings were clipped.

The Raja's brothers-in-law looked black, and shook their heads, saying: "These birds not only lack good sense, but also gratitude!"

With text-book in one hand and baton in the other, the pundits gave the poor bird what may fitly be called lessons!

The kotwal was honoured with a title for his watchfulness, and the blacksmith for his skill in forging chains.

The bird died.

Nobody had the least notion how long ago this had happened. The fault-finder was the first man to spread the rumor.

The Raja called his nephews and asked them, "My dear nephews, what is this that we hear?"

The nephews said: "Sire, the bird's education has been completed."

"Does it hop?" the Raja enquired.

"Never!" said the nephews.

"Does it fly?"

"No."

"Bring me the bird," said the Raja.

The bird was brought to him, guarded by the kotwal and the sepoys and the sowars. The Raja poked its body with his finger. Only its inner stuffing of book-leaves rustled.

Outside the window, the murmur of the spring breeze amongst the newly budded asoka leaves made the April morning wistful.

Francisco Ferrer and
the Modern School

Emma Goldman
From the 1917 edition of Anarchism and Other Essays

Emma Goldman (1869–1940) is perhaps the most famous, and certainly the most t-shirtized anarchist in history. Born in Lithuania, she moved to Russia, then immigrated to the United States at the age of seventeen, where she worked in New York factories and became a revolutionary anarchist after the Haymarket Riot of 1886. After years of volatile activism and several imprisonments, she was deported to Russia, where she witnessed the results of the Russian Revolution, then spent years traveling. She wrote her autobiography, Living My Life, *when living in France and took part in the Spanish Civil War in 1936.*

Francisco Ferrer (1859–1909) was born near Barcelona to Catholic parents. After becoming involved in the Republican movement Ferrer was exiled to Paris returning to Spain in 1901 and opening la Escuela Moderna (The Modern School) to teach radical social values. Between 1901 and 1909, Ferrer organized/inspired scores of radical and liberal schools to open in Spain and established an international journal for anarchist education. In 1906, he was arrested, then released uncharged over a year later, and his school closed while he was incarcerated. In 1908, he wrote The Origins and Ideals of the Modern School *which inspired the creation of Modern Schools around the world, the first and most notable being the Modern School in NYC, then Stelton, New Jersey. Ferrer was arrested and summarily executed in 1909 without proof of any activity beyond being an or organizer of radical schools.*

There lived and worked in Barcelona a man by the name of Francisco Ferrer. A teacher of children he was, known and loved by his people. Outside of Spain only the cultured few knew of Francisco Ferrer's work. To the world at large this teacher was non-existent.

On the first of September, 1909, the Spanish government—at the behest of the Catholic Church—arrested Francisco Ferrer. On the thirteenth of October, after a mock trial, he was placed in the ditch at Montjuich prison, against the hideous wall of many sighs, and shot dead. Instantly Ferrer, the obscure teacher, became a universal figure, blazing forth the indignation and wrath of the whole civilized world against the wanton murder.

The killing of Francisco Ferrer was not the first crime committed by the Spanish government and the Catholic Church. The history of these institutions is one long stream of fire and blood. Still they have not learned through experience, nor yet come to realize that every frail being slain by Church and State grows and grows into a mighty giant, who will some day free humanity from their perilous hold.

Francisco Ferrer was born in 1859, of humble parents. They were Catholics, and therefore hoped to raise their son in the same faith. They did not know that the boy was to become the harbinger of a great truth, that his mind would refuse to travel in the old path. At an early age, Ferrer began to question the faith of his fathers. He demanded to know how it is that the God who spoke to him of goodness and love would mar the sleep of the innocent child with dread and awe of tortures, of suffering, of hell. Alert and of a vivid and investigating mind, it did not take him long to discover the hideousness of that black monster, the Catholic Church. He would have none of it.

Francisco Ferrer was not only a doubter, a searcher for truth; he was also a rebel. His spirit would rise in just indignation against the iron regime of his country, and when a band of rebels, led by the brave patriot, General Villacampa, under the banner of the Republican ideal, made an onslaught on that regime, none was more ardent a fighter than young Francisco Ferrer. The Republican ideal—I hope no one will confound it with the Republicanism of this country. Whatever objection I, as an Anarchist, have to the Republicans of Latin countries, I know they tower high above the corrupt and reactionary party which, in America, is destroying every vestige of liberty and justice. One has but to think of the Mazzinis, the Garibaldis, the scores of others, to realize that their efforts were directed, not merely towards the overthrow of despotism, but particularly against the Catholic Church, which from its very inception has been the enemy of all progress and liberalism. In America, it is just the reverse. Republicanism stands for vested rights, for imperialism, for graft, for the annihilation of every semblance of liberty. Its ideal is the oily, creepy respectability of a McKinley, and the brutal arrogance of a Roosevelt.

The Spanish republican rebels were subdued. It takes more than one brave effort to split the rock of ages, to cut off the head of that hydra monster, the Catholic Church and the Spanish throne. Arrest, persecution, and punishment followed the heroic attempt of the little band. Those who could escape the bloodhounds had to flee for safety to foreign shores. Francisco Ferrer was among the latter. He went to France. How his soul must have expanded in the new land! France, the cradle of liberty, of ideas, of action. Paris, the ever young, intense Paris, with her pulsating life, after the gloom of his own belated country—how she must have inspired him. What opportunities, what a glorious chance for a young idealist.

Francisco Ferrer lost no time. Like one famished he threw himself into the various liberal movements, met all kinds of people, learned, absorbed, and grew. While there, he also saw in operation the Modern School, which was to play such an important and fatal part in his life.

The Modern School in France was founded long before Ferrer's time. Its originator, though on a small scale, was that sweet spirit, Louise Michel. Whether consciously or unconsciously, our own great Louise felt long ago that the future belongs to the young generation; that unless the young be rescued from that mind and soul destroying institution, the bourgeois school, social evils will continue to exist. Perhaps she thought, with Ibsen, that the atmosphere is saturated with ghosts, that the adult man and woman have so many superstitions to overcome. No sooner do they outgrow the deathlike grip of one spook, lo! they find themselves in the thralldom of ninety-nine other spooks. Thus but a few reach the mountain peak of complete regeneration.

The child, however, has no traditions to overcome. Its mind is not burdened with set ideas, its heart has not grown cold with class and caste distinctions. The child is to the teacher what clay is to the sculptor. Whether the world will receive a work of art or a wretched imitation, depends to a large extent on the creative power of the teacher.

Louise Michel was pre-eminently qualified to meet the child's soul cravings. Was she not herself of a childlike nature, so sweet and tender, unsophisticated and generous. The soul of Louise burned always at white heat over every social injustice. She was invariably in the front ranks whenever the people of Paris rebelled against some wrong. And as she was made to suffer imprisonment for her great devotion to the oppressed, the little school on Montmartre was soon no more. But the seed was planted, and has since borne fruit in many cities of France.

(Ed. Note: Here Goldman writes of radical schools founded in the late 1800s by Paul Robin, Madelaine Vernet, and Sebastian Faure. This section has not been included for brevity)

Francisco Ferrer could not escape this great wave of Modern School attempts. He saw its possibilities, not merely in theoretic form, but in their practical application to everyday needs. He must have realized that Spain, more than any other country, stands in need of just such schools, if it is ever to throw off the double yoke of priest and soldier.

When we consider that the entire system of education in Spain is in the hands of the Catholic Church, and when we further remember the Catholic formula, "To inculcate Catholicism in the mind of the child until it is nine years of age is to ruin it forever for any other idea," we will understand the tremendous task of Ferrer in bringing the new light to his people. Fate soon assisted him in realizing his great dream.

Mlle. Meunier, a pupil of Francisco Ferrer, and a lady of wealth, became interested in the Modern School project. When she died, she left Ferrer some valuable property and twelve thousand francs yearly income for the School.

It is said that mean souls can conceive of naught but mean ideas. If so, the contemptible methods of the Catholic Church to blackguard Ferrer's character, in order to justify her own black crime, can readily be explained. Thus the lie was spread in American Catholic papers, that Ferrer used his intimacy with Mlle. Meunier to get possession of her money.

Personally, I hold that the intimacy, of whatever nature, between a man and a woman, is their own affair, their sacred own. I would therefore not lose a word in referring to the matter, if it were not one of the many dastardly lies circulated about Ferrer. Of course, those who know the purity of the Catholic clergy will understand the insinuation. Have the Catholic priests ever looked upon woman as anything but a sex commodity? The historical data regarding the discoveries in the cloisters and monasteries will bear me out in that. How, then, are they to understand the co-operation of a man and a woman, except on a sex basis?

As a matter of fact, Mlle. Meunier was considerably Ferrer's senior. Having spent her childhood and girlhood with a miserly father and a submissive mother, she could easily appreciate the necessity of love and joy in child life. She must have seen that Francisco Ferrer was a teacher, not college-, machine-, or diploma-made, but one endowed with genius for that calling.

Equipped with knowledge, with experience, and with the necessary means; above all, imbued with the divine fire of his mission, our Comrade came back to Spain, and there began his life's work. On the ninth of September, 1901, the first Modern School was opened. It was enthusiastically received by the people of Barcelona, who pledged their support. In a short address at the opening of the School, Ferrer submitted his program to his friends. He said: "I am not a speaker, not a propagandist, not a fighter. I am a teacher; I love children above everything. I think I understand them. I want my contribution to the cause of liberty to be a young generation ready to meet a new era."

He was cautioned by his friends to be careful in his opposition to the Catholic Church. They knew to what lengths she would go to dispose of an enemy. Ferrer, too, knew. But, like Brand, he believed in all or nothing. He would not erect the Modern School on the same old lie. He would be frank and honest and open with the children.

Francisco Ferrer became a marked man. From the very first day of the opening of the School, he was shadowed. The school building was watched, his little home in Mangat was watched. He was followed every step, even when he went to France or England to confer with his colleagues. He was a marked man, and it was only a question of time when the lurking enemy would tighten the noose.

It succeeded, almost, in 1906, when Ferrer was implicated in the attempt on the life of Alfonso. The evidence exonerating him was too strong even for the black crows; they had to let him go—not for good, however. They waited. Oh, they can wait, when they have set themselves to trap a victim.

The moment came at last, during the anti-military uprising in Spain, in July, 1909. One will have to search in vain the annals of revolutionary history to find a more remarkable protest against militarism. Having been soldier-ridden for centuries, the people of Spain could stand the yoke no longer. They would refuse to participate in useless slaughter. They saw no reason for aiding a despotic government in subduing and oppressing a small people fighting for their independence, as did the brave Riffs. No, they would not bear arms against them.

For eighteen hundred years, the Catholic Church has preached the gospel of peace. Yet, when the people actually wanted to make this gospel a living reality, she urged the authorities to force them to bear arms. Thus, the dynasty of Spain followed the murderous methods of the Russian dynasty—the people were forced to the battlefield.

Then, and not until then, was their power of endurance at an end. Then, and not until then, did the workers of Spain turn against their masters, against those who, like leeches, had drained their strength, their very life-blood. Yes, they attacked the churches and the priests, but if the latter had a thousand lives, they could not possibly pay for the terrible outrages and crimes perpetrated upon the Spanish people.

Francisco Ferrer was arrested on the first of September, 1909. Until October first, his friends and comrades did not even know what had become of him. On that day a letter was received by L'Humanite, from which can be learned the whole mockery of the trial. And the next day his companion, Soledad Villafranca, received the following letter:

"No reason to worry; you know I am absolutely innocent. Today I am particularly hopeful and joyous. It is the first time I can write to you, and the first time since my arrest that I can bathe in the rays of the sun, streaming generously through my cell window. You, too, must be joyous."

How pathetic that Ferrer should have believed, as late as October fourth, that he would not be condemned to death. Even more pathetic that his friends and comrades should once more have made the blunder in crediting the enemy with a sense of justice. Time and again they had placed faith in the judicial powers, only to see their brothers killed before their very eyes. They made no preparation to rescue Ferrer, not even a protest of any extent; nothing. "Why, it is impossible to condemn Ferrer; he is innocent." But everything is possible with the Catholic Church. Is she not a practiced henchman, whose trials of her enemies are the worst mockery of justice?

✳ ✳ ✳

October 13th, 1909, Ferrer's heart, so brave, so staunch, so loyal, was stilled. Poor fools! The last agonized throb of that heart had barely died away when it began to beat a hundredfold in the hearts of the civilized world, until it grew into terrific thunder, hurling forth its malediction upon the instigators of the black crime. Murderers of black garb and pious mien, to the bar of justice!

Did Francisco Ferrer participate in the anti-military uprising? According to the first indictment, which appeared in a Catholic paper in Madrid, signed by the Bishop and all the prelates of Barcelona, he was not even accused of participation. The indictment was to the effect that Francisco Ferrer was guilty of having organized godless schools, and having circulated godless literature. But in the twentieth century men can not be burned merely for their godless beliefs. Something else had to be devised; hence the charge of instigating the uprising.

In no authentic source so far investigated could a single proof be found to connect Ferrer with the uprising. But then, no proofs were wanted, or accepted, by the authorities. There were seventy-two witnesses, to be sure, but their testimony was taken on paper. They never were confronted with Ferrer, or he with them.

Is it psychologically possible that Ferrer should have participated? I do not believe it is, and here are my reasons. Francisco Ferrer was not only a great teacher, but he was also undoubtedly a marvelous organizer. In eight years, between 1901–1909, he had organized in Spain one hundred and nine schools, besides inducing the liberal element of his country to organize three hundred and eight other schools. In connection with his own school work, Ferrer had equipped a modern printing plant, organized a staff of translators, and spread broadcast one hundred and fifty thousand copies of modern scientific and sociologic works, not to forget the large quantity of rationalist text books. Surely none but the most methodical and efficient organizer could have accomplished such a feat.

On the other hand, it was absolutely proven that the anti-military uprising was not at all organized; that it came as a surprise to the people themselves, like a great many revolutionary waves on previous occasions. The people of Barcelona, for instance, had the city in their control for four days, and, according to the statement of tourists, greater order and peace never prevailed. Of course, the people were so little prepared that when the time came, they did not know what to do. In this regard, they were like the people of Paris during the Commune of 1871. They, too, were unprepared. While they were starving, they protected the warehouses, filled to the brim with provisions. They placed sentinels to guard the Bank of France, where the bourgeoisie kept the stolen money. The workers of Barcelona, too, watched over the spoils of their masters.

How pathetic is the stupidity of the underdog; how terribly tragic! But, then, have not his fetters been forged so deeply into his flesh, that he would not, even if he could, break them? The awe of authority, of law, of private property, hundredfold burned into his soul—how is he to throw it off unprepared, unexpectedly?

Can anyone assume for a moment that a man like Ferrer would affiliate himself with such a spontaneous, unorganized effort? Would he not have known that it would result in a defeat, a disastrous defeat for the people? And is it not more likely that if he would have taken part, he, the experienced ENTREPRENEUR, would have thoroughly organized the attempt? If all other proofs were lacking, that one factor would be sufficient to exonerate Francisco Ferrer. But there are others equally convincing.

For the very date of the outbreak, July twenty-fifth, Ferrer had called a conference of his teachers and members of the League of Rational Education. It was to consider the autumn work, and particularly the publication of Elisee Reclus' great book, *L'Homme et le Terre*, and Peter Kropotkin's *Great French Revolution*. Is it at all likely, is it at all plausible that Ferrer, knowing of the uprising, being a party to it, would in cold blood invite his friends and colleagues to Barcelona for the day on which he realized their lives would be endangered? Surely, only the criminal, vicious mind of a Jesuit could credit such deliberate murder.

Francisco Ferrer had his life-work mapped out; he had everything to lose and nothing to gain, except ruin and disaster, were he to lend assistance to the outbreak. Not that he doubted the justice of the people's wrath; but his work, his hope, his very nature was directed toward another goal.

In vain are the frantic efforts of the Catholic Church, her lies, falsehoods, calumnies. She stands condemned by the awakened human conscience of having once more repeated the foul crimes of the past.

Francisco Ferrer is accused of teaching the children the most blood-curdling ideas—to hate God, for instance. Horrors! Francisco Ferrer did not believe in the existence of a God. Why teach the child to hate something which does not exist? Is it not more likely that he took the children out into the open, that he showed them the splendor of the sunset, the brilliancy of the starry heavens, the awe-inspiring wonder of the mountains and seas; that he explained to them in his simple, direct way the law of growth, of development, of the interrelation of all life? In so doing, he made it forever impossible for the poisonous weeds of the Catholic Church to take root in the child's mind.

It has been stated that Ferrer prepared the children to destroy the rich. Ghost stories of old maids. Is it not more likely that he prepared them to succor the poor? That he taught them the humiliation, the degradation, the awfulness of poverty, which is a vice and not a virtue; that he taught the dignity and importance of all creative efforts, which alone sustain life and build character. Is it not the best and most effective way of bringing into the proper light the absolute uselessness and injury of parasitism?

Last, but not least, Ferrer is charged with undermining the army by inculcating anti-military ideas. Indeed? He must have believed with Tolstoy that war is legalized slaughter, that it perpetuates hatred and arrogance, that it eats away the heart of nations, and turns them into raving maniacs.

However, we have Ferrer's own word regarding his ideas of modern education:

"I would like to call the attention of my readers to this idea: All the value of education rests in the respect for the physical, intellectual, and moral will of the child. Just as in science no demonstration is possible save by facts, just so there is no real education save that which is exempt from all dogmatism, which leaves to the child itself the direction of its effort, and confines itself to the seconding of its effort. Now, there is nothing easier than to alter this purpose, and nothing harder than to respect it. Education is always imposing, violating, constraining; the real educator is he who can best protect the child against his (the teacher's) own ideas, his peculiar whims; he who can best appeal to the child's own energies.

"We are convinced that the education of the future will be of an entirely spontaneous nature; certainly we can not as yet realize it, but the evolution of methods in the direction of a wider comprehension of the phenomena of life, and the fact that all advances toward perfection mean the overcoming of restraint—all this indicates that we are in the right when we hope for the deliverance of the child through science.

"Let us not fear to say that we want men capable of evolving without stopping, capable of destroying and renewing their environments without cessation, of renewing themselves also; men, whose intellectual independence will be their greatest force, who will attach themselves to nothing, always ready to accept what is best, happy in the triumph of new ideas, aspiring to live multiple lives in one life. Society fears such men; we therefore must not hope that it will ever want an education able to give them to us.

"We shall follow the labors of the scientists who study the child with the greatest attention, and we shall eagerly seek for means of applying their experience to the education which we want to build up, in the direction of an ever fuller liberation of the individual. But how can we attain our end? Shall it not be by putting ourselves directly to the work favoring the foundation of new schools, which shall be ruled as much as possible by this spirit of liberty, which we forefeel will dominate the entire work of education in the future?

"A trial has been made, which, for the present, has already given excellent results. We can destroy all which in the present school answers to the organization of constraint, the artificial surroundings by which children are separated from nature and life, the intellectual and moral discipline made use of to impose ready-made ideas upon them, beliefs which deprave and annihilate natural bent. Without fear of deceiving ourselves, we can restore the child to the environment which entices it, the environment of nature in which he will be in contact with all that he loves, and in which impressions of life will replace fastidious book-learning. If we did no more than that, we should already have prepared in great part the deliverance of the child.

"In such conditions we might already freely apply the data of science and labor most fruitfully. I know very well we could not thus realize all our hopes, that we should often be forced, for lack of knowledge, to employ undesirable methods; but a certitude would sustain us in our efforts—namely, that even without reaching our aim completely we should do more and better in our still imperfect work than the present school accomplishes. I like the free spontaneity of a child who knows nothing, better than the world-knowledge and intellectual deformity of a child who has been subjected to our present education."

Had Ferrer actually organized the riots, had he fought on the barricades, had he hurled a hundred bombs, he could not have been so dangerous to the Catholic Church and to despotism, as with his opposition to discipline and restraint. Discipline and restraint—are they not back of all the evils in the world? Slavery, submission, poverty, all misery, all social iniquities result from discipline and restraint. Indeed, Ferrer was dangerous. Therefore he had to die, October 13th, 1909, in the ditch of Montjuich.

Yet who dare say his death was in vain? In view of the tempestuous rise of universal indignation: Italy naming streets in memory of Francisco Ferrer, Belgium inaugurating a movement to erect a memorial; France calling to the front her most illustrious men to resume the heritage of the martyr; England being the first to issue a biography—all countries uniting in perpetuating the great work of Francisco Ferrer; America, even, tardy always in progressive ideas, giving birth to a Francisco Ferrer Association, its aim being to publish a complete life of Ferrer and to organize Modern Schools all over the country; in the face of this international revolutionary wave, who is there to say Ferrer died in vain?

That death at Montjuich—how wonderful, how dramatic it was, how it stirs the human soul. Proud and erect, the inner eye turned toward the light, Francisco Ferrer needed no lying priests to give him courage, nor did he upbraid a phantom for forsaking him. The consciousness that his executioners represented a dying age, and that his was the living truth, sustained him in the last heroic moments.

A dying age and a living truth,
The living burying the dead.

SECTION II

Sweet Land of Liberty

Grace Llewellyn

Grace taught school for three years before unschooling herself and writ-ing the first edition of The Teenage Liberation Handbook *in 1991. She has since edited* Real Lives: Eleven Teenagers Who Don't Go to School Tell Their Own Stories *and* Freedom Challenge: African American Homeschoolers, *and, with Amy Silver, co-authored* Guerrilla Learning: How to Give Your Kids a Real Education With or Without School. *In 1996, she founded Not Back to School Camp, a gathering for unschooled teenagers which she contin-ues to direct each summer. A passionate student, performer, and teacher of bellydance, and an obsessive student of Argentine tango, she lives in Eugene, Oregon.*

The most overwhelming reality of school is control. School controls the way you spend your time (what is life made of if not time?), how you behave, what you read, and to a large extent what you think. In school you can't control your own life. Outside of school you can, at least to the extent that your parents trust you to. "Comparing me to those who are conven-tionally schooled," writes twelve-year-old unschooler Colin Roch, "is like comparing the freedoms of a wild stallion to those of cattle in a feedlot."

The ultimate goal of this book is for you to start associating the concept of freedom with you, and to start wondering why you and your friends don't have much of it, and for you to move out of the busy prison into the meadows of life. There are lots of good reasons to quit school, but in my idealistic American mind, the pursuit of freedom encompasses most of them and outshines the others.

If you look at the history of "freedom," you notice that the most frightening thing about people who are not free is that they learn to take their bondage for granted, and to believe that this bondage is "normal" and natural.

Right now, a lot of you are helping history to repeat itself; you don't believe you should be free. Of course you want to be free in various ways, not just free of school. However, society gives you so many condescending, false, and harmful messages about yourselves that most of you wouldn't trust yourselves with freedom. It's all complicated by the fact that the people who infringe most dangerously and inescapably on your freedom are those who say they are helping you, those who are convinced you need their help: teachers, school counselors, perhaps your parents.

Why should you have freedom?

Why should anyone? To become human, to live fully. Insofar as you live what someone else dictates, you do not live. Choice is a fundamental essence of life, and in the fullest life, each choice is deliberate and savored.

Another reason you should be free is obvious. You should learn to live responsibly and joyfully in a free country.

Recently, school people talk a lot about "experiential education." Educators have wisely realized that the best way to teach anything includes not only reading about a subject, but also practicing it. For example, my colleague Gary Oakley taught science by having students rehabilitate a polluted pond. Naturally, learning this way sinks in deeper than merely reading, hearing lectures, and discussing. It means participating—being a scientist or musician rather than watching from the outside.

What the educators apparently haven't realized yet is that experiential education is a double-edged sword. If you do something to learn it, then what you do, you learn. All the time you are in school, you learn through experience how to live in a dictatorship. In school, you shut your notebook when the bell rings. You do not speak unless granted permission. You are guilty until proven innocent, and who will prove you innocent? You are told what to do, think, and say for six hours a day. If your teacher says sit up and pay attention, you had better stiffen your spine and try to get Bobby or Sally or the idea of Spring or the play you're writing off your mind. The most constant and thorough thing students in school experience—and learn—is the antithesis of democracy.

Authority

Regardless of what the law or your teacher have to say about this, you are as human as anyone over the age of eighteen or twenty-one. Yet "minors" are one of the most oppressed groups of people in the United States, and certainly the most discriminated against legally.

It starts at home. Essentially, your parent can require you to do almost anything and forbid you to do almost anything. Fortunately, most parents try hard not to abuse this power. Yet, from a legal standpoint, the reason schools have so much tyrannical power over you is that they act *in loco parentis*—in place of the parent. As legal parental substitutes, they can search your locker or purse, tell you to be quiet, read your mail (notes), sometimes hit or "spank" you, speak rudely to you, and commit other atrocities—things I hope your parent(s) would not do with a clean conscience, and things no sensible adult would do to another adult, for fear of losing a job or ending a friendship.

Many teenagers, of course, do clash with their parents to some extent. But most parents like and love their children enough to listen to their side, grant them most freedoms as they grow, back off when they realize they're overbearing, and generally behave reasonably. The schools may do this with some "rebellious" students, but not usually, and not after a second or third "offense." Schools are too big, and the adults in them too overworked, to see "rebels" as people—instead, they'll get a permanent-ink "bad person" label and unreasonable treatment. Even in a small private school, authority is often unyielding and unfairly judgmental.

When I was substitute teaching in Oakland, California, I was told I could have a month-long job teaching choir and piano while the regular teacher had a baby. As it happened, I did have a fairly substantial musical background and could have handled at least that aspect of the job just fine. But the administrators showed no interest in my musical knowledge—all they wanted was someone who could maintain order for a month. When the principal introduced me to the choir class, one of the students raised his hand and asked, "Since she's not a music teacher, what are we supposed to do if she's not any good?" The principal launched into a tirade about how it doesn't matter what you think of her teaching, you'll do exactly what she says and I don't want to hear about any problems from any of you; the state board of education decided she was good enough to be certified and that's all you need to know.

One of the worst things about this sort of arbitrary authority is it makes us lose our trust of natural authority—people who know what they're doing and could share a lot of wisdom with us. When they make you obey the cruel and unreasonable teacher, they steal your desire to learn from the kind and reasonable teacher. When they tell you to be sure to pick up after yourselves in the cafeteria, they steal your own natural sense of courtesy.

Many times, I have heard teachers resort defiantly to the proclamation: "The bottom line is, they need to do what we tell them because they're the kids and we're the adults." This concept that teenagers should obey simply because of their age no longer makes any sense to me. I can't figure out what it is based on, except adults' own egos. In this regard, school often seems like a circus arena full of authority-craving adults. Like trained animals, you are there to make them look good, to help them believe they are better than you.

Because they can never make you free, schools can never allow you to learn fully.

Love of Learning

If you had always been free to learn, you would follow your natural tendency to find out as fully as possible about the things that interest you, cars or stars. We are all born with what they call "love of learning," but it dives off into an elusive void when we go to school.

Of course, quitting school doesn't guarantee that you are going to learn more in every subject than you did in school. If you hate math in school, and decide to continue studying it outside of school, it's possible that you won't enjoy it any more or learn it much better, although being able to work without ridicule at your own speed will help. You will see a dramatically wonderful change in the way you learn about the things that interest you. What's more, you will find out that you are interested in things that haven't yet caught your attention, and that you can love at least some of the things which repulsed you in school.

Beyond the love and pursuit of something specific, there's another quality you might also call love of leaning. It's simple curiosity, which kills more tired assumptions than kills cats. Some people move around with their ears and eyes perked open like raccoons, ready to find out something new and like it. Do everything you can to cultivate this characteristic; it will enliven your life immeasurably.

The Public School Nightmare: Why Fix a System Designed to Destroy Individual Thought?

John Taylor Gatto

John worked as a scriptwriter in the film business, an advertising writer, a taxi driver, a jewelry designer, an ASCAP songwriter, and a hotdog vendor before becoming a schoolteacher. He climaxed his teaching career as New York State Teacher of the Year after being named New York City Teacher of the Year on three occasions. He quit teaching on the Op Ed page of the Wall Street Journal *in 1991 while still New York State Teacher of the Year, claiming that he was no longer willing to hurt children. His books include:* Dumbing Us Down: The Hidden Curriculum of Compulsory Schooling *(1992);* The Exhausted School *(1993);* A Different Kind of Teacher *(2000); and* The Underground History Of American Education *(2001).*

I want you to consider the frightening possibility that we are spending far too much money on schooling, not too little. I want you to consider that we have too many people employed in interfering with the way children grow up—and that all this money and all these people, all the time we take out of children's lives and away from their homes and families and neighborhoods and private explorations gets in the way of education.

That seems radical, I know. Surely in modern technological society it is the quantity of schooling and the amount of money you spend on it that buys value. And yet last year in St. Louis, I heard a vice-president of IBM tell an audience of people assembled to redesign the process of teacher certification that in his opinion this country became computer-literate by self-teaching, not through any action of schools. He said forty-five million people were comfortable with computers who had learned through dozens of non-systematic strategies, none of them very formal; if schools had pre-empted the right to teach computers use we would be in a horrible mess right now instead of leading the world in this literacy.

Now think about Sweden, a beautiful, healthy, prosperous and up-to-date country with a spectacular reputation for quality in everything it produces. It makes sense to think their schools must have something to do with that. Then what do you make of the fact that you can't go to school in Sweden until you are seven years old? The reason the unsentimental Swedes have wiped out what would be first and seconds grades here is that they don't want to pay the large social bill that quickly comes due when boys and girls are ripped away from their best teachers at home too early.

It just isn't worth the price, say the Swedes, to provide jobs for teachers and therapists if the result is sick, incomplete kids who can't be put back together again very easily. The entire Swedish school sequence isn't twelve years, either—it's nine. Less schooling, not more. The direct savings of such a step in the United States would be $75–100 billion—a lot of unforeclosed home mortgages, a lot of time freed up with which to seek an education.

Who was it that decided to force your attention onto Japan instead of Sweden? Japan with its long school year and state compulsion, instead of Sweden with its short school year, short school sequence, and free choice where your kid is schooled? Who decided you should know about Japan and not Hong Kong, an Asian neighbor with a short school year that out-performs Japan across the board in math and science? Whose interests are served by hiding that from you?

One of the principal reasons we got into the mess we're in is that we allowed schooling to become a very profitable monopoly, guaranteed its customers by the police power of the state. Systematic schooling at-tracts increased investment only when it does poorly, and since there are no penalties at all for such performance, the temptation not to do well is overwhelming. That's because school staffs, both line and management, are involved in a guild system; in that ancient form of association no single member is allowed to outperform any other member, is allowed to adver-tise or is allowed to introduce new technology or improvise without the advance consent of the guild. Violation of these precepts is severely sanc-tioned—as Marva Collins, Jaime Escalante, and a large number of once-brilliant teachers found out.

The guild reality cannot be broken without returning primary decision-making to parents, letting them buy what they want to buy in schooling, and encouraging the entrepreneurial reality that existed until 1852. That is why I urge any business to think twice before entering a cooperative relationship with the schools we currently have. Cooperating with these places will only make them worse.

The structure of American schooling, twentieth-century style, began in 1806 when Napoleon's amateur soldiers beat the professional soldiers of Prussia at the battle of Jena. When your business is selling soldiers, losing a battle like that is serious. Almost immediately afterwards, a German philosopher named Fichte delivered his famous "Address to the German Nation" which became one of the most influential documents in modern history. In effect, he told the Prussian people that the party was over, that the nation would have to shape up through a new utopian institution of forced schooling in which everyone would learn to take orders.

So the world got compulsion schooling at the end of a state bayonet for the first time in human history; modern forced schooling started in Prussia in 1819 with a clear vision of what centralized schools could deliver:

* obedient soldiers to the army;
* obedient workers to the mines;
* well subordinated civil servants to government;
* well subordinated clerks to industry;
* citizens who thought alike about major issues.

Schools, according to Fichte, should create an artificial national consensus on matters that had been worked out in advance by leading German families and the head of institutions. Schools should create unity among all the German states, eventually unifying them into Greater Prussia.

Prussian industry boomed from the beginning. Prussia was successful in warfare and her reputation in international affairs was very high. Twenty-six years after this form of schooling began, the King of Prussia was invited to North America to determine the boundary between the United States and Canada. Thirty-three years after that fateful invention of the central school institution, at the behest of Horace Mann and many other leading citizens, we borrowed the style of Prussian schooling as our own.

You need to know this because, over the first fifty years of our school institution, Prussian purpose—which was to create a form of state socialism—gradually forced out traditional American purpose, which in most minds was to prepare the individual to be self-reliant.

In Prussia, the purpose of the *Volksschule*, which educated ninety-two percent of the children, was not intellectual development at all, but socialization in obedience and subordination. Thinking was left to the *Real Schulen*, in which eight percent of the kids participated. But for the great mass, intellectual development was regarded with managerial horror, as something that caused armies to lose battles.

Prussia concocted a method based on complex fragmentations to ensure that its school products would fit the grand social design. Some of this method involved dividing whole ideas into school subjects, each further divisible, some of it involved short periods punctuated by a horn so that self-motivation in study would be muted by ceaseless interruptions.

There were many more techniques of training, but all were built around the premise that isolation from first-hand information, and fragmentation of the abstract information presented by teachers, would result in obedient and subordinate graduates, properly respectful of arbitrary orders. "Lesser" men would be unable to interfere with policy makers because, while they could still complain, they could not manage sustained or comprehensive thought. Well-schooled children cannot think critically, cannot argue effectively.

One of the most interesting by-products of Prussian schooling turned out to be the two most devastating wars of modern history. Erich Maria Remarque, in his classic *All Quiet on the Western Front*, tells us that the First World War was caused by the tricks of schoolmasters, and the famous Protestant theologian Dietrich Bonhoeffer said that the Second World War was the inevitable product of good schooling.

It's important to underline that Bonhoeffer meant that literally, not metaphorically: schooling after the Prussian fashion removes the ability of the mind to think for itself. It teaches people to wait for a teacher to tell them what to do and if what they have done is good or bad. Prussian teaching paralyses the moral will as well as the intellect. It's true that sometimes well-schooled students sound smart, because they memorize many opinions of great thinkers, but they actually are badly damaged because their own ability to think is left rudimentary and undeveloped.

We got from the United States to Prussia and back because a small number of very passionate ideological leaders visited Prussia in the first half of the nineteenth century, and fell in love with the order, obedience, and efficiency of its system and relentlessly proselytized for a translation of

Prussian vision onto these shores. If Prussia's ultimate goal was the unification of Germany, our major goal, so these men thought, was the unification of hordes of immigrant Catholics into a national consensus based on a northern European cultural model. To do that, children would have to be removed from their parents and from inappropriate cultural influences.

In this fashion, compulsion schooling, a bad idea that had been around at least since Plato's Republic, a bad idea that New England had tried to enforce in 1650 without any success, was finally rammed through the Massachusetts legislature in 1852. It was, of course, the famous "Know-Nothing" legislature that passed this law, a legislature that was the leading edge of a famous secret society which flourished at that time known as The Order of the Star Spangled Banner, whose password was the simple sentence, "I know nothing"—hence the popular label attached to the secret society's political arm, the American Party.

Over the next fifty years, state after state followed suit, ending schools of choice and ceding the field to a new government monopoly. There was one powerful exception to this: the children who could afford to be privately educated. It's important to note that the underlying premise of Prussian schooling is that the government is the true parent of children—the state is sovereign over the family. At the most extreme pole of this notion is the idea that biological parents are really the enemies of their own children, not to be trusted.

How did a Prussian system of dumbing children down take hold in American schools? Thousands and thousands of young men from prominent American families journeyed to Prussia and other parts of Germany during the nineteenth century and brought home the PhD degree to a nation in which such a credential was unknown. These men pre-empted the top positions in the academic world, in corporate research, and in government, to the point where opportunity was almost closed to those who had not studied in Germany, or who were not the direct disciples of a German PhD, as John Dewey was the disciple of G. Stanley Hall at Johns Hopkins.

Virtually every single one of the founders of American schooling had made the pilgrimage to Germany, and many of these men wrote widely circulated reports praising the Teutonic methods. Horace Mann's famous "Seventh Report" of 1844, still available in large libraries, was perhaps the most important of these. By 1889, a little more than a hundred years ago, the crop was ready for harvest. In that year the U.S. Commissioner of Education, William Torrey Harris, assured a railroad magnate, Collis Huntington, that American schools were "scientifically designed" to prevent "over-education" from happening. The average American would be content with his humble role in life, said the commissioner, because he would not be tempted to think about any other role. My guess is that Harris meant he would not be able to think about any other role.

In 1896, the famous John Dewey, then at the University of Chicago, said that independent, self-reliant people were a counterproductive anachronism in the collective society of the future. In modern society, said Dewey, people would be defined by their associations—not by their own individual accomplishments. In such a world, people who read too well or too early are dangerous because they become privately empowered, they know too much, and know how to find out what they don't know by themselves, without consulting experts.

Dewey said the great mistake of traditional pedagogy was to make reading and writing constitute the bulk of early schoolwork. He advocated that the phonics method of teaching reading be abandoned and replaced by the whole word method, not because the latter was more efficient (he admitted that it was less efficient) but because independent thinkers were produced by hard books, thinkers who cannot be socialized very easily. By socialization, Dewey meant a program of social objectives administered by the best social thinkers in government. This was a giant step on the road to state socialism, the form pioneered in Prussia, and it is a vision radically disconnected with the American past, its historic hopes and dreams.

Dewey's former professor and close friend, G. Stanley Hall, said this at about the same time, "Reading should no longer be a fetish. Little attention should be paid to reading." Hall was one of the three men most responsible for building a gigantic administrative infrastructure over the classroom. How enormous that structure really became can only be understood by comparisons: New York State, for instance, employs more school administrators than all of the European Economic Community nations combined.

Once you think that the control of conduct is what schools are about, the word "reform" takes on a very particular meaning. It means making adjustments to the machine so that young subjects will not twist and turn so, while their minds and bodies are being scientifically controlled. Helping kids to use their minds better is beside the point.

Bertrand Russell once observed that American schooling was among the most radical experiments in human history, that America was deliberately denying its children the tools of critical thinking. When you want to teach children to think, you begin by treating them seriously when they are little, giving them responsibilities, talking to them candidly, providing privacy and solitude for them, and making them readers and thinkers of significant thoughts from the beginning. That's if you want to teach them to think. There is no evidence that this has been a state purpose since the start of compulsion schooling.

When Friedrich Froebel, the inventor of kindergarten in nineteenth century Germany, fashioned his idea, he did not have a "garden for children" in mind, but a metaphor of teachers as gardeners and children as the vegetables. Kindergarten was created to be a way to break the influence of mothers on their children. I note with interest the growth of daycare in the United States and the repeated urgings to extend school downward to include four-year-olds. The movement toward state socialism is not some historical curiosity but a powerful dynamic force in the world around us. It is fighting for its life against those forces which would, through vouchers or tax credits, deprive it of financial lifeblood, and it has countered this thrust with a demand for even more control over children's lives, and even more money to pay for the extended school day and year that this control requires.

A movement as visibly destructive to individuality, family, and community as government-system schooling has been might be expected to collapse in the face of its dismal record, coupled with an increasingly aggressive shakedown of the taxpayer, but this has not happened. The explanation is largely found in the transformation of schooling from a simple service to families and towns to an enormous, centralized corporate enterprise.

While this development has had a markedly adverse effect on people and on our democratic traditions, it has made schooling the single largest employer in the United States and the largest granter of contracts next to the Defence Department. Both of these low-visibility phenomena provide monopoly schooling with powerful political friends, publicists, advocates, and other useful allies. This is a large part of the explanation why no amount of failure ever changes things in schools, or changes them for very long. School people are in a position to outlast any storm and to keep short-attention-span public scrutiny thoroughly confused.

An overview of the short history of this institution reveals a pattern marked by intervals of public outrage, followed by enlargement of the monopoly in every case.

After nearly thirty years spent inside a number of public schools, some considered good, some bad, I feel certain that management cannot clean its own house. It relentlessly marginalizes all significant change. There are no incentives for the "owners" of the structure to reform it, nor can there be without outside competition.

It cannot be overemphasized that no body of theory exists to define accurately the way children learn, or which learning is of most worth. By pretending the existence of such, we have cut ourselves off from the information and innovation that only a real market can provide. Fortunately our national situation has been so favorable, so dominant through most of our history, that the margin of error afforded has been vast.

But the future is not so clear. Violence, narcotic addictions, divorce, alcoholism, loneliness—all these are but tangible measures of a poverty in education. Surely schools, as the institutions monopolizing the daytimes of childhood, can be called to account for this. In a democracy, the final judges cannot be experts, but only the people.

Trust the people, give them choices, and the school nightmare will vanish in a generation.

Learning? Yes, of course. Education? No, thanks.

Aaron Falbel

Aaron is still figuring out how to live a decent life in an absurd society. In the interim, he works at various organic farms in western Massachusetts and at his local public library. He had the great fortune of knowing both John Holt and Ivan Illich personally, both of whom have profoundly affected the course of his life.

In 1982, a British interviewer asked John Holt how he defined the word "education." He responded: "It's not a word I personally use ... The word 'education' is a word much used, and different people mean different things by it. But on the whole, it seems to me what most people mean by 'education' has got some ideas built into it or contains certain assumptions, and one of them is that learning is an activity which is separate from the rest of life and done best of all when we are not doing anything else, and best of all where nothing else is done—learning places, places especially constructed for learning. Another assumption is that education is a designed process in which some people do things to other people or get other people to do things which will presumably be for their own good. Education means that some A is doing something to somebody else B. I guess that, basically, is what most people understand education to be about."

The interviewer pressed John further: "Very well, but what is your definition?" John replied, "I don't know of any definition of it that would seem to me to be acceptable. I wrote a book called *Instead of Education*, and what I mean by this [title] is instead of this designed process which is carried on in specially constructed places under various kinds of bribe and threat. I don't know what single word I'd put [in its place]. I would talk about a process in which we become more informed, intelligent, curious, competent, skillful, aware by our interaction with the world around us, because of the mainstream of life, so to speak. In other words, I learn a great deal, but I do it in the process of living, working, playing, being with friends. There is no division in my life between learning, work, play, etc. These things are all one. I don't have a word which I could easily put in the place of 'education,' unless it might be 'living.'"

I wrote the following statement at the request of Ivan Illich to try to explain the difference between learning and education. I realize that "education" is a difficult word to pin down—some people may use it in the way that I use the word "learning." But I believe that John Holt is right in saying that most people use "education" to refer to some kind of *treatment*. (Even "self-education" can reflect this: a self-administered treatment.) It is this usage that I am contrasting with learning, and this idea of people needing treatment, whether carried out in schools or homes or wherever, that I wish to call into question.

✳ ✳ ✳

Many people use the words "learning" and "education" more or less interchangeably. But a moment's reflection reveals that they are not at all the same. I invite you to take this moment and reflect with me on this idea.

Learning is like breathing. It is a natural, human activity: it is part of being alive. A person who is active, curious, who explores the world using all his or her senses, who meets life with energy and enthusiasm—as all babies do—is learning. Our ability to learn, like our ability to breathe, does not need to be improved or tampered with. It is utter nonsense, not to mention deeply insulting, to say that people need to be taught how to learn or how to think. We are born knowing how to do these things. All that is needed is an interesting, accessible, intelligible world, and a chance to play a meaningful part in it.

If the air is polluted, then it can become difficult to breathe. We cough, wheeze, and gasp for air. Similarly, if our social environment is polluted, it can become difficult to learn. Today our social environment is thoroughly polluted by education—a designed process in which one group of people (educators, social engineers, people shapers) tries to make another group (those who are to be educated) learn something, usually without their consent, because they (the educators) think it will be good for them. In other words, education is forced, seduced, or coerced learning—except that you can't really make another person learn something that he or she doesn't want to learn, which is why education doesn't work *and has never worked*. People have always learned things, but education is a relatively recent innovation, and a deeply destructive one at that.

It is ironic that education, carried out by well-meaning people hoping to produce or enhance learning, ends up attacking learning. But this is precisely what happens, despite all the good intentions. In the climate of education, learning is cut off and disembedded from active life. It is divorced from personal curiosity and is thus profoundly denatured. Learning shrivels as it becomes the result of a process controlled, manipulated, and governed by others. It deteriorates into empty actions done under the pressure of bribe and threat, greed and fear. We all know this to be true from our own "educational" experiences.

When I speak of education, I am not referring only to that which goes on in schools. Today education takes place in many guises and settings: through the mass media, in the workplace, and in the home. We adopt the educative stance when we feel it is our right and duty to manipulate others for their own good.

Let me be clear: I am not against all forms of teaching. It is a privilege and a joy to help someone do something he or she has freely chosen to do, provided that we are invited to help. I am against unasked-for, I'm-doing-this-for-your-own-good teaching.

I do have a problem with professional teachers—people who try to turn whatever knowledge they might have into capital, into a commodity. I want to live in a society where casual, asked-for teaching is a matter of courtesy, not a quick way to make a buck. Sure, there are times when it is proper to compensate a teacher for his or her time and effort. But the new educational supermarkets, which offer courses (for a fee) on everything from breastfeeding to sensitivity training, are a step in the wrong direction. Though such courses are not compulsory, they end up convincing people that learning through living is inferior to instruction. For instance, why learn to diaper a baby by watching Granny do it when you can receive "parental education" from a professional parental instructor?

Most of us have forgotten what it was like to follow our own noses, to ask our own questions and find our own answers. Years of educational treatment have convinced us that learning is, and can only be, the result of teaching. We grow up into adults who insist that our children "receive" an education. We trust neither ourselves nor our children to learn.

The last thing I want to do is improve education: rather I want to escape its noxious fumes, to offer my help to anyone seeking similar detoxification, and to clean up the environment where I can. If you are interested in joining me, there are some steps that you and I can take that will help clear the air of education and create a cleaner social environment supportive of learning.

First, let us rid our own minds of the prejudice that views others who opt out of educational treatment as "delinquents," "failures," or "dropouts." Let us view them instead as wise refuseniks, as conscientious objectors to a crippling and dehumanizing process. Let us act in a way that removes the stigma currently hanging over the heads of educational underconsumers.

Second, if we agree that children are good at learning, let our attitude and dealings with young people bear this out. Let us resist the temptation to become educators, to rub the noses of the young in our greater experience by adopting the roles of teacher, helper, and instructor at the drop of a hat. Let us trust people to figure things out for themselves, unless they specifically ask for our help. (As it turns out, they ask frequently. Small children, whose curiosity has not been deadened by education, are usually brimming over with questions.) The nature of the toxicity inherent in education is precisely that so much of the teaching that goes on is unasked for. Let us endeavor to rid our own behavior of unasked-for help.

Third, let us not discriminate against the uncertified when it comes to the matter of employment. Several landmark studies have shown that there is no correlation between educational training and performance on the job. (See especially Ivar Berg's *The Great Training Robbery*, Beacon Press, 1971.) If we must assess competence for a given job, let us assess it as directly as we can, and not conflate competence with length of sitting done in educational institutions. We can also deflate the value of educational currency by refusing to talk about our own educational credentials. Take them off your résumé! Demand that others judge you by your actual talents and accomplishments, as you would judge others.

Fourth, let us do our own part to create a more open and accessible society, where knowledge and tools are not locked up in institutions or hoarded as closely guarded secrets, by offering (not imposing) to share our skills with others. Take on an apprentice. Hang a shingle outside your home describing what you do. Let your friends and neighbors know that you are making such an offer to any serious and committed person.

Fifth, let us outlaw exploitative labor, not child labor, the prohibition of which currently denies many forms of meaningful participation to the young. This will help end the policy of age discrimination, which mandates that the young be taught about the world before they are allowed to learn from it by participating in it.

Sixth, let us support libraries, museums, theatres, and other voluntary, non-coercive community institutions. (Many libraries, for example, are open only during working hours, when only those with the luxury of a research stipend may use them. With more support, they could be open evenings and weekends.) Additionally, let us create more spaces in our communities where young and old (and those in between), can get together to pursue unprogrammed activities of all sorts: arts, crafts, sports, music, hobbies, discussion groups, etc. Let us end the policy of shunting young and old into separate institutions "for their own good."

Finally, think up more ideas of your own! As a society that has been addicted to education for several generations, we have lost the ability to imagine what it might be like to grow up and live in a world free of pedagogical manipulation.

If you agree with this statement, or just find it provocative, make copies and discuss it with your family, friends, neighbors, and fellow workers. Send a copy to distant friends and invite them to do the same.

Unschooled Kids'
Comments II:

3. Those of you in schools now (or who have been in the past), how does your non-traditional background effect you in a regular school environment? Does it make school harder, easier, weirder? If you are planning on going to school, do you think not doing the regular thing will be a help or a burden?

Fyona DeBalasi Brown: When I started grade ten at a 1,700-student high school I was ludicrously nervous.

Not only were the numbers huge but I had never completed a curriculum course or done an academic test. I had been told by friends who had moved from alternative backgrounds into regular school that getting good grades wasn't difficult as long as you paid attention; my experience has been that it isn't difficult to get good grades, as long as you are willing to give up all other aspects of your life.

For my first four months of Grade Ten, I worked hard, got good grades, made Honour Role, and participated in a very intense theatre program. By the time winter break came along, I was completely burnt out. The day before school was to begin again, I had a total breakdown, I realized I wasn't up for another four months of full-time school.

I would now call what I'm doing "deschooling school." I go to three classes which I particularly enjoy, and I have the opportunity to get more out of my classes because I'm focusing on only the three rather than the traditional eight. I can say quite confidently that my alternative background has given me a huge advantage over other students; I have good self esteem, I'm not constantly stressed about grades and unfinished work, and most of all I have the opportunity to and have practiced making my own choices. I've heard many teachers say that school is not so much about the curriculum, but that it "teaches people to learn." I thoroughly disagree. The regular school system instead teaches students to resent learning, and to ignore the important learning that goes on outside the classroom.

Mari Piggott: I have never been enrolled in a regular school, but I think if I ever did go I would have lots of social skills (like skills in resolving conflict and working with people). I think it would be hard to be so coerced and not have so much of a say in my education.

Sadie Couture: I go to Templeton Mini School currently and I am really liking it. The program is an "academically advanced" program within Templeton Secondary. When I came, I realized that I had a real competitive streak and that I hated doing badly on something. I think psychologically, it makes school easier for me, as I am not doing this for my parents, I am doing it for me. It also helps that I chose the school myself and am not being forced into anything. At first, school was really hard and really weird. I didn't really know how to act or what to do. Math was really hard for me at first, but academically everything else was fine, and eventually Math worked itself out.

Maizy Thorvaldson: I went to a mainstream school for a little while and at first I had an excellent teacher, so it was great (even though I thought she was talking gibberish sometimes).

Gen Robertson: I think in high school, my non-traditional background affected me hugely. All my peers had learned how to play the school game way back in Grade Two or Three. Not many kids really cared about school anymore. They knew how to ride the line, suck up to the teachers, and generally get by without doing much at all. Partly because of my nature, and in part due to my naiveté about the system I was in, I did not have a developed bullshit filter. I worked so hard without much discretion between what I actually liked and what I didn't actually care about. I think at the time I thought I was just an avid learner and everyone else had lost their love for learning. Perhaps this is a small bit true, but I think it was more about the fact that I had not learned to play the required game. Considering I don't remember anything from those two years except for some Spanish, I think that my true love for learning was getting hidden away somewhere and replaced by these meaningless, short-lived feelings of accomplishment after writing a test or an essay. The relief that comes when you realize you can forget everything you just learned.

However, post-secondary education was a very different story. A year ago, I graduated from an amazing two-year studio art program. There, I found that my enthusiasm for learning was still intact. However, some of the kids around me, many of them having just graduated from high school, seemed very stuck. They had learned how to get by doing very little, and now could not turn that habit off. Many of them had decided to come to art school because they had a genuine desire to follow their interest/talent, yet they were treating self-directed art projects as if they were uninteresting high school essay assignments. It seemed to me like they had forgotten that they came on their own accord, to develop further as artists. At that point in my life, I felt incredibly grateful that my independent thought and work ethic had not been squeezed out of me by years of repetitive learning.

David Gagnon: Having never gone from alternative to mainstream, the post-secondary situation is the best answer I have for this question. I am fairly certain that my alternative school experiences will be an asset in a post-secondary environment. I have seen this be the case with most of my old school peers and it makes sense. Having been given responsibility for my life early on, I have already had plenty of experience with what that means. College and university dropout rates are pretty high, not surprising given that many folks registering are using that as their first experience in making a big decision.

4. How has your non-traditional approach to schooling affected your relationships with other kids?

Daisy Couture: No one has ever cared. I'm just me to them, why would they care? I'm just another kid.

Maya Motoi: I have almost never had friends living close to me, except when I was little, so I usually see my close friends about three times a year and write letters often. None of the few kids living close to me in rural Japan were my friends or people who I hung out with, except for when I went to school with them. But I rarely ever feel lonely because, while I no doubt have fewer friends than most people, I am sure that the ones I have are a lot closer to me than the many friends everybody else has.

Maizy Thorvaldson: I am a very social person. I have friends who are eighteen because we are not restricted to classrooms. We are much freer to choose our friends. My Best Friend is only nine and I am twelve and we have another close friend who is fourteen. I think that's very cool!

David Gagnon: I certainly felt some of that "you're dumb cause you don't go to real school" kind of crap from other kids. As a result, I didn't really interact with other kids from traditional school. At present I tend to interact largely with older adults or other young people who were also deschooled. I have a handful of friends my age from traditional schooling, but not many.

Mari Piggott: In truth, I don't feel like it's made me a lot different than the other kids, like when I talk with or hang out with them. Sometimes I feel really weird when they talk about what they have to do at their school because I don't really have to do anything if I don't want to at mine.

Gen Robertson: As a young child, I think I struggled a bit justifying my "weird" school to other kids. A couple of my best friends did not go to alternative school, and didn't understand what it was all about. I think they were influenced by their parents, who did not agree with my mother's approach to educating my brother and me. Anyways, at a very early age, I remember my friends quizzing me on stuff they were doing in school. "Genny, can you do long division? How do you spell "kaleidoscope"? What were the names of King Henry the Eighth's wives?" etc. I remember explaining that my school did not follow the same prescribed curriculum that theirs did, but I think the constant questioning and testing made me feel like I always had to defend something.

The last time I remember feeling really singled out for my alternative upbringing was in Grade Ten, while I was at Trek. I was walking through the soccer field during a lunch break with my friend Claire. We were having a long conversation about alternative education and deschooling. She looked at me and said "Let's put it this way: You are a success story in a sea of failures." I remember thinking that I was tired of defending myself and my views, and wondering if I would always feel like I had to prove that my school was not just a hippie school for losers and dropouts who couldn't play the game. And if I didn't "succeed," would my education be to blame in other people's eyes?

Now as a young adult I never feel like I have to prove anything, and none of my traditionally educated friends ever question the validity of my education. Most of the time when I talk about Windsor House to people who don't know about it, they are fascinated and end up saying that they wish they had the freedom I did.

To answer this question in a whole other way: Many of the kids that did go to Windsor House with me are still good friends. I think there is a strong bond between us because we did really get to do some crazy, amazing things together that you would *never* get to do in a regular school. With these kids, I never feel like I have to explain anything. They know me really well, even if we don't see each other all the time anymore, or we don't have much in common. There is a certain familial comfort that hovers around the room when we get together.

Nigel Boeur: I have friends in and out of school, and I feel at ease in lots of different social situations. If it has affected me at all, I think it was in a good way.

Russ Gendron: In high school, I remember some students being standoffish to different ways of thinking such as: school with no homework, choosing every class you take, and having a friendly personal relationship with your teachers. However, many of my friends expressed feelings of loss and missing out when I would tell them of my past schooling, as if it were impossible for them to ever have something so good.

Most of the conflict I came across was with teachers. Many times, we would disagree and it was new for them to hear a young person state their point or a challenge, what some teachers would call, "talking back." That always sucked. Going from an environment of total encouragement to a place where your voice didn't want to be heard was a shitty transition. The unfortunate result of this is learning how to "suck it up" and realize you're in the "real world" now. I should point out that this is not always the case; the public system does have an abundance of awesome, hard working, and fun teachers who are a joy to be around.

Sadie Couture: It's hard not coming from a traditional schooling background and I found it hard to really connect with some people my age at school. It's hard for them to realize where you are coming from and your background. Of course, I also find I tend to gravitate towards older friends/people. Maybe this is because of my personality or maybe my non-traditional schooling background.

5. How about your relationships with your parents and family?

Nigel Boeur: Unschooling has had a huge impact on my relationship with my parents, because I got to spend way more time with them than a normal kid would. My parents have been incredibly supportive of all the things I've been interested in throughout the years, and even though they wouldn't always let me do exactly what I wanted, they were always willing to explain "why." They never used the reward system, which I'm really grateful for because now, I participate in things because I want to, not because of the prize at the end. I also have two awesome unschooling sibs that have always been there for me.

Russ Gendron: My parents were the ones who tossed me into the alternative system, so they were into it most of the time. Sometimes a parent or a family member (a distant aunt or some other random relative) would express concerns about my future and worry on my behalf about how successful I would turn out to be. No biggy.

Maya Motoi: I don't know most of my extended family very well, but I feel like I am unusually close to my parents, especially my mom who doesn't seem so much like a parent, but more like a close friend to me.

David Gagnon: My parents did a pretty good job of doing the research to back what they were doing. My dad is a teacher and comes from an all-teacher family. I don't doubt that they gave him a hard time for pulling me out of school and I don't doubt that he held his ground well.

The flip side of that is that I know my parents were pretty scared a lot of the time. When I was fourteen and still not reading I know it was hard on them. Despite their feelings, they sure did a great job of (almost) never letting it show. They were behind me all the way, which was worth more than I think I will ever know.

Gen Robertson: My mother got her teaching certificate in order to become a teacher at Windsor House. My brother attended and my sister still goes there. Our entire circle of family friends, neighbours, and acquaintances are all somehow involved in the Windsor House or the home schooling community. My mother believes in the alternative deschooling philosophy with conviction, as do most of the people I bump into on the street, and am involved with in life in general. It is nice to know that there is an unspoken understanding and no need to prove or explain anything. It is also comforting to know that my peers and I have a huge amount of support from almost every older person that is in our lives.

My grandmother is the only adult that I never felt supported me. Every time we saw our grandmother as children, she would ask us questions like "So, what are you learning in math class right now? How are your grades? When do you get your end of year report cards?" She spent at least ten years unable to admit to herself that we didn't get report cards. I think she's finally warming up to alternative education now, fifteen years too late.

From Untouchables to Conscientious Objectors

Daniel Grego

Dan is the Executive Director of TransCenter for Youth, Inc., the non-profit agency that operates Shalom High School, the Northwest Opportunities Vocational Academy (NOVA), El Puente High School for Science, Math, and Technology, The CITIES Project High School, and the Technical Assistance & Leadership Center (TALC New Vision) in Milwaukee. One of his major interests is exploring the confluence of the ideas of Mahatma Gandhi, Ivan Illich, and Wendell Berry. He lives with his wife, choreographer Debra Loewen, and their daughter, Caitlin Grego, on a small farm in the Rock River watershed in Dodge County, Wisconsin.

1.

As the sun rose, I saw Nick in a new light. Away from the classroom, he was relaxed and amiable. On the pier extending into Lake Michigan from the McKinley Marina, he was in his element. He was an accomplished fisherman. I was a novice. So now our roles were reversed. He was the teacher. I was the student. We met that morning so he could show me how to cast with spoons and spinners in an attempt to catch lake or rainbow or brown trout or coho salmon—and so I could mull over a decision I had to make.

I do not remember catching any fish that day. But I do remember enjoying the sunrise, the quiet, the vastness of the lake, and getting to know a little better a fellow traveler on this earth.

Nick and I were first introduced the year before (in 1980), when I began teaching math at Shalom High School. Shalom had been founded seven years before as an alternative school for what were then called "marginal students," those students who were not succeeding in traditional high schools and who were potential dropouts. The school survived on a shoestring budget and depended on volunteers and people willing to work for low wages and no benefits. Not surprisingly, there was high staff turnover. When my wife and I moved to Milwaukee so she could pursue graduate studies at the University of Wisconsin, Shalom had an opening for a math teacher. On our first day in town, I applied for the job. I had previous experience teaching "marginal students" in the Chicago area and when Shalom's personnel committee discovered I enjoyed working with joukers, jiggers, kippers, tickers, mitchers, plunkers, scivers, school skippers, attendance spoilers, excusers, and dirty dodgers, I was hired on the spot.[1]

My first day in the classroom that Fall was right out of a Hollywood movie, something like *Stand and Deliver* or *Dangerous Minds*. About eighty students were enrolled at that time. They had all started ninth grade in one of the large public high schools but had stopped attending for one reason or another. Some were bored. Some were lost. Some felt unsafe. Some just could not tolerate it any longer.

On a given day, about three-quarters of the students enrolled at Shalom dropped by the school. Most of them were African-Americans, but there were Latinos, Native Americans, and some students from the German families who had hung on in the neighborhood. Nick was from this latter group.

I had been hired to teach algebra and geometry, but many of the students had not mastered basic arithmetic. Nick had already taken algebra at his former high school and although he understood it, he had failed the class because he had refused, as he put it, "to kiss the teacher's ass." That first day, he sauntered into my room, found a desk by the window, and slouched so low in his chair he was more lying down than sitting.

I gave the students a diagnostic test to find out what they knew. They interpreted it as an attempt to expose their ignorance and to embarrass them. Nick wrote his name on the test paper and that was all. During those first weeks his main contributions to my class, on those occasions when he was present, were obnoxious remarks. The thought crossed my mind that the best way to deal with him would be to hang him out the second story window by his ankles. But being a disciple of Mahatma Gandhi, I decided against it.

One day, after he had been particularly disagreeable, I asked Nick to stay after class. I inquired about his behavior. At first, he was reluctant to say anything. Finally, he told me about his previous algebra class and some of his feelings about school. He hated it. He hated being cooped up inside all day. At the age of sixteen, he had "waived out" of public school. (In Wisconsin at that time, children were required to attend school until they were eighteen unless they had earned their diplomas or had formally "waived out," which they could do at sixteen.) Nick was one of dozens of students in those days who told me that on their sixteenth birthday, they had been met at the door of their high school by an administrator who explained to them that if they signed a waiver form, one of which the administrator just happened to have with him, they could legally drop out of school. Nick signed.

He had enrolled at Shalom under pressure from his family who knew about the school because one of his older siblings had attended. Repeating the conventional wisdom, they told him he would need some kind of credential to get a good job. He was just biding his time there until he figured out what he wanted to do.

I asked him if he understood the material we were covering in class. He said he did, so I tried to enlist his help in explaining it to some of the other students who did not.

"I'll think about it," he said and started for the door.

As he was leaving, an inspiration came to me.

"Nick," I called after him, "student government elections are coming up. Why don't you run for president?"

He was startled by my suggestion. Later, I learned that, in all his years of schooling, no one had ever asked him to do anything like that before. Most of the attention he had received from teachers and other school personnel had been in the form of punishment. His *modus operandi* in school had been to disrupt class and then affect indifference. This made him look doubly cool in the eyes of his friends.

"I'll think about it," he said and left.

Following the Hollywood script, Nick decided to run for president and won. He started to come to my class more often and helped his classmates with their math. He even made the honor roll once or twice. I do not remember him ever sitting up straight in a chair, however.

After my first year of teaching at Shalom, I was asked to become the school's director—a combination of principal, spokesperson, fundraiser, bookkeeper, personnel manager, teacher, counselor, and janitor. I hesitated. In the school's first eight years, there had been six directors. Sustaining alternative schools for "marginal students" was not easy, then or now. I was not sure I wanted the responsibility or the stress. I was not sure my wife and I would stay in Milwaukee after she finished graduate school. I was not sure it was what I was called to do.

I sought the advice of family and friends, board members and staff. I also asked Nick if he thought I should take the job. He wondered if I liked to fish. I told him I had never been fishing, but that I would be interested in trying.

"I always do my best thinking when I'm fishing," he explained.

So we agreed to rendezvous the next morning on the pier at the McKinley Marina. Nick lent me a rod and reel, showed me how to cast and how to set the hook if I got a bite. After a while, we started talking. He told me about himself. He said he enjoyed working with his hands. He enjoyed taking things apart and putting them back together. He loved being outdoors. He loved to hunt and to fish. He dreamed someday of owning a cabin in northern Wisconsin, a part of the world he referred to simply as "up north."

When we grew quiet again, I thought about Nick and his classmates. Each one of them had special gifts and interests, hopes and fears, joys and sorrows. And all of them had been tossed aside by the System as uneducable failures or troublemakers. Shalom's eighty students were like thousands more in Milwaukee in the same circumstances, the young men and women who today are labeled "at risk."

In Milwaukee, as in other large cities in the United States, for every ten bright, curious, enthusiastic children who enter the System, only about five graduate.[2] As I thought more about this plight, I was haunted by the following questions: Are the children (and their families) who do not make it through the System still part of the "public"? If they are, why are educational resources not made available to them in some other way? What happens to those other five kids?

As the sun rose, the lake began sparkling. I looked at Nick whose face glowed in the early light.

"I might be crazy," I said. "But I think I'm going to take the job."

"You won't get an argument from me," my friend grinned. "Not about that first part anyway."

2.

A few years after I began my tenure as director of Shalom High School, I attended a conference about "at risk" children in Madison, Wisconsin. The keynote speaker was Gary Wehlage who was at the time the Associate Director of the Center on Organization and Restructuring of Schools at the University of Wisconsin. Wehlage told his audience that the basic question that had to be asked about "at risk" students was why so many of them dropped out of school. He suggested two possible answers: either something was wrong with the students or something was wrong with the schools.

For many years, I assumed the problem was the schools. They were too big and impersonal. The curriculum was arbitrary and irrelevant to the students' lives. The pedagogy favored students with certain intelligences and learning styles and frustrated others. There was little opportunity for students to do real work and have it recognized in their communities.

One of Shalom's students was once asked by a prominent politician why so many young people drop out of school. He thought for a moment and then responded: "I think you're asking the wrong question. Given what high school is, the question you should ask is why anyone bothers to stay." After further reflection, he added, "I guess some students tolerate school better than others."

Schools have never served poor and minority children well. As Colin Greer noted in *The Great School Legend*:

> The rate of school failure among the urban poor, in fact, has been consistently and remarkably high since before 1900. The truth is that the immigrant children dropped out in great numbers—to fall back on the customs and skills their families brought with them to America. It was in spite of, and *not* because of, compulsory public education that some eventually made their way.[3]

For many years, I used Wehlage's question as a way to introduce the work we were doing at Shalom. The schools were the problem and we were part of a movement to create alternatives to them.

It never occurred to me that Wehlage had omitted a third possibility. Perhaps the reason the schools fail so many students is that they are doing exactly what they were designed to do: sort people into winners and losers, perpetuate an elite group to run the world, and maintain a class of "untouchables" to complete the shitwork, the dirty work, the work Wendell Berry has called "fundamental and inescapable" that no one else wants to do. And since we persist in our desire "to rise above the sweat and bother of taking care of anything—of ourselves, of each other, or of our country," some method for assigning these tasks had to be invented.[4]

One of the "at risk" students Murray Levin interviewed at Greater Egleston Community High School in Boston understood the sorting function of schools:

> What do we do when we finish here? Slap hamburgers at Mc-Donald's or Burger King? Clean up shit at hospitals? Drive buses? Janitor? Handyman? Dealer? They gotta get this shit done. Who going to do it? We're at the bottom of the pyramid so we do this. And for them to stay at the top, we got to stay at the bottom.[5]

Whether compulsory schooling was *intended* to divide students into winners and losers or not, that has been its inevitable effect, as has been pointed out by Ivan Illich and Everett Reimer among others. Twenty years after he published *Deschooling Society*, Ivan Illich summarized his findings:

> In the minds of the people who financed and engineered them, schools were established to increase equality. I discovered that they really acted as a lottery system in which those who didn't make it didn't just lose what they had paid in but were also stigmatized as inferior for the rest of their lives.[6]

Illich's critique was continued by John Holt and more recently by Madhu Suri Prakash and Gustavo Esteva. The latter expose the duplicity of those of us engaged in schooling:

> Educators continue espousing radical democracy, justice, equality, and excellence as the goal of their project, while enjoying the privileges of the global educational system, designed to spew and vomit out millions of Ds, dropouts, and failures while providing to a few a socially recognized certificate—a *patente de corso*. This legitimizes the As and other "successes" in their disposition to impose, control, and oppress, for consuming at the expense of the majorities they doom to the life of failures.[7]

John Holt concluded his book, *Instead of Education,* with his characteristic directness:

> Education—compulsory schooling, compulsory learning—is a
> tyranny and a crime against the human mind and spirit. Let all
> those escape it who can, any way they can.[8]

3.

After thirty years of working with "at risk" teenagers in Chicago and Milwaukee, I have come to the conclusion that Holt was right. Compulsory schooling is a tyranny. I understand now that the educational alternatives and alternative schools to which I have given so much time and energy "cover up the fact that the project of education is fundamentally flawed and indecent."[9] In spite of the best intentions of reformers, schooling will continue to be "a worldwide soul-shredder that junks the majority and burdens an elite to govern it."[10]

But I am terribly conflicted about these conclusions, for I have looked into the eyes of hundreds of young men and women like Nick who are stuck in *this* society and who have been designated "untouchables." And as long as children are still compelled by law to attend school and can be harassed by the police (and their parents fined) if they fail to do so; as long as economic opportunities are divvied up according to school credentials (even though there is no evidence linking successful job performance with school performance); as long as people are taxed to pay for a System that many of them cannot use because it continues "to spew and vomit out millions" of children, places like Shalom can be justified.

I have attempted to escape my own cognitive dissonance by challenging the definitions of "education" employed by both its defenders and its critics. The philosophy of Mahatma Gandhi and the writings of Wendell Berry have led me to consider "education" not as an individual accomplishment, not as some *thing* that a person "gets" (nor as something done to someone for his or her own good), but as a community practice.

A more benign conception of "education" is to think of it as the process by which people become responsibly mature members of their communities. In non-industrial cultures, this educational process is inseparable from the life of the community. Children are "educated" by the example of their elders, by stories, by initiation rituals, and by performing the daily tasks required for subsistence. Schools are not necessary for education defined in this way, although communities might decide to use them as tools. *Compulsory schooling*, which is inextricably connected to what Esteva and Prakash call "The Global Project," the blight that is devastating communities around the world, clearly thwarts the educational process.[11]

The schools I administer in Milwaukee—Shalom, the Northwest Opportunities Vocational Academy (NOVA), El Puente High School, and The CITIES Project High School—attempt to embed their activities as much as possible in their communities. In addition to academic work, the students plant gardens in vacant lots and share their produce with the hungry, organize food and clothing donations for the homeless, visit the incarcerated, document the stories of elders in nursing homes, tutor younger children at nearby elementary schools, write and produce plays, create art exhibits for the public, initiate neighborhood clean-ups and recycling programs, conduct voter registration drives, and advocate for educational opportunities for other "at risk" children. Elders from the community are invited into the schools to share their knowledge, to mentor the students, and to guide their rites of passage into adulthood.

In the mid-1980s, I convened a philosophy seminar at Shalom in which I asked the students to analyze "The Global Project." (Back then, we spoke of the monstrous abstraction called "The Economy.") By the end of the course, my young friends concluded they had three choices: they could resign themselves to the status of "untouchables" and endure, if they could, the crushing weight of "The Global Project" on their backs; they could learn "to play the game" of schooling and make their way into the exploiter class and pay (or force) someone else to do their shitwork for them; or they could rebel and become conscientious objectors to the System, using it if and when they chose for their own purposes.

Of course, the authorities who monitor schools like Shalom consider only students who make the second choice as "positive outcomes." And Shalom has had many of those. But I have taken greater personal satisfaction from knowing those young people who decided to redefine themselves from "untouchables" to conscientious objectors whether they graduated or not.

Nick's story did not have a Hollywood ending. After a couple of years, he dropped out of Shalom. He cannot be counted, therefore, as one of the school's "successes." But I think he made the third choice. Nick used Shalom to avoid the truant officers and the police and to placate his parents until he was ready to leave home. He made some good friends. He thought deeply about what he wanted out of life. When he quit, he may not have known what he was called to do, but he knew he had tolerated school long enough.

A few years ago, Nick stopped by to see me. He told me he is married with two children. He has a job he loves: building motorcycles for Harley-Davidson. He is saving money to buy his cabin "up north." And, on his days off, he takes his kids fishing.

Notes

1. For various names for truants, see: Opie, Iona and Peter. 2001. *The Lore and Language of Schoolchildren*. New York: New York Review of Books. pp. 371–372.

2. Dropout data are difficult to analyze and compare because school officials are so adept at fudging the numbers and nebulously and variously defining "dropout." A more accurate way to capture the problem of school failure is to look at what is being called "the cohort survival rate." Pick a given year's ninth grade class and check to see how many graduated four years later. For example, in the 1992–93 school year, the Milwaukee Public Schools reported 6,874 students were enrolled in ninth grade. Four years later, in 1996, 2,434 students or 35% of the original number graduated. According to *City Kids Count*, a 1997 publication of the Annie E. Casey Foundation, Milwaukee's dropout rate was 17th among the 50 major cities in the United States. There were 33 cities where the dropout problem was worse than in Milwaukee

3. Greer, Colin. 1972. *The Great School Legend*. New York: Basic Books. p. 4. Italics in the original.

4. Berry, Wendell. 1989. *The Hidden Wound*. San Francisco: North Point Press. p. 112.

5. Levin, Murray. 2001. *Teach Me!: Kids Will Learn When Oppression Is the Lesson* (expanded edition). Lanham, MD: Rowman & Littlefield. p. 28.

6. Cayley, David. 1992. *Ivan Illich in Conversation*. Concord, Ontario: Anansi. p. 63.

7. Prakash, Madhu Suri and Esteva, Gustavo. 1998. *Escaping Education: Living as Learning within Grassroots Cultures*. New York: Peter Lang. p. 104.

8. Holt, John. 1976. *Instead of Education*. New York: Dutton. p. 222.

9. Prakash and Esteva, 1998, p. 97

10. Illich, quoted in Prakash and Esteva, 1998, p. 97.

11. Esteva, Gustavo and Prakash, Madhu Suri. 1998. *Grassroots Post-Modernism: Remaking the Soil of Cultures*. London: Zed Books.

Challenging the Popular Wisdom: What Can Families Do?

Geraldine and Gus Lyn-Piluso

The Lyn-Pilusos have been thinking and writing about education, child-rearing and social justice issues for twenty years. They both have doctorates in education and teach undergrad and grad students in education at Goddard College. Their research interests include emancipatory relationships, critical pedagogy, anarchist theory, and the role domestic values play in social change. Gus is avid gardener, a reluctant weightlifter, longtime coach, and a biker. Geraldine is a certified Spinning instructor and personal trainer, is always interested in pushing herself, and is now learning various kinds of dance. They have two daughters, Joei and Caileigh.

Family. What do we talk about when we talk about the family? Our lives—our past or present circumstances, our loves, our hurts, our life choices, and philosophies. A mélange of stories and people and relations, richly diverse, sometimes tender, often not. The nervous (and increasingly nasty) struggle by cultural conservatives to force their own narrow definition of the family on this shifting assortment of living arrangements signifies a bundle of hot-button anxieties: about gender and sexual orientation, abortion, sex, race and class, male privilege. Not coincidentally, these same issues have served to catalyze major modern movements of liberation; consequently, "family values" has become a coded phrase for the home front in the ongoing culture wars.

And "family values" means, of course, kids—precious, obedient, little spittin' images. But the Right's attempt to dictate their retrograde ideology betrays a suspicion that no amount of sentimental rhetoric can hide: a fear that children—the heart of the nuclear family—are potentially radical.

This suspicion is well-founded. Kids, as anyone who takes them seriously can attest, often demonstrate an ability to draw attention to the underlying political dimension of everyday life, to the dubious pretences by which authority, including parental authority, establishes itself.

Without censure, with the room to be confidently inquisitive and direct, kids may discern the fundamentals of social relations by unearthing the root, or radical, details which betray the reality of those relations—reminding us, time and again, of the hidden strangling roots of power from which our society draws its authority. Spying that loose edge, they may just pry it back to ask: Why? Why do my sneakers say "Made in Pakistan"? Why are the sidewalks in this part of town crumbling? Why are we supposed to go to school?

What does this ability mean? It means that children haven't quite consented to a society organized on the basis of oppression, for one thing. It also presents parents and other caregivers with a definite choice. On the one hand, we can induce children to blunt their concerns, to concede to domination as an inevitable and immutable state of affairs in the home or the classroom, and so secure our own rule (and ultimately, hierarchy itself). In short, we can crush the radical potential of childhood the moment it arises.

On the other hand, we may nurture this ability which, as it matures, makes it possible to imagine a better world. Nurture it how? By allowing and encouraging children to challenge any authority which would compel them to surrender their consent.

This means that we commit ourselves to nothing short of a dialogue, since by agitating our certainties with perfectly sensible questions, kids prod us to examine our own authority. They also remind us that, in the face of unjustifiable authority, we adults too often and too easily acquiesce. The result? A cooperative exploration of power, society, and the natural world—an adventure which constitutes deschooling.

Here we ought to distinguish deschooling from homeschooling. Deschooling begins with the radical appraisal of compulsory schooling. In common with other educational reform movements, the inability of the present school system to actually "educate" is exposed. However, deschoolers reject the present schooling system because of its inherently authoritarian nature; and this staunchly anti-authoritarian critique is where deschooling parts ways with the "homeschooling" movement. Many homeschooling families reject the school system, yet maintain authoritarian family structures and in fact implement authoritarian pedagogical techniques within the home. While such families admittedly challenge the school system, the intent of the challenge is to demand that schools adhere more rigidly to their authoritarian ways, in order to annihilate the child's subversive inclinations.

This reactionary position may offer short term advantages, but in the long run it serves to strengthen our hierarchical society. Deschooling does not simply move the school to home—it rejects the school and its authoritarian nature completely. It aims at the full development of human beings who "own" themselves, who are critically conscious, free individuals committed to social transformation.

Deschooling, then, means more than just protecting kids from the coercive policies of the school. It's a way of parenting, a critique of the family, and a genuinely mutual endeavor—requiring a dialogue among parents (or other caregivers) and children, as well as a conscious effort to de-professionalize learning by acknowledging it as a lifelong, cooperative project of questioning and discovery, thinking and rethinking. In stark contrast to the traditional authoritarian family structure, deschooling demands egalitarian relations between parents and kids—a family organization which accommodates the radical curiosity of childhood, even (perhaps especially) when it challenges authority. Parenting, in the deschooling family, becomes a revolutionary activity.

The Challenges of Deschooling

The hurdles deschoolers face are formidable. For instance, working vigorously to discourage kids from questioning anything deeply are institutions of explicit power, such as school and government and capitalist business, which rationalize their exploits with a credo so effective it eventually becomes simple, incontrovertible, common sense. What's common sense? That set of implicit assumptions which is not to be doubted—that bedrock of unyielding and unexamined convictions we may run up against when, for instance, we attempt to explain deschooling to a resistant friend or colleague or grandparent.

"But you've got to think about socialization," we hear, "you've got to think about academics!"—as if the basic childhood activities of learning and socializing depended on state-mandated institutions. Absurd? Of course. Among adults, this impasse—encountered when we question what is generally acknowledged as unquestionable—bears testimony to the power that dominant institutions employ in shaping our view of the world.

Until they're "properly" trained, however, kids don't know what not to question; as a result, their artless queries can cut deep, exposing authority's most damning contradictions. As we've pointed out, this indicates a radical potential in childhood. At the very least, such questions deserve our honest response. Scorned, or deterred, the inquisitive child learns to regard the world as incomprehensible, not worth questioning—and thus unchangeable.

Here the challenges of deschooling become intricate, because, before receiving an answer, children deserve something even more basic: the opportunity to ask the question. We would be naive to consider this a simple, naturally-occurring thing. It takes a good deal of savvy, as well as a sense of humor, to give a child's searing, point-blank curiosity its due; and as we know, occasions for genuine inquiry are routinely obstructed by professionalized education and the corporately-dispensed culture of the various mainstream media, with the goal of confining the child's potentially subversive curiosity to suit their own purposes.

In other words, the opportunity to ask the radical question is the very opportunity these institutions struggle to interrupt; and it is the opportunity that we—as caring adults—ought to provide and nurture, so that curiosity may flourish. Because it forces us to side either with or against institutions of power, the way we care for children is, among other things, a political act.

It's also a responsibility which demands a detailed awareness of the political landscape. To cite an example: in the United States, Federal Communication Commission (FCC) rulings of 1983 and 1984 lifted all children's programming guidelines, including those restricting the length and number of TV commercials aimed at kids. As a direct result, increasingly sophisticated marketing efforts targeting pre-teens have painstakingly constructed a universe of products whose every loose corner has been seemingly nailed tight: films tied in to television series tied in to action figures tied in to cereal box loot tied in to video game cartridges tied in to school lunch packs tied in to fast food prizes tied in to blanket sleepers tied in to disposable dinnerware, and on and on. The goal, obviously, is to diminish the child's opportunity to pose any questions which may spoil the plastic pretense—to obliterate all traces of those strangling roots of power. Take a look around, kid. It's a Disney world—you just live in it. So join the fun, shut up, and buy.

A Space for Creative Inquiry

Caught in the shadow of such institutional monoliths, how can we live according to our principles, especially beyond the confines of our home? Let's admit that retreating to a safe haven—through isolation, avoidance of mass culture, unplugging the TV—hardly solves the problem. Not only is it a quixotic goal, a kind of self-delusion, it also fails to answer the simple question of what we do when a niece requests a Sun Beach Barbie for her birthday.

Maybe we give in—buy it, make her happy, and win temporary status as a favorite uncle or aunt. Or we flat out refuse, take a deep breath, and—at the risk of sounding tedious—explain that the purchase of one Barbie doll reinforces our sexist society, perpetuates consumerism, exploits the labor of underpaid wage workers, and secures yet another piece of plastic for an overflowing landfill.

Or, less pedantically, we draw out the radical potential in this fragile moment, not with a lecture or an interrogation, but with candid, open-ended talk. That is, we gently rouse the spirit of critical inquiry which Mattel, with its vision of pink, polished, ecstatic blondness, has struggled to obliterate from our niece's psyche.

Why Sun Beach Barbie? Uh-huh. And where did you hear about her? What do you think of the actors in the Barbie commercial? Yeah, me, too. How much do you think Barbie costs? How many hours do you think an employee in a Barbie factory would have to work in order to afford a Barbie doll? No, I don't quite know either. Does it matter? And what kind of lifestyle would Sun Beach Barbie lead? How would she pay for it? Would it be fun? What's "fun" mean?

The issues are the fundamental sort that children regularly contemplate. Trying to make sense out of a paradoxical world, kids are neither completely free nor wholly dominated; after a few playful exchanges, even the most TV-addled kid may begin disputing corporate authority with considerable enthusiasm. Our responsibility lies in providing a space for creative inquiry. And, of course, for dialogue—for in the end, we might find ourselves facing a few equally pointed questions. ("Uh yeah, I used to have a Barbie. Yeah, I guess she was kind of fun...") Admittedly, a life of sand, surf, and endless leisure has some appeal. We may even be forced to rethink our political convictions, as well as our parental authority, since a child's eye for the hidden political dimension is guileless—it can unmask all sorts of pretense, including principled affectation.

Family, Politics, and Authority

The political dimension of childrearing comes to the fore in such encounters, which are obviously risky. They are also rarely discussed. For example, while general-interest bookstores are well stocked with an abundance of childrearing and educational manuals, the standard glossy trade paperback offers very little on the political nature of parenting. Rather, we're instructed how to toilet train our children in a day, help them read in thirty, hone their competitive edge by enrolling them in this week's computer whiz-kid class, and so forth. All this depends, of course, on our becoming proficient in the latest behavior management techniques. Deeper questions concerning our existence, our society and its relation to the natural world, and the nature of our institutions remain largely unacknowledged.

This oversight shows a misunderstanding of children, who are captivated by the deeper questions. But the subject of authority is regularly neglected, even by genuinely caring parents; and this is at least understandable. For when children are encouraged to ponder the legitimacy of power and authority, the authority of family structure inevitably comes under scrutiny. And there, for many adults, the conversation ends with, "Because I said so."

This phrase is famously effective; it appeals, after all, to the parents' indisputable might. Here we once again confront the political responsibilities of the deschooling parent, and the reality of an oppressive political institution much closer to home: the family. As numerous radical social thinkers have argued, the conflation of authority with might—the very basis of the patriarchal family—is crucial to the development of the obedient, fearful, authoritarian personality, and the authoritarian personality, in turn, forms the backbone of a society organized according to the hierarchical tenet of dominance and submission.

If the adult caregivers appeal to patriarchal rule and physical force, if they encourage docility and demand unquestioning homage to their own authority, if they express parental love through destructive self-sacrifice, their demands neatly dovetail with the demands of the state and the workplace. In short, the family—even more so than the school—serves the needs of an oppressive social, political, and economic order; historically, it has done so with appalling success, generating millions of pliant citizens quite willing to sacrifice their lives to defend and maintain the instruments of their own oppression.

But as we've seen, the social impact of family structure works both ways. That is, if the traditional family is a powerful force, then a more communal and egalitarian childrearing arrangement can act as a powerfully subversive force, challenging those institutions organized along lines of command and obedience—institutions which propagate the self-serving notion that egalitarian social organization is impractical, if not preposterous. This bleak ideology sediments into a general, widespread belief that any society ensuring collective decision-making is impossible. But what "impossible" really means in this context is: inconceivable to the conventional thinker. The work of people striving to revolutionize family structure allows the suggestion of such a society to take shape in the imagination.

Toward a Deschooled Society

Let's develop our description of this potential society, and its prefiguration in alternative means of childrearing, by explaining a few principles of deschooling. The word "educate" derives from the Latin *educare*, meaning "to nourish, to cause to grow"; originally it retained this organic connotation in English. Deschooling reclaims the origins of the word. Education, then, does not start at the arbitrary age of six, nor does it end with high school or college; education is the act of living and growing, of consciously responding to and manipulating one's environment based on experience and reflection. This definition recalls John Dewey's notion of learning by doing, except that in deschooling, the child—not the teacher—ultimately directs the process.

Gandhi referred to an analogous unified process as "education by the craft," insisting that education arises from life itself through doing what one must, in order to survive. For Gandhi, this meant craft work, which would then serve the child, the family, and the community as an economic resource. Unlike the busy work prescribed in schools, the craft is not a mere exercise detached from life, but a vital means of participating in the life of the community. Similarly, for the deschooler, curriculum emerges from the relationship of the learner with others, and with the natural world.

We ought to define conscientiously what we mean by freedom. Freedom means much more than leaving kids alone; as social beings, we cannot be free without the love and support of others. Freedom requires the individual's conscious participation in the self-generative process of creating society, a collective undertaking in which the individual recognizes his or her duty to others, as well as a right to individuality. In Bakunin's words,

"I can feel free only in the presence of and in relationship with other men [sic] ... I am not myself free or human unless I recognize the freedom and humanity of all my fellow men." As recognized members of this communal endeavor, children become responsible for the well-being of one another—an awareness of duty which thereby contributes to their own personal freedom. For the radical educator A. S. Neill, this is quite simply "freedom, not licence." To be free as a member of a community, one must respect the freedom of others. Deschoolers recognize that a child's development thrives upon this kind of freedom.

By encouraging questioning and rethinking, discussion and debate, exploration and discovery, disagreement and dissent—practices which lead to disequilibrium and, in turn, growth—deschooling requires us to face profound ambiguities. In turn, it allows us to recognize that society is a human creation—that it has no ultimate, articulate basis to which we can appeal, other than our own interdependency, and our powers of thought and imagination. This awareness frees us, and our children, to work toward transforming society as it stands.

Since deschooling aspires to develop not only the free individual, but ultimately a free society, let's locate our description of this potential society in the framework of a body of political thought. It's democratic, in the actual sense of self-managed; and it's communal, taking root and developing within the local community. It derives from a long history of largely anarchist practice and from the ideals of social ecology. And it depends, ultimately, not on perfect and steadfast harmony, but on constant public scrutiny, open evaluation and reevaluation, discussion, collective restructuring. Community members engage in regular dialogue in order to arrive at joint decisions and plans of action. Their concern is, of course, with the final outcome, but they are always deeply aware of the process through which they, as conscious members of a group, make changes in their own lives and social circumstances, recognizing their own communal interdependence, and their interdependence with the natural world. Since the form of such a society is regularly put into question, this activity is profoundly creative. It is also plainly analogous to the activity of deschooling.

This image, in fact, is what a community might look like if it were to embrace the ideas of deschooling. In the ongoing attempt to restructure family life, tentative steps are currently being taken toward such a society; for instance, many families are rejecting the medicalization of birth, choosing their own homes as the ideal setting for the birth process, ensuring that control rests with the mother and child, not with a doctor. We can cite the growing popularity of a number of practices: holistic health care; intentional communities and co-housing; childrearing philosophies emphasizing cooperation and intimacy over obedience and discipline; alternative family arrangements and shared childcare; and, of course, deschooling—all choices which reject the combination of patriarchal authority, sexual repression, and professionalized indoctrination employed in conventional family organization, opting instead for a fuller, richer, more generous range of social possibilities. (We should point out that, as long as we allow ourselves to be intimidated by economic or social pressure to participate in the traditional institutions of marriage and the family, the prospects of "choice" in living and childrearing arrangements will remain blighted.)

Our role as parents and caregivers is not to ensure that our children develop the capacity to survive the rigors of modern life. Our task is to establish ways of childrearing so that children develop in a non-hierarchical relationship with others, and with the natural world—so that they genuinely regard freedom as education's ultimate end. We might even define deschooling as the development of a sensibility—nurturing a keen consciousness and appreciation of social and individual freedom, cultivating an unaffected capacity to imagine a communal, authentically democratic society with this image in mind, beginning with the creation and development of institutions such as freer, more humane, and more diverse alternatives to the family. With this definition, we embrace deschooling as a revolutionary opportunity.

From a Pedagogy for Liberation to Liberation from Pedagogy

Gustavo Esteva, Madhu Suri Prakash, and Dana L. Stuchul

Gustavo Esteva is a grassroots activist and deprofessionalized intellectual. For the last twenty-five years, he has associated his life and work with indigenous peoples, particularly in the South of Mexico, where he lives in a small Indian village. The author, co-author, or editor of more than thirty books and many essays, and a columnist in Mexican newspapers, he is affiliated with Centro de Encuentros y Diálogos Interculturales and Universidad de la Tierra, two coalitions of grassroots organizations.

Madhu Suri Prakash is Professor-in-Charge of the Education Theory and Policy Program at the Pennsylvania State University and is the recipient of the Eisenhower Award for Distinguished Teaching. Co-author with Gustavo Esteva of Grassroots Post-modernism: Remaking the Soil of Cultures *(Zed, 1998) and* Escaping Education: Living as Learning Among Grassroots Cultures *(Lang, 1998), Dr. Prakash is currently co-editing a collection of essays and stories in a book titled,* Ahimsa: Beyond War, Violence, and Counterviolence.

Dana L. Stuchul is Assistant Professor of Education Studies at Berea College in Berea, Kentucky. Her publications have included the following topics: education as a technology, friendship, and criticism of the sustainability paradigm. Her on-going research interests focus on the writings of Ivan Illich, while attempting to formulate a philosophy of technology consistent with the Gandhian and Illich inspired idea of "modern subsistence." In this endeavor, she also celebrates peoples living at the grassroots.

Paulo Freire was a prominent member of a group of brilliant intellectuals and activists, who revealed—particularly to privileged audiences—the horrors of modern oppression. In the steps of Franz Fanon, they fostered a new awareness of the condition of the world's social majorities after World War II.

In Latin America, Freire was inspired by the revolutionary ethos stimulated by Fidel Castro and Che Guevara in the 1960s. Like many others, however, Freire searched for an alternative to guerrilla warfare and terrorism to promote profound social change: Revolution would arise neither by pen nor by sword, but via enlightened literacy.

Freire gained fame and fortune for his ideas on literacy and education. Banking education—the dominant curriculum and pedagogy of classrooms and campuses for credentials, careers, social caste, or pedigree—came under Freire's critical scrutiny. He denounced its flaws with great effectiveness. Thousands, perhaps millions, of young people found in his writings a source of inspiration for their activism on behalf of peoples' liberation. His many followers applied his method with courage and ingenuity all over the world. In the years following the publication of his pedagogy, Freire remained highly fashionable, particularly within certain professional educational circles of industrial countries.

Given the well-established image of Freire as a progressive, radical or even revolutionary educator, it may seem preposterous, outrageous or even ridiculous to present him—as we do in this essay—as a conservative thinker and practitioner. Even more, on both theoretical and political grounds, we present him as a colonizer.

We strongly believe that Freire was a man of integrity, faithful to his beliefs and possessing profound social commitments. He was particularly committed to deep social transformation for liberating the "oppressed," as he called them. Yet, in spite of his intentions, we observe that he adopted assumptions or presuppositions, which served the system he wanted to change. Instead of its transformation, his ideas nourished its conservation and reproduction. In making this claim, we hope that our observations may help to explain the frustration we have sensed in many of his followers and practitioners of his ideas—frustration arising from their accommodation within the very system against which they were courageously rebelling after being educated by Freire. We also hope that these will help those involved in learning societies develop greater clarity about their own efforts.

I. The Corruption of Awareness

During the 1960s, a new awareness emerged among sections of the educated elite across the world. Surveying their social, political, and environmental landscapes, they recognized serious wrongs in it: growing social injustice; wars like the one being waged in Vietnam; the failure of the progress promised for the post World War II period. They wanted change.

Yet, if you want to change the world, you need to be aware of the direction of the global change you think is needed. You need a catholic (universally human) vision of both the desirable outcome for everyone and the way to achieve it. And if you do not suffer the illusion of being god, such consciousness should include the identification of the actors, subjects, agents who would produce the global change of which you are "aware."

Freire's pedagogy was born out of this kind of universal conscience. Freire had it. He imagined the direction and nature of change. He identified the agents for that change. And, he dedicated his life to promoting the change he conceived. The way which would enable that change was education. Freire's catholic mission: secular salvation via education.

The unsatisfactory conditions of the world had already a universal name, even a global identity by the 1960s: underdevelopment. The Peace Corps, the Point Four Program, the War on Poverty, and the Alliance for Progress contributed to root into both popular and enlightened perception the notion of underdevelopment, coined by Truman on January 20, 1949. These programs also deepened the disability created by such a perception. None of those campaigns, however, were comparable to what was achieved by Latin American dependency theorists and other leftist intellectuals dedicated to criticizing all and every one of the development strategies that the North Americans successively put into fashion to counter underdevelopment everywhere (Esteva, 1992). For them, as for many others, Truman had simply substituted a new word for what had already been there: backwardness or poverty. They attributed such conditions to past looting (a.k.a. colonization), as well as to the continued raping caused by capitalist exploitation. The neologism coined by Frank aptly summarized the prevailing political perception: development (capitalism) develops underdevelopment (1969).

Trapped within an ideological dispute, very virulent at the time, many activists took sides: to get cured of underdevelopment, their countries needed to get cured of capitalism. Instead of a party, to develop the conscience or organization necessary for leading the people to their emancipation, guerrilleros will conscienticize the people—through word and praxis—in the nature of their oppression: leading them in the struggle to dismantle the dominant system; bringing them the right and appropriate kind of development; offering them the promise of their emancipation.

While sharing the critique and purposes of the guerrilleros, Freire drew a line separating his thinking and action from theirs. He explicitly rejected the use of violence for seizing political power, in the name of revolution and liberation, and its usual outcome: an authoritarian state. Freire wanted the change to start with the people themselves, with their conscientization, their awareness. Convinced that both oppressors and oppressed were dehumanized by oppression, he assumed that a new consciousness would enable both to be fully human again. This consciousness, by itself, would give them the capacity to dissolve the oppression.

According to Freire, "the oppressors, who oppress, exploit and rape by virtue of their power, cannot find in this power the strength to liberate either the oppressed or themselves. Only power that springs from the weakness of the oppressed will be sufficiently strong to free both" (1996). The oppressed, however, cannot liberate themselves by themselves. They are submerged within oppression, in the world of the oppressor; they are dehumanized, divided, inauthentic beings. They need an outside critical intervention.

According to Freire, a pedagogy was needed to conceive and implement such intervention—a pedagogy of the oppressed. Such pedagogy could not be developed by the oppressors. "It would be a contradiction in terms if the oppressors not only defended but actually implemented a liberating education" (1996). It can neither be implemented through "systematic education which can only be changed by political power" (1996). The oppressed neither have that political power nor should they seize it. What is thus needed is a group of liberated pedagogues, fully conscienticized themselves in the pedagogy of the oppressed. The liberated would conceive educational projects, which should be carried out with the oppressed in the process of organizing them. At first a pedagogy of the oppressed, this pedagogy would then become a pedagogy of all people in the process of permanent liberation, a pedagogy of humankind.

Freire used many titles for his mediators, his agents of change, in different moments of his life and work, describing them in different ways. Yet, he always wrote for them. He did not address himself to the oppressed, who had lost their humanity. Instead, he addressed the mediators. Freire's pedagogy is, therefore, best understood as a pedagogy for mediators *qua* liberators. Freire wrote for critical educators, revolutionary leaders, social workers, organic intellectuals, a motley crowd of characters who in his view could and would dedicate themselves to the liberation of the oppressed. He attempted to teach them the moral and political virtues, as well as the technical tools, that would enable them, through their own liberation, to perform the function he ascribed to them. They become a substitute for a revolutionary party or for guerrilla activities. Once liberated, they become, for Freire, the new enlightened vanguard that would make possible the desirable change.

There is no need to assume, like Peter Berger, that Freire's consciousness raising implies the arrogance of higher-class individuals with respect to the lower-class population (Berger, 1974). Neither does he attribute to them an ontological or existential sickness. He is most certainly not a racist. Freire merely assumes that the oppression suffered by the oppressed has radically disabled them. The oppressed can neither liberate themselves from oppression, nor can they even perceive fully this oppression. Thus, the mediator must endow the oppressed with both awareness and conscience. In both cases, what is supposedly needed is a abstract, rational perception, with a specific theory about the oppression and its causes. Such theory takes for granted: 1) that such awareness defines "true" reality, 2) that the oppressed lack such awareness and conscience, and 3) that such awareness and conscience are preconditions for liberation and transformation to occur.

Freire's position belongs to a distinctly modern (and therefore, Western) tradition. At the beginning of modernity, Hegel stated it in very clear terms: people cannot govern themselves; someone needs to govern them. This apothegm has been the premise, the point of departure, for all the dominant political theories and practices of the last two centuries. It implies that if people cannot govern themselves, they cannot change by themselves. They cannot, therefore, liberate themselves from any form of oppression. The underpinnings of this tradition and conviction are well known. They are embedded in the unilinear, evolutionist vision of the world, which presupposes the equally Western conception of the autonomous individual and of Western rationality/science. An enlightened elite should guide the masses of individuals along their evolutionary path, sometimes controlling them, sometimes subordinating them to the dominant system, and at other times, leading them in the process of substituting one system for another.

This perspective, however, implicitly or explicitly dismisses, suppresses, or disqualifies the abundant historical evidence of how people have governed themselves or have rebelled by themselves against all sorts of oppressors, through what Teodor Shanin calls "vernacular revolutions" (1983). The term "vernacular" means native, indigenous, not of foreign origin or of learned formation (OED). The antonyms of vernacular are: cosmopolitan and worldly-wise, artificial and subtle, expert, official, universal and scientific.

According to the dominant modern perception, vernacular initiatives and movements—expressing the rebellion of the oppressed against their oppressors or at least their resistance—are unseen, irrelevant, or non-existent. Or, even worse, they are viewed as counterproductive, traditionalist, parochial, fundamentalist, reactionary, or counter-revolutionary, because they do not follow the official program. The only movements or initiatives taken into account are those conceived and promoted by cosmopolitan, universal, educated agents of change, agents who educate the people towards progress, pointing the way out of the vernacular towards the universal ... the global.

Yet, no longer can the existence of vernacular revolutions be denied. With the insurrection of dominated knowledge, as Foucault (1992) calls it, a whole corpus of revisionist literature provides documentation of changes, initiatives and movements born among the people themselves, in their vernacular realms (Frank 1987, Eyerman and Jamison 1991, The Ecologist 1992, Esteva and Prakash 1998, Negri 1999).

What is therefore increasingly in question is the real nature and potential for transformation of the conscience which all sorts of revolutionaries have attempted to instill in the people in order to promote their own projects. For some, this has been but another form of colonization, not of liberation. As Wendell Berry puts it: "In the formula Power to the People, I hear 'Power to me, who am eager to run the show in the name of the People.' The People, of course, are those designated by their benevolent servant-to-be, who knows so well what is good for them" (1972).

Often, when it becomes impossible to deny the very presence and the social and political impact of peoples' initiatives or vernacular revolutions, the dominant reaction is to associate them with prominent characters or charismatic leaders. Such attributions of the origins and orientations of peoples' movements to enlightened or educated leaders legitimizes the prejudice that nothing progressive can happen without mediators.[1]

The construction of mediators, intrinsic to Freire's pedagogy for liberation, expresses thus a corruption of his awareness of oppression. It operates as a veil, hiding from the supposedly "liberated" agents of change their own oppression—the fact that their conscience is still embedded in an oppressive system and thus becomes counterproductive—adding oppression to the oppressed, disabling them while dismissing, denying, or disqualifying the fullness of their initiatives. This operation does not only imply a specific, untenable arrogance: the hubris of possessing the true, universal conscience. It also serves the purpose of legitimizing the right of intervention in the lives of others.

II. The Corruption of Love

Similar to liberation theology (an option for the poor) courageously adopted by an important sector of the Catholic Church in Latin America, Freire finds a foundation and a destiny for his theory and practice in the ideal of solidarity. Solidarity expresses an historical commitment based on a universal ethics. Solidarity legitimizes intervention in the lives of others in order to conscienticize them. Derived from charity, *caritas*, the Greek and Latin word for love, and motivated by care, by benevolence, by love for the other, conscientization becomes a universal, ethical imperative.

Certainly, Freire was fully aware of the nature of modern aid; of what he called false generosity. He identified clearly the disabling and damaging impact of all kinds of such aid. Yet, for all of his clarity and awareness, he is unable to focus his critique on service. Freire's specific blindness is an inability to identify the false premises and dubious interventions—in the name of care—of one specific class of service professionals: educators.

In its modern institutional form, *qua* service, care is the mask of love. This mask is not a false face. The modernized service-provider believes in his care and love, perhaps more than even the serviced. The mask is the face (McKnight 1977). Yet, the mask of care and love obscure the economic nature of service, the economic interests behind it. Even worse, this mask hides the disabling nature of service professions, like education.

All of the caring, disabling professions are based on the assumption or presupposition of a lack, a deficiency, a need, that the professional service can best satisfy. The very modern creation of the needy man, a product of economic society, of capitalism, and the very mechanism through which needs are systematically produced in the economic society, are hidden behind the idea of service. Once the need is identified, the necessity of service becomes evident.

In this way, Freire constructed the human need for the conscience he conceived. In attributing such need to his oppressed, he also constructed the process to satisfy it: conscientization. Thus, the process reifies the need and the outcome: only conscientization can address the need for an improved conscience and consciousness and only education can deliver conscientization. This educational servicing of the oppressed, however, is masked: as care, love, vocation, historical commitment, as an expression of Freire's universal ethic of solidarity. Freire's blindness is his inability to perceive the disabling effect of his various activities or strategies of conscientization. He seems unaware that the business of modern society is service and that social service in modern society is business (McKnight 1997). Today, economic powers like the USA pride themselves in being post-industrial: that is, smokestacks and sweatshops have moved to the South in an economy retooled for global supremacy in providing service. With ever-increasing needs, satisfaction of these needs requires more service, resulting in unlimited economic growth.

Freire was also unaware that solidarity, both the word and the idea, are today the new mask of aid and development, of care and love. For example, in the 1990s, the neoliberal government of Mexican president Carlos Salinas used a good portion of the funds obtained through privatization to implement the Programa Nacional de Solidaridad. The program was celebrated by the World Bank as the best social program in the world. It is now well-documented that, like all other wars against poverty, it was basically a war waged against the poor, widening and deepening the condition it was supposed to cure, a condition that, in the first place, was aggravated by the policies associated with the neoliberal credo.

Freire could not perceive the corruption of love through caring, through service, and particularly the impact of the corruption which occurs when the oppressed are transformed into the objects of service: as clients, beneficiaries, and customers. Having created a radical separation between his oppressed and their educators, Freire was unsuccessful in bringing them together, despite all his attempts to do so through his dialogue, his deep literacy—key words for empowerment and participation. All these pedagogical and curricular tools of education prove themselves repeatedly to be counterproductive: they produce the opposite of what they pretend to create. Instead of liberation, they add to the lives of oppressed clients, more chains and more dependency on the pedagogy and curricula of the mediator.

During the last several centuries, all kinds of agents have pretended to "liberate" pagans, savages, natives, the oppressed, the under-developed, the uneducated, under-educated, and the illiterate in the name of the Cross, civilization (i.e. Westernization), capitalism or socialism, human rights, democracy, a universal ethic, progress or any other banner of development. Every time the mediator conceptualizes the category or class of the oppressed in his/her own terms, with his/her own ideology, he is morally obligated to evangelize: to promote among them, for their own good, the kind of transformation he or she defines as liberation.

In response to colonization, Yvonne Dion-Buffalo and John Mohawk recently suggested that colonized peoples have three choices: 1) to become good subjects, accepting the premises of the modern West without much question, 2) to become bad subjects, always resisting the parameters of the colonizing world, or 3) to become non-subjects, acting and thinking in ways far removed from those of the modern West (Quoted in Esteva and Prakash 1998).

The assumption of Freire is that his oppressed are trapped within the dominant ideology, that they have been de-humanized by the system, that they are its subjects. But his rebellion, as much as his solidarity, succeeds at best in creating the condition of a bad subject, a rebel subject. In this way, neither Freire nor his conscienticizers can perceive their own oppression. By reducing his definition of himself, of his own being, to the terms of the oppressor, even to resist or oppose him, Freire can not even conceive of the possibility of becoming a non-subject.

In rejecting the need of mediators and the dominant paradigm which holds that the people cannot govern themselves or change and rebel by themselves autonomously, we are of course affirming the opposite: that the people can govern themselves. Even more, it is our contention that people liberate themselves from oppressors only when both the initiative and the struggle come from them; from within themselves rather than from external agents of change. Instead of pro-motion (which operates under the assumption that the people are paralyzed or are moving in the wrong direction), those taking initiatives at the grassroots to govern themselves autonomously or democratically speak of co-motion—moving with the people, rather than moving the people. In Spanish, the word *conmover*, *conmoción*, is instructive and strong in its denotation. *Conmoción* means not only to dance with the other the common tune (which does not necessarily define a common conscience). It also denotes moving together with the heart and stomach, not only with the brain, with rationality. The real plurality of the world is manifest in a pluralist attitude, fully respecting both the radical otherness of the other and their visions and initiatives. Co-motion may thus operate as a vaccine against the corruption of love.

III. Resisting Awareness: The Case of Literacy

Like Marx, Freire professed a profound fascination for modern technology. Like Marx, he recognized that technology is not neutral; that it can be used as a vehicle of oppression. But like Marx, he seemed unable to discover the nature of technological society and to find in *la technologie* itself, as defined by Ellul (1964), a source of oppression and alienation.

In no other aspect is his silence or denial more evident than in the case of the alphabet: the tool of literacy. It is to the alphabet and to literacy that Freire dedicated his life. Literacy was his chosen field and, until his end, he dedicated himself to promoting it and its tools. Courageously, he denounced the deficiencies and perversions of the literacy promoted and imposed by banking education. From these critiques followed Freire's proposed paths to liberation: the appropriation of the tool, its pedagogy and curricula, as well as the skills engendered by the oppressed themselves. He insisted on the importance of a "critical appropriation" of literacy so that oppressors can no longer oppress the oppressed.

Here, Freire confines himself to the critical question of who owns the tools and curricula of literacy as well as to their means and ends. He does not venture the distance required to see how the tool itself tames people, reducing and confining them to the operations of the textual mind. Freire's historical perspective does not extend itself to examine the social construction of the textual mind. Neither does he reflect upon the implications of the textual mind for the human condition, including social organization and its system of domination (Illich 1993).

In his denunciation of the discrimination suffered by the illiterate, Freire does not see, smell, imagine or perceive the differential reality of the oral world. While aspiring to eliminate all these forms of discrimination from the planet, he takes for granted, without more critical consideration, that reading and writing are fundamental basic needs for all humans. And he embraces the implications of such assumptions: that illiterate people are not full human beings.

Freire's pedagogic method requires that literacy should be rooted in the socio-political context of the illiterate. He is convinced that in and through such a process, they would acquire a critical judgement about the society in which they suffer oppression. But he does not take into account any critical consideration of the oppressive and alienating character implicit in the tool itself, the alphabet. He cannot bring his reflection and practice to the point of establishing clear limits to the alphabet, like with many other modern tools, in order to create the conditions for the oppressed to critically use the alphabet, instead of being used by it.

As Plato suggested, the text is radically uprooted from any concrete, living experience, no matter how much it evokes living and concrete experiences or is written or read in a very concrete and alive situation. The textual mind is constructed according to that model. The textual mind thinks of speech as frozen; of memories as things that can be saved and recovered; of secrets that can be engraved within the conscience and thus examined; and of experiences that can be described. In writing texts, the modern individual "looks" for the proper word to say what he wants to say. He thinks that he can fix in line what has happened—in his life, his job, his country—and mummify them, only to resurrect them later. A text is in a sense past speech, but speech which has suffered a radical transformation, so radical that perhaps it can no longer be called speech.

In the world of orality, where the oath is law, words are the fabric of human interaction. Modern men are men in context. The word context still describes the weaving of words, the connection between the parts of a discourse, the parts around a "text" which determine its meaning. But it also means today how men and woman are woven together, connected. They are connected through texts. Their minds are constructed in the shape of texts—uprooted, homeless texts. And they feel unbearable loneliness unless they find their contexts, to connect themselves to others through pertinent texts.

Modern mentality—whether that of Freire's oppressor or oppressed—is inextricably shaped by the alphabet. Liberation cannot come from literacy—not even critical literacy, Freirean style. Liberation comes with the autonomy of assuming a critical distance from the alphabet, from the recovery and regeneration of our minds, currently trapped and embedded within texts.

We recognize and celebrate that most people on earth are either functionally or absolutely illiterate: that is, non-alphabetized. Tragically, with each and every literacy campaign, their way of life and cosmovision are at risk of being disqualified. Thus, in departing from Freirean pedagogy and liberation, interest in the autonomy or liberation of the non-alphabetized by the literate must also be accompanied by the sense and feeling of the association between our texts and their oppression.

IV. Resisting Love: The Case Against Education

Freire's central presupposition: that education is a universal good, part and parcel of the human condition, was never questioned, in spite of the fact that he was personally exposed, for a long time, to an alternative view. This seems to us at least strange, if not abhorrent.

Freire was explicitly interested in the oppressed. His entire life and work were presented as a vocation committed to assuming their view, their interests. Yet, he ignored the plain fact that for the oppressed, the social majorities of the world, education has become one of the most humiliating and disabling components of their oppression: perhaps, even the very worst.

Education creates two classes of people: the educated and the uneducated or undereducated. The educated, a minority, receive all kinds of privileges from their position. The rest get all kinds of deprivation and destitution. No literacy campaign or educational project has or can overcome that deprivation and destitution in any society. Why did Freire close his eyes to such facts? Like all other educational reformers, he concentrated his efforts on polishing and cosmetizing people's chains. This further legitimized and deepened the oppression he was supposedly struggling against.

The uneducated are not able to read the texts of the educated. But they are not stupid. They retain their common sense. In the era of accelerated educational reforms, the uneducated are better equipped to accept the fact denied by the educated: the foolishness of placing faith in the possibility of secular salvation through education. The growing awareness among the illiterate, the uneducated, and the undereducated about this situation, coupled with many other facts, is allowing an increasing number of them to think that perhaps the beginning of the end of the era of education has already begun.

For the experts, the contemporary state of education is dire. The educational system becomes more oppressive to those enrolled within it, even as it expands. With every step of its expansion, teaching becomes more mechanical, monotonous and irrelevant. Students discover faster than their teachers how irrelevant their learning is; how little it prepares them to do useful work or to live.

Despite this, the reform proposals proliferate. Grouped into three categories of reformers, some look to improve the classroom: its methods, equipment or personnel. Others attempt to liberate it from any bureaucratic imposition: promoting teachers, parents, and communities as the principal decision-makers for determining the content and methods of education. Still others attempt to transform the whole society into a classroom: with new technologies substituting for the closed space of the classroom, providing for open markets and remote teaching. Whether reformed, free or a world-wide classroom, these reforms represent three stages in the escalation of interventions to increase social control and to subjugate people.

The most dangerous reformers are today those who promote the substitution of the classroom for the massive distribution of knowledge packages via global communication technologies. These reformers go further in establishing knowledge consumption as a basic need for survival. While traditional reformers are still promising more and better schools, these current reformers are at this moment winning the race. They present themselves as the only ones who will be able to achieve the goal, accepted by everyone: equality of access. Rather than diminishing the need for classrooms, these reformers extend its function. Theirs is an attempt to transform the global village into an environmental womb in which pedagogic therapists will control, under the appearance of a free market, the complex placenta necessary for nourishing every human being.

Furthermore, the regulation of intellectual rights, now being negotiated in international institutions, will serve to protect the corporations which produce and distribute the knowledge packages that from now on will define education in the global campus.

Educators continue to educate the world in the fallacy that education is as old as the hills. However, the idea of education is exclusively modern. Born of capitalism, education perpetuates it. The past is colonized every time the cultural practices or traditions for learning or study of pre-modern or non-modern peoples are reduced to that category understood as education.

Education, like capital, was initially promoted through force. Today, police and armies are still used to extend and deepen educational control. However, education has now been established as a personal and collective need. Like other needs, it has been transformed into a right. More than bureaucratic imposition, education has become a legitimate and universally accepted social addiction—it stimulates knowledge consumers to freely, passionately, and compulsively acquire their chains, thus contributing to the construction of the global Big Brother.

Globalized markets simply cannot absorb the masses. Increasingly, people become disposable human beings—unavailable for capital to exploit them. However, by giving them, with public funds, access to knowledge packages, capital educates them as consumers and prepares them for the moment in which it can subsume them again in the system of exploitation.

These "disposable" people have started to react everywhere. There is a proliferation of initiatives escaping the logic of capital. Everywhere, disposable people are transforming the drama of exclusion into an opportunity to follow their own path and to create by themselves their own life. One of their first steps is to escape education.

Given the fact that education is the economization of learning, transforming it into the consumption of a commodity called knowledge, people are recovering their own notions of learning and living free of educational mediation. Since the noun "education" imposes a completely passive dependence on the system which provides education, people are substituting this noun with the verbs "to learn" and "to study." Unlike the noun, these verbs reestablish the autonomous capacity for building creative relationships with others and with nature—relationships which generate knowing, wisdom. People are again acknowledging that to know is a personal experience, and that the only way to know, to widen the competencies for living, is to learn from the world, not about the world. Their hope: that the extinction of the ritual of schooling and of the myth of education is appearing on the horizon—the beginning of an era ending privilege and license (Illich 1971).

Freire was entirely unable to anticipate such evolution or even to perceive the nature of the problem. He was thus unable to perceive the victimization created by schooling and education and to derive the pertinent conclusions. He was unable to bring his brilliant critique of "banking education" to education itself.

The very modern idea of teaching everything to everyone, of providing the same knowledge to every member of a society, of educating all of them to give to them vital competence, transformed learning and knowledge into a commodity. It applied to learning the premise of scarcity: the economic principle that man's wants are very great, not to say infinite, but his means are limited, although improvable. The logic of this assumption defines the economic problem par excellence: to allocate resources (limited means to alternative, unlimited ends). Once defined as education, the conditions for learning, always sufficient in every culture for its own requirements, became scarce. Once the premise of scarcity became the main principle of organization for society, with modernity and capitalism, the allocation of means for learning and for the distribution of the new commodity called knowledge, always limited, started to follow the pattern of injustice: some had access to them; others did not. Furthermore, the ways and means of learning still available for the destitute were restricted, eliminated, or radically devalued. The very experience of knowing was transmogrified into the mechanical consumption of abstract, unfleshed, disembodied, genderless texts, now called "knowledge."

Freire's pedagogy of liberation, viewed with archeological eyes, is yet another modern tool and technology used against vernacular probity and honor. The universal conscience and the institutional rules guarding it are doomed to colonize, standardize, and tame the wilderness of what still remains vernacular.

V. Liberation from Pedagogy

There are teachers—past and present—whom we admire. We admire them for different reasons and in different ways. They come from completely different worlds. We admire the kind of impact each of them has had or is having in their worlds; an impact so profound and powerful on their people that it spills over into other worlds; of the Other who does not belong to the world of each of these.

The teachers we admire have not prided themselves in being professional teachers. In fact, even those who were professionals chose to abandon their profession: to become, so to speak, professional dropouts. Here, for matters of variety and spice, we will limit ourselves to identifying only three. Three de-professionalized teachers, belonging to three worlds so different ... they might as well be three distinct planets.

For clarifying the issues of this essay, we chose to reflect on the life, the work, and the teachings of Mahatma Gandhi, Subcomandante Marcos, and Wendell Berry. Purposely, we juxtapose them to exacerbate their radical and dramatic differences—personal and cultural: an international teacher of peace from India; a ski-masked combatant in an indigenous,

Zapatista army from Mexico; and a North American farmer-poet from Kentucky.

Is it absurd to even place them under the same umbrella of public and private virtues we dwell on as we reflect on the kind of impact they have had upon others ... even as they have said a firm No! to all the symbols of modern power? Particularly the power of the modern agent of secular salvation: education?

We cannot call them educators. Even less can we call them Freirean educators. Emancipators. Conscienticizers. Empowerers. Liberators. Humanizers. Undeniably, each of them has put up the good fight for freedom from colonizers, from corporations, from the oppressive system of the State. Undeniably, their courage has infected others with the contagion needed to swim upstream against the global current. Each lives a life so compelling that it becomes their message—let me be the change I wish for the world. Each is literally an enfleshment of these words. Words made flesh. Each reveals in his own fashion what it means to buck the modern madness called Progress. Each has been cured of modern man's mad love for The Machine. Each goes against the grain of modernity, not to be novel, not as a fashion, but because his wisdom suggests the significance of breaking free from the radical rupture imposed by modern man on tradition. And, each reveals the art of enriching, enlivening tradition; they possess the traditional knowledge for changing tradition from within, thus ensuring its historical continuity.

Each of them suffered a radical transformation, once they became aware of their condition as subjects. First, they became good subjects. Next, they became bad subjects in an oppressive system. In so doing, each was able to perceive and conceive a way out of such oppression. And each of them fell into the temptation to transform their awareness into the agency of change, leading others towards that way. But each recovered after that fall and transformed their culturally rooted awareness into the decision to incarnate, in their own lives, the way out of oppression, while embracing their own personal limits under pervading social constraints.

Finally, each of them became non-subjects and attributed the agency of change to the people themselves, rather than to any kind of mediator. They do not see others' awareness as something created or constructed by them: their intermediation, their leadership. They are only articulating peoples' experiences and traditions, through which people recognize the foundation for their own thinking and action. Instead of using such awareness to preach ideals of life, they transform it into living ideals which they attempt to incarnate and regenerate, in ashrams in India; in the jungle of Chiapas in Southern Mexico; or on a farm in rural Kentucky in North America.

These non-teacher, non-conscienticizer teachers give us a glimpse of what it means to be non-subjects; what is involved in the recovery and the regeneration of vernacular worlds. They do not do it in any nostalgic, sentimental way. Their living, rather than a going back, are worthy of emulation precisely because they live full of hope, in the present. Their lives are attempts to heal the brutal rupture caused by modernity while they break free from it in order to re-connect themselves to real people in their soil cultures.

VI. Reclaiming Awareness and Love

As victims, we have been seduced into believing that schooling and education are prerequisites for living a good life. We have been deceived by the cult of experts to accept that living, learning, and growing require expert expertise. We have been schooled into accepting one kind of institutional arrangement (for example the school)—hierarchical, centralized, compartmentalized, and normalized—which provides programmed choice behind the guise (and using the language) of freedom. Through curricularized learning, we know how to measure, assess, and rank knowledge (as well as ourselves and others), increasingly devoid of real-life experience. And, we have resolved that schooling yields learning, that school-learning yields wisdom, and that school-wisdom ought to yield quantitatively improved living. Yet, most fail to consider the ill-effect that an over-emphasis on "quantity" or "quality" (education, not to mention career, income, "toys" and the like) must have on spirit, body, culture, and nature.

Having despaired over the deceit perpetrated by schooling and education, we are, we believe, ready to hope. The gods of schooling and education no longer hold possession of us. They no longer bind us to expectations of a world or society made better as a result of their functioning—whether reformed, revolutionized, humanized, conscienticized, multi-culturalized, democratized, or greened.

We prevent our hope from being transmogrified into a program or an expectation—the hubris of pretending to control the future. As Vaclav Havel affirms, "Hope is not the conviction that something will turn out well, but the conviction that something makes sense, regardless of how it turns out" (1991).

Our hope is continually nourished by the Zapatistas, who have inspired thousands, millions of globaphobics all over the planet. The Zapatistas continue to offer a radical refutation to all modern fanatics, self-styled cosmopolitan individuals, still dismissing all vernacular initiatives and movements as parochial, fundamentalist, and as going-back-in-time. We find parochialism in all globaphilics, like international institutions or transnational corporations, and in their reductionist science. All of them are constrained by their lenses, which reduce the richness of the world, in all its diversity and complexity, to the homogeneous, abstract quantities of their statistics, always associated with a very parochial, self-serving interest.

As defined by the deeds of the Zapatistas as well as by the words of Marcos, localization is the opposite to both localism and globalization. True, traditional resistance to all kinds of colonizers often implied forms of localism in which people were forced to entrench themselves in their own places. Such entrenchment implied the danger of short sighted and even fundamentalist localism. In the epoch of economic and technological globalization, people realize that all isolated localisms will be razed to the ground. But instead of abandoning their roots and places, as global forces push them to do—in order to better gut them in the shapeless space of the market and the State—they affirm themselves in them while at the same time opening their hearts and hands to others like themselves.

In our own struggles to become non-subjects, we find inspiration in the words of Paul Goodman:

> Suppose you had had the revolution you are talking or dreaming about. Suppose your side had won, and you had the kind of society you wanted. How would you live, you personally, in that society? Start living that way now! Whatever you would do then, do it now. When you run up against obstacles, people, or things that won't let you live that way, then begin to think about how to get over or around or under that obstacle, or how to push it out of the way, and your politics will be concrete and practical. (Quoted in Holt 1970).

Notes

1. A case in point is the Zapatista movement. For the government, the political parties, many analysts, and even many of its followers or sympathizers, the
Zapatistas are in fact reduced to the now famous subcomandante Marcos. They
thus express their racist prejudice: the only educated white man of the movement,
who has performed a brilliant role as speaker (a kind of cultural bridge between
the indigenous peoples and the educated world), should be the one conceiving and
leading the movement. Time and again, the Zapatistas have declared, or dem-
onstrated with facts, that their uprising came from people's own initiative, from
their communities, that have since then been in control of it. Marcos himself has
explained how the communities cured him of the ideological burden he brought to
the jungle. But the Zapatistas are still seen, by the elite, as a group of manipulated
Indians, under the control of a mestizo.

References

Berger, P.L. 1974. *Pyramids of Sacrifice: Political Ethics and Social Change*. New
York: Basic Books.

Berry, W. 1972. *A Continuous Harmony: Essays Cultural and Agricultural*. New
York: Harcourt Jovanovich.

_____. 1990. *What Are People For?* San Francisco: North Point Press.

_____. 1998. *A Timbered Choir: The Sabbath Poems, 1979–1997*. Washington,
D.C.: Counterpoint.

_____. 2000. *Life is a Miracle: An Essay against Modern Superstition*. Washing-
ton, D.C.: Counterpoint.

Cayley, D. 1992. *Ivan Illich: In Conversation*. Concord, Ontario: Anansi Press.

_____. 2000. *The Corruption of Christianity: Ivan Illich on Gospel, Church and
Society*. Toronto: Canadian Broadcasting Corporation.

Dietz, S. 1992. Quoted by Tom Pruiksma, personal correspondence.

The Ecologist. 1993. *Whose Common Future? Reclaiming the Commons*. London:
Earthscan.

Ellul, J. 1964. *The Technological Society*. New York: Alfred A. Knopf.

Esteva, G. 1992. "Development," in *The Development Dictionary: A Guide to Knowledge as Power*. W. Sachs (Ed.). London: Zed Books.

Esteva, G., Prakash, M.S. 1998. *Grassroots Postmodernism: Remaking the Soil of
Cultures*. London: Zed Books.

Eyerman, R., Jamison, A. 1991. *Social Movements: A Cognitive Approach*. University Park, PA: The Pennsylvania State University.

Frank, A.G. 1969. *Capitalism and Underdevelopment in Latin America*. New York:
Monthly Review.

Frank, A.G., Fuentes, M. 1987. *Nine Theses on Social Movements*. Amsterdam: IS-
MOG.

110   ...   Everywhere All the Time

Foucault, M. 1992. *Microfísica del poder*. Madrid: La piqueta.

Freire, P. 1972. "Education: Domestication or Liberation," in *Prospects*, Vol.II, No. 2 (Summer). Reproduced in Lister, I. 1993. *Deschooling—A Reader*. Cambridge: Cambridge University Press.

_____. 1970, 1996 ed. *Pedagogy of the Oppressed*. New York: Continuum.

_____. 1997. *Pedagogía de la autonomía*. México: Siglo XXI. (First published in Portuguese, 1996)

Gandhi, M.K. 1970. *Essential Writings*. V.V. Ramana Murti. (Ed.). New Delhi: Gandhi Peace Foundation.

Gatto, J.T. 1992. *Dumbing Us Down: The Hidden Curriculum of Compulsory Schooling*. Philadelphia: New Society Publishers.

Goodman, A. Feb. 1, 2001. "'I sell goats': Knowledge and Education in a Borderless World." Address at the Pennsylvania State University.

Havel, V. 1991. Quoted in *In Context*, No.30, Fall/Winter.

Holt, J. 1970. *What Do I Do Monday?* New York: Dutton.

_____. 1976. *Instead of Education*. New York: Dutton.

Illich, I. 1970. *Celebration of Awareness*. New York: Doubleday.

_____. 1971. *Deschooling Society*. New York: Harper & Row.

_____. 1973. *Tools for Conviviality*. New York: Harper & Row.

_____. 1978. "In Lieu of Educationl," in *Towards a History of Needs*. New York: Harper & Row.

_____. 1982. *Gender*. New York: Pantheon.

_____. 1986. *La alfabetización de la mentalidad: un llamamiento a investigarla*. Cuernavaca: Tecnopolítica.

_____. 1993. *In the Vineyard of the Text: A Commentary to Hugh's Didascalicon*. Chicago, IL: The University of Chicago Press.

Illich, I., Sanders, B. 1988. *The Alphabetization of the Popular Mind*. San Francisco, CA: North Point Press.

Kumar, K. 1998. "*Freire's Legacy*." *Economic and Political Weekly*, No. 46.

McKnight, J. 1977. "Professionalized service and disabling help," in I. Illich, Zola, I.K., McKnight, J., Caplan, J. and Shaikeb, H., *Disabling Professions*. London: Marion Boyars.

Negri, A. 1999. *Insurgencies*. Minneapolis, Mn.: University of Minnesota Press

Panikkar, R. 1993. *La diversidad como presupuesto de la armonía entre los pueblos*. Barcelona: Wisay Marka.

_____. 1996. "The defiance of pluralism," in *Soundings*, 79.1–2 (Spring/Summer), 170–191.

Prakash, M.S., Esteva, G. 1998. *Escaping Education: Living as Learning within Grassroots Cultures*. New York: Peter Lang.

Sachs, W. 1992. "One World," in *The Development Dictionary: A Guide to Knowledge as Power*. W. Sachs (Ed.). London: Zed Books.

Sbert, J.M. 1992. "Progress," in *The Development Dictionary: A Guide to Knowledge as Power*. W. Sachs (Ed.). London: Zed Books.

Shanin, T. 1982. *Late Marx and the Russian Road*. Berkeley: University of California Press.

Stuchul, D. 1999. *Schooling as Ritual and as Technology: Explorations in the Social Thought of Ivan Illich*. Ph.D. diss., The Pennsylvania State University.

SECTION III

Getting Busy

Matt Hern

Matt lives and works in East Vancouver with his partner and daughters. He directs the Purple Thistle Centre and founded Car-Free Vancouver Day. His writing has been published on all six continents and translated into many languages. He continues to lecture widely, including at both UBC and SFU in Vancouver. His books include Field Day: Getting Society Out of School *and* Watch Yourself: Why Safer Isn't Always Better.

There's one small argument I want to add to this collection and I think it fits here at the beginning of these next two sections which highlight excellent projects from around the world. It is this:

To my mind, deschooling has to be about freedom—and that cannot be just a simple liberty, but a social freedom—a freedom *to something* not just a *freedom from*.

In large part, when I talk about deschooling, I am not talking about doing away with schools per se, but extinguishing monopoly state schooling and compulsory education. I love and admire the homeschooling movement (and you'll find a lot of it in this book), but most kids need a place to go during the day: we need to be talking about counter-institutions.

It is really important for kids to have a place where their parents aren't around all the time. Somewhere they will encounter a lot of other kids who are not like them. Somewhere they can run into ideas and people and values that they won't find in their kitchens. Contemporary schools provide those possibilities only to a very limited extent, and vastly more is possible outside the confines of compulsory schooling.

We need a viable, publicly-supported and broadly articulated homeschooling movement so that pretty much any family can make homelearning work. But we also need networks of learning centres, community projects, libraries, youth centres, parks, pools, gyms, playgrounds, and museums of every possible variety. We need those networks to be alive in every neighbourhood, and they have to be commonly-held and democratically controlled by everyday people.

We just can't be waiting for politicians, administrators, leaders, or anyone else: we need to be building everyday alternatives right now, right where we live.

* * *

The truth is that no guru, no academic, no bureaucrat, no curriculum expert knows how all kids will learn best, or what they need to learn and when. It just can't be right that having kids stuck inside institutions, confined to classrooms of thirty peers for five days a week, six hours a day, ten months a year, for twelve years of their childhood is the best way for kids to be spending their time. There are just better ways to grow up, and better places for kids to grow up in. But its more than that.

Schools both construct and reflect larger society: they are in a dialectic relationship with each other, and by building more democratic, freer, and more respectful places in our communities we build a more democratic, freer, and more respectful world. And that's why I think the writing in this book matters so much—not because it's not just some cool families with interesting ideas, or some innovative schools or alternatives-to-school—but because these writings represent a radical reimagining of our society.

And if that's what we're after—and I'm arguing that it has to be—then deschooling can't be just another lifestyle option for the most privileged people in world history. We have to take common responsibility for making alternatives to compulsory schooling commonly available—especially to the least fortunate folks in our communities—otherwise deschooling just becomes another brick in the wall of white privilege

* * *

So what does a good place for kids look like then? Attempting to define specific characteristics of The Good School is a project that has become popular in recent years among school people, academics, and researchers. The fundamental presumptions of the question though, reveal a pedagogical and philosophical arrogance that points, ironically, towards an answer.

After a little more than 150 years of compulsory state schooling in North America, our culture has moved no closer to the school fantasy of a educationally-leveled populace. There is a deep antagonism to mandatory schooling (what is more cliché than "kids hate school"?), and yet our culture clings to the illusion that schools can globalize their canonical vision of knowledge and skills.

The reality is that our schools are not making our kids smarter, more knowledgeable, more capable or more skilled. Did you know, for example that literacy levels in Massachusetts, where compulsory schooling first took root on this continent were 95% in 1850, two years before sending kids to school was made law?[1] It has never reached those levels since. Or that in the U.S., in 2004, a country that has so enthusiastically and bombastically swallowed the compulsory school pill, still only 32% of fourth graders could read at grade level?[2] Despite an explosion of funding in the past few decades ("Even when accounting for inflation, [U.S.] funding has doubled since 1985") North American school performance, using *their own evaluative standards*, continues to flounder. [3]

The basic aspects of everyday school life have emerged and continue to evolve not as a response to the needs of students, but as driven by institutional needs.[4] Contemporary pedagogical thinking is almost entirely constrained by classroom requirements, and it is of little use for teachers to ask broad questions about their students' well-being. Students are required to fit into the apparatus of school days, times, schedules, agendas, curricula, and class order, and it is their flexibility and adaptivity that is assumed, not the institutions'. Why do we demand that children fit into schools and not the other way round?

Forcing children to adapt to a pre-described institutional model has given rise to a whole teaching industry of carrots and sticks, bribes, threats, rewards, surveillance, monitoring, drugging, therapy, counseling, and much more, desperately trying to ensure that all students can learn the same curriculum, in the same fashion, at the same rate. The reality is that all kids are uniquely enigmatic creatures with constantly changing learning patterns, needs, interests, passions, family circumstances, capacities, and quirks.

And that's why it is impossible to describe The Good School, as if it were a magic formula that could be applied and reapplied anywhere. It is the technocratic fantasy of imposing industrial production models everywhere. Kids need places to gather and places to meet interested and interesting adults who care about them and their lives. Beyond that, there is an endless array of possibilities, and how these places are constructed is a matter for local conversation and debate. Kids and families need to come together and create the kinds of institutions that best serve their children, their families and their communities. The resources, the facilities, the people, the knowledge, the skill are all there.

The point I'd say, is to get busy. Start asking those questions of your kids, their friends, your neighbours' kids, kids you see on the street. What kind of place would they come to? What kinds of projects would get them excited? Start asking questions and then get working. If it ain't you, who's going to do it? If not now, then when?

✳ ✳ ✳

When we start thinking about building new places for and with kids, I think we should be using the same evaluative criteria that we use to describe libraries, parks, pools, plazas, bike trails, community centres and rinks: the kinds of places that people all over the world use and love. These are public places, widely available, open for a variety of uses, free when possible, and do not have a coercive agenda. These institutions are community resources and widely admired for their utility and broad value.

So instead of trying to figure out what a theoretical Good School might look like, let's just get busy building local places that ask "what will it take for these kids to flourish?" And let's not ask this of the abstract kids of theory, but pose real questions to the kids we know and love. That's a complex and meandering set of questions that are pretty similar to parenting. It is imperative for people who want to work with kids to turn their backs on the manipulative intents of "education," wash themselves of the impulse to mould students in their idealized image and begin to create community institutions that are flexible enough to evolve with the needs of participants.

Notes

1. Ron Koetzsch, *A Handbook of Educational Alternatives* (Boston: Shambhala, 1997) p. 4.
2. From www.nclb.gov/next/stats The US Dept. of Education *No Child Left Behind* website. Do note the boggling array of stats attesting to the lack of literacy and numeracy, and the shocking degree to which they plummet for low-income and minority children.
3. See www.nclb.gov/next/overview/presentation/slide004.html

4.   Which pretty much everyone everywhere recognizes near-instinctually. Ivan
     Illich defines school as "Compulsory attendance in groups of no more than fifty
     and no less than fifteen, of age-specific cohorts of young people around one person
     called a teacher, who has more schooling than they." From David Cayley, *Ivan Illich
     in Conversation* (Concord, Ont.: Anansi, 1992) p. 66.

Summerhill School

Zoe Readhead

Zoe is the daughter of A.S. Neill. She was born and educated at Summerhill, the best known free school in the world, located in England. In 1971, she married Tony Readhead, a local farmer. They have four children, all of whom attended Summerhill. Zoe worked for some time at Lewis Waldham Free School in New York State. A qualified riding teacher, she managed and ran a riding stables near Summerhill, and took over the headship of the school in 1985. "My main accomplishments in life are being able to light a really good camp-fire and peeling oranges like a professional! I am also a pretty good dancer."

A. S. Neill was born is Forfar, Scotland in 1883. He was the fourth of thirteen children of the village schoolmaster or "Dominie," a stern, puritanical man who ruled his classroom with a rod of iron. In those days the strap or "tawse" was commonly used in schools in Scotland and when at the age of fifteen, Neill was taken on as a pupil-teacher by his father, he was expected to use it on the other children. His father cared little for him and made it clear that he thought him both dull and unworthy.

At the age of twenty-five, Neill went to Edinburgh University and took a degree in English. Afterwards he became a journalist and then Head of a small school in Gretna Green. It was there that he wrote his first book, *A Dominie's Log*, and began to form his ideas on freedom for children. After a year in the school, he wrote:

> I have converted a hard-working school into a playground, and I rejoice. These bairns have had a year of happiness and liberty. They have done what they liked; they have sung their songs while they were working at graphs, they have eaten their sweets while they read their books, they have hung on my arms as we rambled along in search of artistic corners.

In 1913, Neill visited Homer Lane's Little Commonwealth, a community for delinquent adolescents, and saw self-government at work. A firm believer in the innate goodness of children, Lane acquainted Neill with Freud's New Psychology and later became his psychoanalyst. Thus ,he introduced Neill to two elements that were essential to the founding of Summerhill: the self-government meeting and the importance of a child's emotional well-being over academic development.

Summerhill was founded in 1921 in Germany, in Hellerau, a suburb of Dresden, as part of an international school, The Neue Schule. There were wonderful facilities there and a lot of enthusiasm, but over the following months Neill became progressively less happy with the school. He felt it was run by idealists—they disapproved of tobacco, foxtrots, and cinemas—while he wanted the children to live their own lives. He said:

> I am only just realizing the absolute freedom of my scheme of Education. I see that all outside compulsion is wrong, that inner compulsion is the only value. And if Mary or David wants to laze about, lazing about is the one thing necessary for their personalities at the moment. Every moment of a healthy child's life is a working moment. A child has no time to sit down and laze. Lazing is abnormal, it is a recovery, and therefore it is necessary when it exists.

Together with Frau Neustatter (later to be his first wife), Neill moved his school to Austria. The setting, on top of a mountain, was idyllic, but the local people—a Catholic community—were hostile. By 1923, Neill had moved to a town in the South of England, Lyme Regis, and a house called Summerhill where he settled down until 1927, when he moved to the present site at Leiston in the county of Suffolk. Neill continued to run the school with his second wife, Ena, until he died in 1973. She then took over until her retirement in 1985 when their daughter, Zoe, and her husband took over.

Summerhill today has not changed fundamentally since it was first started. Its aims could be described as the following:

* To allow children freedom to grow emotionally;
* To give children power over their own lives;
* To give children the time to develop naturally;

* To create a happier childhood by removing fear and coercion by adults.

Allowing children freedom helps to develop self-motivation. Emotionally healthy individuals are not inhibited in their learning process. Giving children power over their own lives promotes a feeling of self-worth and of responsibility to others. They learn from an early age that what they think is important and that others will listen to what they have to say.

Giving children time to develop means letting them play and play and play for as long as they want to. Only through free, imaginative play can a child develop the skills needed for adulthood. Just as a kitten learns to hunt by chasing leaves and insects, so a child prepares for adult life by playing with other children. Within the group, all the qualities, good and bad, that will be encountered later, are present. By making mistakes, the child grows and matures without the need for morals to be taught. Neill constantly stressed the innate goodness of children and urged us to have patience and trust that they would learn these things for themselves.

Summerhill is a community of approximately eighty people, adults and children. There are usually twelve staff and an international group of children. At the present time about a third are from Japan, while the rest are divided between English and European. Summerhill is less well known in its own country than anywhere else.

It is a self-governing community—which means that all the decisions regarding daily life are made by the whole group. An important aspect of this is that the business side, the hiring and firing of staff, the intake of pupils, etc., is not the responsibility of the children. They are not asked to take on responsibilities which would be inappropriate or arduous for them. Children have a very real interest in what time they go to bed at night but little in who pays the electricity bills!

The school decision-making process is democratic. Each adult and child has an equal vote. Thus the youngest child has the same voting power as a staff member. Not only do the children have equal power in school meetings, they also vastly outnumber the adults. Most teachers' reaction to this is one of fear—imagine what would happen in a conventional school if all the pupils outnumbered the staff in a vote! Total anarchy? Loss of all moral codes? Possibly—but in Summerhill, because of the freedom they have experienced, most of the pupils are already socially responsible and are used to thinking about the needs of the group rather than their own. This does not mean that there are never disputes or disagreements; one of the important lessons learned has been that the needs of children and adults are very different indeed!

The following is an example of a typical School Meeting. The older kids in the school wanted to have no bedtime and proposed that they could stay up as late as they liked, provided that they stick to the silence hour which is 10:30 p.m. There was a long discussion about it as many people had things to say on the subject. Some were worried about the possible noise, others about lack of sleep. Eventually, the vote was taken and the motion was carried that they try it for one week to see if it could work. A week or so later, there was a special meeting because one of the staff had been woken up several times with noise in the night. The community decided that the older kids had had their chance and should get their bedtimes back again.

Occasionally there are rebellious children who want to break all the school laws and go against the community in whatever way they can. Sometimes such a child can whip up enough support to get some school laws dropped or changed. Obviously, it can be a bit disruptive, but it is a good learning experience and in most cases is quickly put right. What better way to learn to be a law-abiding citizen than to try living without laws?

Summerhill believes in freedom but not license. This means that you are free to do as you like—but you must not interfere with somebody else's freedom. You are free to go to lessons or stay away because that is your own personal business and you can make the choice. But you cannot play your drum kit at four in the morning because that would interfere with the freedom of others. Within this structure, there are probably more laws in Summerhill than any other school in the country—about 190 at the last count! They range from what time you have to be in bed at night to where you are allowed to shoot bows and arrows. Here is a random selection of them:

* Only twelve-year-olds and over are allowed sheath knives.
* You must have a working front and back brake on your bike. You can't ride little kids' bikes—even with permission.
* You can't watch TV during lessons or meal times.
* Writing graffiti—E1 .00 fine (but there is a special wall where you are allowed to).
* Breaking bedtime laws—half hour community work.

There are School Meetings twice a week, one on Friday afternoon and one on Saturday evening. The Friday meeting is called Tribunal and is used for people to bring cases against one another. Thus, if somebody has been riding your bike without permission or has broken into your box to nick your cash, you can bring it up in the tribunal.

Chairing the meeting is a difficult task. Although nobody is exactly unruly, it is demanding to keep up to seventy people of different ages sitting quietly for about an hour at a time. The Chairperson has ULTIMATE power! You can be fined for making noise, moved, or thrown out altogether. It is a strangely formal occasion and visitors have often remarked how much more ordered it is than the House of Commons!

Sometimes teachers bring up children for being unruly in class. One such case recently carried the fine that the culprit should be banned from lessons for three days—but the child appealed it on the grounds that it was too severe! Naturally the staff can be brought up, too. It is a very leveling experience to be brought up before the whole community—especially if you have been teaching in the conventional system. Some new staff find it too much and are very embarrassed about it. But it is a valuable experience for grown-ups to be put in a position where they can be brought up by children and fined accordingly.

Possibly the whole educational system would benefit if all teachers were put into that situation, if only for the experience of it. The face of teaching would change if all teachers had a class that could get up and walk out if they were not interested, as they do at Summerhill. Teaching to a captive audience is one thing; having to hold people's interest is quite another!

Summerhill is now an old and respected institution among progressive-minded educationalists. It continually struggles both financially and with the Department of Education but so far, it is keeping its head above water! A proud place with many friends throughout the world, Summerhill is eager to make new connections and very willing to share any helpful experiences.

A History of the Albany Free School and Community

Chris Mercogliano

Chris was a teacher at the Albany Free School, a unique, freedom-based inner-city alternative school from 1973 to 2007, and was co-director from 1985. His essays, commentaries, and reviews have appeared in numerous newspapers, journals, and magazines, as well as in four anthologies: Challenging the Giant *(Down to Earth Books),* Deschooling Our Lives *(1996),* Creating Learning Communities *(2000), and* Field Day: Getting Society Out of School *(2003). He is also the author of* Making It Up As We Go Along, the Story of the Albany Free School *(1998),* Teaching the Restless, One School's Remarkable No-Ritalin Approach to Helping Children Learn and Succeed *(2004),* How to Grow a School: Starting and Sustaining Schools That Work *(2006), and* In Defense of Childhood: Protecting Kids' Inner Wildness *(2007).*

Founded in 1969 by Mary Leue, the Free School in Albany, New York, is one of the oldest inner-city independent alternative schools in the country. Operating on a sliding tuition scale that slides all the way to zero when necessary, we are a learning community of about forty-five children, with many from low-income families, and eight full-time teachers supported by numerous talented and creative volunteers and interns. We have thrived by developing an internal economy which enables us to avoid dependence on outside grants from government or the private sector, or on prohibitively high tuitions. (Never in our history have we turned a single child away for financial reasons.)

Over the years, a group of about thirty-five (at last count) Free School teachers, parents, children, and others interested in exploring the realities of living and working together in community has coalesced around the school and has gradually developed a more consciously spiritual dimension which has nourished deeper and more permanent community roots. Our still-evolving "spiritual tradition" is multifaceted, drawing from many diverse paths as we continue to seek out ways to draw ourselves closer to God and to each other. Our guiding principle could best be called what has been known through the ages as the Perennial Philosophy, whose tenets lie at the core of all forms of religious practice.

According to Aldous Huxley, in his introduction to a 1944 translation of the Bhagavad-Gita, the Perennial Philosophy consists of four central doctrines:

> The material world is a manifestation of the Divine Ground from which it derives its being;
>
> Human beings are capable of a direct experience of that Divine Ground, in such a way that the knower unites with the known;
>
> Human Beings have a double nature, a temporal ego and an eternal self, which is the divine spark within each of us, and which we can identify with at any time;
>
> Human life on earth has but one true purpose: to identify with our eternal selves and seek out a unitive understanding of the Divine Ground.

As I will attempt to portray in this brief sketch, The Free School has acted like the dust particle at the center of every rain drop—or the irritating grain of sand which inspires the growth of the pearl! The story of how this meandering, organic development has occurred will best explain the what and the why of our school and community. At no point has there been a five-year plan or a single guiding philosophy or model; rather at every step, function and necessity—with occasional outside inspiration—have dictated form and process, and there has always been a fascinating parallel between the internal growth of each participating individual and the external growth of the school and the community.

Put more simply, from day one we've been making it up as we go along. Lacking money, we've had to become our own experts, hashing out our own solutions together, and learning from our numerous mistakes along the way. As Rabbi Zalman Schachter-Shalomi, a wonderfully sage leader of the Jewish Renewal Movement, once said to us in one of our workshops, "The only way to get it together is together!" The eternal challenge seems to be trying to live out, on a daily basis, the basic principles of love, truthfulness, emotional honesty, peer-level leadership, and cooperation which are at the heart of the Free School's philosophy of education. (Reb Zalman calls this "Walking your talk.")

The term "community" is grossly over- and ill-used these days and therefore, I think, it's important first to define it carefully. As far as I'm concerned, M. Scott Peck has written *the* book on community, and I always like to refer back to one of his definitions in *The Different Drum* :

> If we are going to use the word meaningfully we must restrict it to a group of individuals who have learned how to communicate honestly with each other, whose relationships go deeper than their masks of composure, and who have developed some significant commitment to rejoice together, mourn together and to delight in each other, making others' condition our own.

The Free School was born, of necessity, when Mary returned to Albany with her husband, Bill, and their five children, from Oxford, where Bill had been studying while on sabbatical from the State University of New York where he was a professor of philosophy. Mary's youngest son, Mark, was miserable in his fifth grade class at one of the "better" Albany Public Schools. Mary made every attempt to address the problem with both the teacher and principal, and with no change in sight, Mark began refusing to go at all, asking if, instead, his mother would teach him at home. At this moment, the Free School's basic operating strategy was born: Do it first, ask permission later.

When Mary received a threatening call from the principal, she sprang into action to establish the legality of teaching her son at home. She managed to find a man in the curriculum department of the State Education Department who told her that her decision was legal and who offered to give "state guidelines" to any school official who hassled her. Sure enough, the school district's truant officer called Mary the next day and began issuing all sorts of final warnings. Mary calmly gave him the name of the official in State Education and then, not long after, the truant officer, who is actually the head of the district's Bureau of Attendance and Guidance, called again to apologize and to offer assistance. Ironically, this man, Joe Markham, would later become our official liaison with the superintendent of schools and a trusted and powerful ally! Thus Mark Leue became perhaps New York State's first legal homeschooler.

But not for long. Two weeks later, Mary ran into a friend who had three children who were suffering in another of Albany's finest schools and she immediately begged Mary to take them on. Mary agreed on the spot, not wanting her son to be isolated alone with her at home, and, presto! a school was born. At that point, Mary decided to visit other "free schools" such as Jonathan Kozol's Roxbury Community School in Cambridge, Massachusetts, and Orson Bean's Fifteenth Street School in New York City, and then to hold alternative education forums around town. Suddenly four students became seven, two teachers climbed aboard, and the need for a building was obvious.

For both pragmatic and socio-political reasons, Mary decided to locate the new school in the inner-city. First of all, property in the ghetto was cheap; and secondly, Mary wanted a fully integrated school, with the onus placed on white, middle-class families to bring their children out of their uptown enclaves. So an old church building was rented temporarily until Mary found and purchased an abandoned parochial school building in the same South End neighborhood.

Two important developments occurred in the early tumultuous years of rapid growth, with parents struggling over educational philosophy and practice and with kids from opposite ends of the socio-economic spectrum thrashing out their own issues. A firm policy was established that only those actually present day-to-day in the building could determine the school's operating policy. Others were welcome to attend meetings and to advise and suggest, but that would be the extent of their power. This absolute internal autonomy remains a cornerstone of our methodology—such as it is.

Next, in order to empower the kids to hold up their end of the bargain, and to give them a way to work out their differences (which were many in that initial period) nonviolently, Mary and the other teachers instituted a "council meeting" system, whereby anyone with a serious problem could call a meeting at any time, with everyone dropping what they were doing to attend. Meetings were run by Roberts' Rules and therefore anyone, with sufficient support, could set policy, make or change rules, etc. The council meeting structure provided a measure of safety for all, and ensured that, borrowing A. S. Neill's phrase, freedom didn't become license. Later, the "stop rule" was borrowed from Jerry Mintz's Shaker Mountain School in Vermont. The rule is quite simple: if you want someone to stop doing something to you, you just tell them firmly to stop and, if they don't, you then call a council meeting to get support in dealing with the aggressor.

One of the valuable lessons Mary learned from Jonathan Kozol was the importance of freeing the school from becoming tuition-dependent (and therefore essentially middle-class), by developing some sort of business. Mary had the vision, bolstered with a small inheritance from her mother, to buy and fix up some of the abandoned buildings on the same block as the school building. We have rehabilitated ten of them so far, for use as teacher housing and for generating income in various ways.

Teaching at the young school was an intense experience, with all of us who were working there full-time truly living on the edge. Salaries, when we got paid at all, were minuscule, and many of the kids we were working with were in crisis most of the time. A number of us were attempting to live together semi-communally in school-owned housing, and so the interpersonal dimension of the whole enterprise was pretty frothy, to say the least. It gradually became apparent that a forum was needed in which the adults could resolve conflicts and deepen their communication with and understanding of each other. Mary suggested we start a weekly "group" where we could both clear up unfinished interpersonal issues, and safely delve into areas of intrapersonal emotional (and later spiritual) growth. Our four-to-five-hour Wednesday evening group has now been meeting continuously since 1974 and is another absolute cornerstone of both school and community, and unquestionably is the key to the longevity of both.

Over the next few years, some of the teachers as well as Free School parents began buying dilapidated houses on the block for themselves and then applying the rehabilitation skills that we had learned while repairing the school buildings toward the creation of our own homes. A number of us were able to qualify for low-income, "sweat equity" Housing and Urban Development grants, which largely solved the financial aspect of this important step. We helped each other on our houses a great deal during this time, and a budding sense of real community began to grow, fed by the shared labor, risk, and excitement.

This expanding group energy, combined with a growing set of practical needs, led to the establishment of several "community institutions." As a number of us began to have children of our own, Mary, with assistance from my wife Betsy, also a teacher in the school who dreamed of becoming a midwife (and now is a fine one), started the Family Life Center. The Center provides pregnancy and childbirth support of all kinds and teaches a variety of forms of medical self-care for both adults and children.

With home-ownership and growing families came the need to manage carefully what little money we had and the need for loans at affordable rates: hence what Mary named "The Money Game," which is part credit union and part cooperative investment group, for those of us who would otherwise be shut out from such mysterious rites of post-industrial capitalism. Then Mary and another Free School teacher, Nancy, each of whom had started a natural foods store in their past lives, collaborated on one for the community; we now have twenty-four-hour a day access to whole foods at low cost. A small book store and crafts co-op were later added on, managed by yet another teacher, Connie.

Finally, we all began yearning for a place away from the city where we could vacation together and where we could retreat as needed. Larry, a Free School parent and community member and a master bargain hunter, found a "camp" on a small lake about twenty-five miles outside of Albany. With two forty-foot living rooms, six large bedrooms and two kitchens, it was just what we were looking for; furthermore, the owner was looking to sell quickly because it was beginning to need substantial repairs. We practically bought it on the spot! Rainbow Camp, as we christened it, is now a multi-purpose facility, used by the community for retreats and vacations, by the school for day- and week-long trips with the kids, and by Rainbow Camp Association for its weekend workshop programs focusing on personal, relational, and spiritual growth, and on ecology and earth survival. Any profit from the workshops goes toward paying for camp upkeep and taxes.

To make one final long story short, the purchase of Rainbow Camp led to us meeting an older man, Hank Hazelton, who dreamed of turning his 250 acres of woods, located just over the hill from our new camp, into a wilderness living center and sanctuary. After several crippling strokes, Hank decided to give his land to the Free School so that we would carry out his vision for him. Currently, we are in the process of building an octagonal "teaching lodge," twenty-four feet in diameter, in the heart of the forest, and are working with the Audubon Society of New York State to open a cooperative wildlife sanctuary on the land. A significant piece of the future of both the Free School and the community seems to lie in this direction, though, as before, there is little in the way of a long range plan. We will continue to trust in God (but tie our camels!), and let one step lead us to the next.

Unschooled Kids'
Comments III:

6. How about your relationship with traditional academic knowledge? The typical knock on deschoolers, homeschoolers, and alternative schoolers is that they just don't learn enough academic stuff—that they are too isolated from important knowledge and information. Do you agree?

Maizy Thorvaldosn: I feel pretty up to speed on everything except Math, but that's my choice. My real passion is Drama so I do a lot of that!

Gen Robertson: Well, I definitely think that there are some holes in my education or my general knowledge now. But I think that most of the people I know, regardless of their educational backgrounds, have some pretty big holes. I did learn how to do long division eventually. I also learned the names of all the Canadian Prime Ministers, and an in-depth history of World War II, along with a lot of other stuff that has faded from my mind. I don't think I have more holes than anybody else. It is natural that you remember what you care about and forget the things that you don't think about.

If I do find a particularly thin spot in my general knowledge, I can learn or re-learn it now, so I don't find the argument that deschoolers missed out on important knowledge very valid. It's not like the seven years you spend in elementary school are the only years you have to learn about everything important in life.

Daisy Couture: No, I don't. I may not know some things they do, but I probably know some things they don't know too.

David Gagnon: I didn't read a book till I was seventeen years old. Years of shame and "failure" in regular school ensured I never wanted to read, ever! I got past most of that by age fourteen (when I got the internet at home) and started teaching myself to read. It was around that time that I began to understand what my dyslexia was and how it affected me. Reading was tricky, but my teenage mind was developed enough that I could use my reasoning skills to hammer things out (which I had not been able to do at age eight). I suspect that I could have done this and learned to read by age ten or twelve if I hadn't been running from past experiences.

As a result of the academic freedom I had, I would definitely say that I am missing huge chunks of curriculum knowledge that kids in regular schools are exposed to. However, the things I have learned experientially that fit into the curriculum are things that I know and likely won't ever forget. I had real experiences around those pieces of knowledge and I really know them. The rest I can pick up when I need it. I can read a chemistry book and look up a bunch of words in the dictionary if I don't understand the terms or other pieces of specialized knowledge. Having been put in charge of my own learning, I have already learned how to learn. I know which ways do and don't work for me to acquiring information and I can use them to build new bodies of knowledge when I need to. On the other side of things, I would say that the human experiences I had, instead of cramming knowledge, were priceless. They are not something I can look up in the dictionary or on Google, and I consider them to be worth far more.

Mari Piggott: Definitely not, I can see why people might though. The thing I don't think they get is that, if you've been in an alternative situation your whole life, academics are very intriguing as a challenge, not daunting and scary.

Nigel Boeur: No. For me, the benefits of learning tons of life skills from a young age far outweighed the benefits of memorizing information that I wasn't interested in at the time. I started taking the Grade Nine curriculum this year, and it's pretty much the first schoolwork I've ever done. I don't notice myself falling behind, or not being able to answer questions. I know quite a few people (my older brother and sister included) that have never attended high school, and they are all living happy, fulfilling lives.

Russ Gendron: My knowledge of academia is somewhat "normal." I gained most of this knowledge in high school and college. Also, before entering alternative school, I learned how to read, write, and complete basic mathematical problems, which I found extremely helpful later, during my transition to regular school from my alternative one. I know a lot of youth who learned these skills later than I did and their attempts to integrate themselves into the regular system has been very troublesome at times.

It really depends what you deem to be important knowledge and information. If you want to check out university or college for academia, then yes, I would suggest banking some knowledge about essay writing, paragraph and sentence structure, etc. And any trade school demands a basic knowledge of math as well as writing, so these can be useful as well. It is certain that one could attain this type of knowledge outside of the regular school system and if one is dedicated, their methods would probably be much more efficient than the regular school's.

I would argue that most regular schoolers are the ones who are more isolated from the "important knowledge and information" one uses in life. To state briefly some of the things one may be isolated from while attending public school are: designing your own education, practicing a realistic model of self-reliance on a daily basis, healthy relationships with people of all age groups (including your teachers), fun adventures in the outdoors that teach hands-on experience, being interested in what you're learning, and the list goes on...

7. What do you think about university, college, or training institutions? Do you feel like not taking the regular approach to school has helped or hurt you, or neither? What are your feelings about post-secondary education?

Maya Motoi: I do not know at this point whether I will do any post-secondary studies and I do not know if my education has helped me or not. But I really think that the idea of college or university, or even continuing education is very interesting and I think that style of education should be offered to all ages. There are many courses that sound very interesting, but I do not know if I will want to pursue any of them.

Russ Gendron: Post-secondary education is a relief once you reach it. Suddenly, people treat you with more respect, as an equal even! Classes are direct and lack a lot of useless bullshit. You meet cool people and pretty much run your own schedule the way you want it. I'll be back.

Maizy Thorvaldson: I would like to go to university and become a teacher because I have met so many wonderful people who are teachers—that made me decide that's what I want to do.

David Gagnon: There really aren't a lot of things I would choose to learn in a learning institution. It just takes too long, costs too much, and isn't useful for me. I think they play an important role, however, for people who have never learned how to learn. People who have been lectured to and fed information for twelve grades don't actually know how to learn something (exceptions excepted). They would be lost if you dropped them in a machine shop and told them to learn to be a machinist. The trouble is classroom learning and the dependency that it creates in people to be presented with information. Being told by a teacher to do a research project on X by Y in Z format doesn't help people develop their ability to learn independently.

More and more people throw around this idea of the "life long learner." As even machine shops jump into the rapidly changing flow of digital technology, their employees are expected and needed to be "life long learners." I think as this demand grows, the advantage that my deschooled peers and I have will become more and more apparent.

Nigel Boeur: I don't think that taking an irregular approach to schooling has hurt me. At the moment, I'm planning on getting my grad certificate and at some point, taking post-secondary education to study music or photojournalism.

8. How about your employment life—future and/or current? How has not taking a traditional school path affected your approach to getting jobs?

Gen Robertson: I have never had trouble getting a job because of my alternative school background, although I did graduate.

The other day, I realized that I have never factored money into any decision about my future or my education that I have ever made. I think this is because I have been brought up within a community of people that do not particularly see great value in making tons of money. Because of this, and a belief that I will make it somehow, I have chosen to pursue art—in some form—as a career. I know this is a tough choice but I feel like I have the tools (self-motivation, self-confidence) to somehow figure out a way that art will keep me happy and full of food. I think one of the most important things that self-directed learning taught me is that it doesn't really matter exactly what degree you graduate with (if you decide to do post-secondary education): it matters how you use your knowledge and skills to shape your own career (and life) afterwards.

As for the jobs I've had so far, most of them have been pretty casual. I have not formally applied for a job (with a resumé) in quite some time. I tend to begin working at a new job without knowing much about what I'm doing, and being open about that. I approach jobs hoping to learn a lot from the experience, and it seems to work well. I've had luck getting jobs that I'm interested in.

David Gagnon: No one has ever asked me if I went to school. People have asked if I have any post-secondary degrees, to which I answer no. This sometimes turns people away, but this says more about them than it does about me. I think it's unfortunate for those folk that they are not interested in looking beyond the degree and judging people on their own ability.

In my current job as a stage technician, I would say that I've moved "up the ranks" about as fast as anyone can. I've been able to do this because of the work ethic I have and my tendency to start learning/absorbing the details of my situation as soon as I arrive in it. A comment I have often get is that I don't act my age, either by being able to take on responsibility or by not having a lousy attitude. As a person who is now often taking the role of producer, organizer, and coordinator, I see now the ways in which my experiences during these years shaped my ability to lead.

Russ Gendron: No problems. At quite a young age, in alternative schooling, I learned to speak on equal terms with many adults and authority figures. I believe one gains a sense of confidence from this and employers can recognize that as a good quality. That's about it.

Maya Motoi: I don't really know, but the first job I get will probably not require any extraordinary skills. I am interested in all kinds of design, writing, and illustrating. I want to become a pilot. I don't think academic knowledge is critical to any of those fields, or even high school graduation. Although I don't know what they will write in the back of my books— where they usually glorify the author by writing about the grand universities they went to—when I didn't even graduate from high school. In the end I do not believe my education will affect what I do in a negative way and have never even considered it a possible problem, except when asked.

Liberating Education

Satish Kumar

In addition to being the founder of the Small School and the Director of Programmes at Schumacher College, Satish is the editor of Resurgence *(an international magazine promoting peace, non-violence, ecology, sustainability, organic agriculture, and holistic philosophy). He has been a Jain Monk, a campaigner for land reform in the Bhoodan movement with Vinoba Bhave, and a pilgrim for peace, walking from India to America without any money, from 1962–1964. In 1968, Satish established the London School of Non-violence. His autobiography,* No Destination, *was published in 1992 by Green Books. In November 2001, Satish was presented with the Jamnalal Bajaj International Award for "Promoting Gandhian Values Abroad." His two other books—*You Are, Therefore I Am *and* The Buddha and the Terrorist—*are also published by Green Books. In 2005, Satish appeared on* Desert Island Discs *on BBC Radio 4.*

There are two aspects of education which require urgent attention: firstly, the relationship between the state and education; secondly, the size of our schools.

Politics is an arena of short-term strategies. Policies are proposed to win votes and influence elections. These policies are often conceived in the interest of the parties rather than society as a whole. Politics is put before children, teachers, and parents. In my view, education is too important to be left to the politicians. Therefore, I believe that the administration of education in any country ought to be taken completely out of the hands of the politicians and given to an independent body. This kind of independent administration already operates to a limited extent in the higher education sector in Europe and America. As a result, there is less direct interference by the governments in universities. There should be independent educational boards, run by people who are free of vested interest, who are respected for their integrity, wisdom and educational experience.

In all countries of the world we need to mount a campaign to liberate education from governmental control. But governments are not likely to give up voluntarily the enormous power and influence that they exercise. So, the parents, teachers, and citizens will have to demand this liberation in no uncertain terms.

The second point that I am concerned with is the size of schools. In a nutshell, most schools in the world are too large. I believe that the pupils, parents, and teachers are the paramount agents of education. Buildings, gymnasiums, swimming pools, visual aids, modern equipment, and everything else come second. Our schools, for too long, have been governed by the economies of scale. The rule of saving money has forced our schools to grow larger and larger. The casualties of this approach have been the school's relationships with parents and personal attention to pupils. This type of education is managed not by intimate understanding of all involved, but according to the rule book.

Schools have come to resemble factories, whereas they should be extensions of homes. Instead of a trusting and friendly environment, fear and suspicion permeate the atmosphere of our schools. Problems of discipline, vandalism, and truancy are the direct results of this giantism. The teaching staff of a large school do not even know each other well, much less the parents of their pupils. In a large school the pupils are like strangers. How many teachers have time to talk with their pupils informally and often? From my own experience, I know that most teachers are too busy to spare time to answer their parents' spontaneous questions, particularly in secondary schools.

Moreover, beyond a certain size even the economy of scale does not apply, as there are new costs involved. For instance, administrative and bureaucratic costs increase greatly and millions are spent repairing the damage. Even more millions are spent on children who don't get on in large schools and must be sent to special schools. And how many other millions are spent on pupils who fall victim to gangsterism, drug abuse, and theft, ultimately ending up in prisons and hospitals as burdens on society? The cost of uncared-for and unfulfilled children leaving a school cannot be measured in pounds and dollars.

In my view, our deepest social problems stem from our obsession to save money and organize schools on the principle of the economies of scale. What is necessary is that school culture and home culture be made compatible; schools would then be truly extensions of homes, and there would come about a strong partnership between home and school. That cannot be if schools have to deal with thousands of pupils and parents.

Schools must be made smaller, much smaller. Schools should be part of the neighborhood and community, within walking distance of the pupil's homes. Smallness is the road to educational plurality. Some schools may have educational excellence in a particular field. Some may have a farm attached. Others may find excellence through craft or science or the arts.

These questions cannot be raised easily in our present education system. So, in order to explore the crucial questions of human existence and the meaning of life we are going to have to reorganize our educational institutions on a human scale, and those institutions are going to have to be independent of the state. Although this is a huge task, I believe that it is possible to liberate education, and to turn it into one of the highest human endeavors. Let us begin to carry it out now.

It is not enough to criticize the system and leave it at that. It is better to light a candle than to curse the darkness. In 1982, a group of us established the Small School, in England, precisely to make education free from state interference and to bring ecological and spiritual concerns into the life of the school. At present there are thirty children in the Small School. Following this example, six other small schools have been founded in England, and one in France. It is no good waiting for the governments to change their policy. People have to take the matter of education into their own hands, by establishing constructive examples, and by vigorous campaigning.

Democratic Education in Israel

Chris Balme and Dana Bennis

After a traditional schooling in the United States, Chris has studied educational alternatives from around the world, visiting schools in Israel, Europe, and North America. In 2004, he co-founded a non-profit youth empowerment program, Spark, which helps middle-school youth pursue their interests and find personal motivation for education. Chris currently lives and works in San Francisco, California, co-directing Spark's youth programs, playing the cello, and spending as much time outdoors as possible.

A native New Yorker, Dana has worked in a variety of democratic and progressive schools, visited innovative schools in the U.S. and around the world, and worked in the non-profit sector to support a freedom-based approach to education. He has researched the theory and practice of democratic education, including the effects of these schools on students, and co-edited The Directory of Democratic Education *(2006), an international catalogue of democratic schools, colleges, and programs. He is an avid birder, naturelover, and musician, currently works with* The Calhoun School *in Manhattan and lives with his partner Julie in Tarrytown, New York.*

We arrived in Tel Aviv at 4 a.m. on a clear January morning. Yaacov Hecht from the Institute for Democratic Education welcomed us in characteristic Israeli fashion, with an enormous breakfast of fresh vegetables, bread, and cheese. We ate on the beach as the sun rose over Tel Aviv, walked on quiet pathways to the Institute, and an intense month of learning and experiencing democratic education began.

In truth, the experience began six months before, at the International Democratic Education Conference (IDEC) in Troy, New York. Over five hundred democratic educators, scholars, families, and students gathered from some twenty-five countries. During the full week of workshops, discussions, and informal brainstorms, a group of five young educators formed. We all had previous experiences working in education, teaching in a wide variety of settings from conventional to radically progressive and democratic.

What we shared was a deep belief that schools should respect every child and their unique interests, strengths, and challenges. We believed schools ought to be empowering places that support children's curiosity, rather than the oppressive, standardized, and damaging environments unfortunately common in most schools.

We believed, essentially, in the power and significance of "democratic education." Although this term has varying interpretations, to us it means inviting students to participate in creating a school's structure and vision; it means trusting students to control their own lives and learning; it means the adult is an advisor and guide rather than a director of activities. Our educational influences and inspirations included A.S. Neill and Summerhill, John Holt, Paulo Freire, Sylvia Ashton-Warner, Krishnamurti, Sudbury Valley School, and the Albany Free School, among others.

There are examples of democratic schools following these principles in the United States and throughout the world (the latest list of democratic schools includes seventy-five from the U.S. and another hundred around the globe). Still, the reality is one of existing on the fringe—the schools often struggle financially, are forced into a defensive position about their approach to education, and most of all, they are few and far between.

At the IDEC in New York, Yaacov met with our group of young educators and planted the idea in our heads to travel to Israel to study that country's efforts at democratic education. As we knew, democratic education seemed to flourish in Israel more than in any other country, with a prominent network of schools and an Institute that coordinated new projects. For the Institute, such an exchange would strengthen international connections and lead to the creation of English documents describing their work. For us, it was an intriguing opportunity to visit Israeli schools, discover how and why democratic education was such a significant movement in Israel, and gain knowledge about how we can strengthen this educational approach in the United States. After several months of fundraising and planning, the trip finally became a reality.

The Institute

As we walked along the beach that first day in Tel Aviv, we eventually came to the Kibbutzim College of Education and, in a building in one section of the campus, the offices of the Institute for Democratic Education

(IDE). The Institute and its staff of over forty educators and consultants function as a network of schools, an incubator for new initiatives, a consulting group for "democratization" of conventional schools, and a support for international initiatives in democratic education. IDE also directs a degree program for Israeli education students, and has increasingly been working with regional and city officials to bring democratic education to the larger population.

All this in a country the size of New Jersey, and with a population of six million people. Waiting lists to attend Israel's democratic schools have at times stretched into the thousands. By contrast, New York City has a population exceeding that of Israel, but can offer its youth only one democratic school. It was clear that Israel's movement for democratic education has left the fringes and affected the mainstream of education.

At the office of IDE, Yaacov ushered us into a conference room and introduced us to several key staff: Zehava Barkani, who works with low-income groups throughout Israel; Gilad Babchuk, Efrat Ben Zvi, and Eyal Ram, who direct the Democratic Education degree program for aspiring educators; Yael Schwartzberg, who leads democratization programs with conventional schools; and especially Michal Shemesh, who as the office coordinator was integral to the Institute's work.

We were fortunate during our stay in Israel to be led by IDE staff through a series of workshops designed to enable us to reflect, brainstorm, and strategize about the work we hoped to do upon our return to the United States. The Institute conducts this visioning process with schools, businesses, and regional leaders, helping each group consider where they have been, where they are now (a 360-degree mapping of strengths, weaknesses, and growth areas), and where they want to be. The group then creates a strategic plan to achieve their goals and evaluate their efforts. This process is the crux of IDE's approach toward organizational and educational change.

Hadera Democratic School

A few days after arriving in Israel, we walked onto the campus of Hadera Democratic School. In 1987, Yaacov and a group of local parents created this school, the first of its kind in Israel. As we entered the campus, a broad circle of buildings surrounding a field, we were swept away by a dozen middle- and high-school students, some eager to try their English on us and some simply interested in meeting the visitors. We immediately sensed the energy in the school, as mixed-age groups engaged in discussions at the snack bar, played soccer in the field, and talked with staff members. The students' enthusiasm and curiosity were palpable.

Hadera has 370 students aged five to eighteen and fifty staff members. The students have only two requirements: to be present at school from 8:30 a.m. to 1:30 p.m., and to meet regularly with a "honech," an adult advisor who provides the student with advice and support regarding educational and often personal issues. Every morning, each honech meets with all of his/her advisees to check-in, share announcements, and continue their discussions. Each loosely-defined age group also has a "house" of their own, a relaxed, multi-use building filled with students working on projects and talking. Soon after arriving at Hadera, the students led us into one of these buildings and began to explain how the school works.

The students described three approaches to learning embraced by Hadera. First, there are classes offered by staff and community members. These may look fairly conventional, with at least one significant exception: the students have chosen to attend the class. Since there are no required classes at Hadera, attendance at these offerings is optional. Second, there are learning centers throughout the campus, focused on art, music, ceramics, and English, among other domains. Here, students often take the lead in teaching other students. In our walks around the campus, we witnessed many projects taking shape in the centers, from a construction group working on a set of clay stairs to a thunderous band rehearsal.

Finally, and perhaps most commonly seen, is self-directed learning. Students can use the resources of the school to pursue projects and interests individually or with others. These pursuits may arise spontaneously or may continue with dedication for hours, days, or weeks. The Institute for Democratic Education describes this as "pluralistic learning," an educational approach that recognizes the equal right of every individual to express his or her uniqueness regarding goals and ways of learning. IDE continually emphasizes that pluralistic learning, this respect for the uniqueness of each individual, is the core of democratic education. A staffed self-directed learning building is always open at Hadera for students to do computer research or seek help from adults or other students. Two times a year students can propose funding for personal projects, to be debated in Parliament.

Parliament? Yes, one of the most important groups in the school is the Hadera School Parliament. Led by students and consisting of students, staff, and parents, it meets every Friday for two hours. This is a sacred time—no classes can be scheduled during this interval, and many parents, according to Israeli tradition, are not working at this time. Average participation is about thirty to fifty people, varying significantly depending on the issues discussed. Here, the core structures and laws of the school, from the class schedule to funding for the learning centers to behavior policies, are discussed collaboratively and voted on, one vote per person. From Parliament, executive committees are formed with power in such areas as student admissions and judicial action. One meeting we attended discussed, among other issues, whether to offer a biology or an ecology class next year given that there was only funding and time for one of the two. About eighty people—sixty students, seven to eight parents, and the rest teachers—passionately debated this issue.

We continued to stroll around Hadera during our visit, each of us led off in a different direction by a group of students. Many of the students spoke of strong relationships with the staff created by the honech system, which we began to realize was a key component of many Israeli democratic schools. That one-on-one relationship seems to prevent students from slipping through the cracks, and indeed, many conventional schools in Israel have introduced the practice with assistance from the Institute.

Students also spoke to us about conflict resolution, a topic we were to hear about continually during the month. Any student or staff member can write up a complaint and submit it to the Judicial Committee, the school's working court. If the complaint does not involve a school rule that has been broken, the complaint usually goes to a mediation committee which seeks to help the two parties agree to a plan of action. If a rule is suspected of being violated, the Judicial Committee will hear and discuss the issue and make a judgment. A student or staff member who is found guilty has the right to appeal the issue to an appeals committee.

Democratic Schools in Israel

As we continued our visits throughout Israel, we saw many variations on the concept of democratic education. As Yaacov describes, what IDE asks of new democratic schools is simple: first, respect the human rights of the child and include democratic processes in the school; and second, be different from every other democratic school that already exists. According to IDE these practices must not be copied or "replicated" but rather explored, embraced, and lived. Each school thus reflects the community that creates it, and as a result, the themes of respect and democratic process appear in a wide variety of forms.

We spent many days touring schools and discussing Israeli education with students, staff, and parents. Each night, we were hosted by a student's family, and each morning we would strap our luggage on top of the car and set off to another town. We saw schools that blended religious perspectives, and schools that had significant diversity between Arab Israelis and Jews. Some schools, like Hadera, only required attendance at the school, while others required attendance at certain classes. Keshet School in Zichron Yaacov, for example, had responded to its community's concern by requiring English, Hebrew, and Mathematics; all other time was open for students to fill as they pleased with classes, personal projects, discussion, and more. Some schools, such as Hadera and the Democratic School of K'Far Sava, offered a schedule of classes each semester, for which students could choose to enroll. Others schools, such as Kedem in Arad and Kanaf Democratic School in Ramat Ha-Golan, had no class schedule, believing students should be able to schedule their own classes when and how they saw fit.

While all democratic schools in Israel have their unique approaches, we sensed from each a community-wide dedication to the principle of respect for young people's freedoms and human rights, and a commitment to democracy, self-directed learning, and strong personal relationships.

Additional Educational Projects of IDE

Our school visits also took us to conventional schools that were re-evaluating their approach to education with assistance from the Institute's "democratization program." At Ma'ale Shaharut, in the south of Israel, we saw that the popularity of Israeli democratic schools had created a great deal of interest in student-directed learning among teachers and students. After a group of high-school students began refusing to attend conventional classes, the principal of Ma'ale Shaharut responded by creating a "democratic education track" within the high-school curriculum. Democratic-track students have some flexibility in their choice of teacher, fewer exams, and a classroom environment based more on their interests than the education ministry's curriculum. As one student told us, taking this route meant risking less preparation for college matriculation exams in exchange for more interesting classes and greater self-determination. Despite the risk, about a third of students had opted to enroll, and the school had hired the Institute to consult in the process. As with other schools, the Institute takes the approach of facilitating a community visioning process, adding in elements of democratic education according to the needs and interests of the community.

During our travels, we came face to face with the political and social tensions existing between Jewish and Arab Israelis. Arab Israelis, who make up roughly 20% of the Israeli population, face many of the same issues endured by minority groups in the United States—lower wages, towns with poor infrastructure, a lack of political representation, and prejudiced attitudes from some of those in the majority population. Likewise, schools in Arab Israeli areas are often over-crowded, lack basic equipment and supplies, and are plagued by teacher shortages.

IDE is dedicated to helping all communities throughout the country, and has been able to connect Jewish and Arab Israeli communities through peace projects and joint entrepreneurship. Some schools in Arab Israeli towns are putting strong efforts into changing their conventional structures with help from the Institute. We visited an Arab Israeli school in K'far Qara with which IDE has been working for several years. The principal and other school members are attempting to reform the school by providing teachers with more independence in creating their classes, and increasing the amount of parental and community interaction. The change is often slow, but it is happening in all segments of the Israeli population.

In an effort to have a greater effect on the education system in Israel, the Institute initiated a Democratic Education degree program within the Kibbutzim College of Education, the country's largest teacher preparation center. Approximately 175 students currently study in the IDE program, which is designed to educate future teachers about democratic education and alternative approaches to learning. The centerpiece of the program is what the Institute calls the "personal greenhouse," a three-year process through which students contemplate and research various opportunities in the field of education and are aided in the creation of a strategic plan in order to achieve their individual goals. Throughout our time in Israel, we met many of the students and teachers in this program, who live in all areas of the country and travel to Tel Aviv to attend the weekly seminars.

City-Wide Projects and Future Centers

The Institute's work has reached a greater number of people in the past few years, since it began working directly with cities and municipalities. Under their "Democratic Education City" program, IDE and city authorities work together to democratize schools, social services, and cultural centers.

At the time of our visit, the Institute's efforts in Be'er Sheva, the sixth largest city in the country, were well underway. We traveled to Makif Het, an urban public school, and saw this process in action. Through a partnership between IDE and the mayor of Be'er Sheva, Makif Het had been granted five years of funding to act as one of eighteen experimental schools in the city. In order to counter the aggression and low achievement that is prominent in city schools and to provide students with more personal support, much of the experimental efforts at Makif Het focused on improving the quality of relationships. The school instituted a modified honech system, pairing each student with an adult advisor. Classes were led by three adults, each of whom focuses on a difference emphasis—academics, emotional support, or morals and ethics. Moreover, students took only three classes each for six to ten hours per week, instead of six classes at one time.

The efforts in Be'er Sheva are coordinated in part by the city's Future Center, which could be described as a cross between an educational resource center and a community-wide visionary think-tank. As IDE consultant Yael Schwartzberg said, "How often do you walk into a school and hear, 'I'm concerned about X becoming a problem in fifteen years'?" Yael explained that, as educators, we know we have the power to change the future. But first, she advised, we must understand its trends. We must consider our visions, extending them forward into the long-term, and then drawing them back to the present.

Future Centers are physical, organizational, and virtual spaces designed to facilitate this blend of long-term thinking, discussion, and learning. They invite the whole community to join in the process of envisioning, brainstorming, planning, and taking action. IDE sees the concept as an antidote; an attempt to change the short-term, reactionary thinking of school systems driven by crises and political fluctuations. The Future Center can ensure that political and educational changes do not simply become the latest dogma. Thus the goal for each Future Center is to permanently open the process of change to the public, in the hope of fostering a proactive attitude toward educational and social change. In Be'er Sheva, the Future Center is the focal point of the city's process of change, uniting educational organizations and schools, public and private organizations, and the public citizenry. Recently, IDE has entered into a relationship with the city of Hadera to transform the largely low-income neighborhood of Givat Olga and serve as a model for transforming underprivileged communities throughout the country. The Givat Olga Pioneer Program, as it is called, includes the creation of a new tuition-free democratic school, the development of an arts and cultural community center, and a Future Center, which will serve as a forum for residents to dialogue and mutually design the future of the community.[1] Much of the leadership for this new program will come from a group of students and graduates of IDE's Democratic Education degree program, many of whom are re-locating to the area to focus on this initiative.

The Growth of Democratic Education in Israel

As we traveled, we sought to understand how democratic education had become so popular in Israel. We wanted to find out what was particular to Israel and what could be applied in the U.S. and elsewhere. We realized that the Israeli tradition of living in a kibbutz, or cooperative commune, may make Israelis more likely to see education as a community action that embodies social dimensions in addition to academics. Moreover, the small size of the country seems to allow for a great deal of awareness of new ideas such as democratic schools.

More importantly than any one trend, we began to feel confident that the education system in the U.S. and in any country can be influenced by having well-established examples of democratic schools, such as Hadera in Israel. Even more significantly, it became clear that a strong networking organization with well-thought-out strategies and approaches toward expanding democratic education can greatly enhance a country's efforts. And, of course, we could not overlook that IDE's impact in Israel depended on a healthy dose of courage—to persistently speak one's mind, to pursue innovative ideas, and to carry one's message to the educational and political leaders who can help bring about change on a grander scale.

Conclusion

During our visit to Israel, we saw example after example of schools that respect the rights and freedoms of young people, and which value self-determination, shared-decision-making, and strong personal connections. We witnessed a dedicated group of educators at IDE who are striving to create a more democratic, just, and empowered society. We left Israel with the conviction to expand and strengthen democratic education in our respective communities, throughout the United States, and around the world.

Yaacov Hecht and the Institute for Democratic Education have continued to expand their work of inspiring, creating, and connecting democratic education projects in Israel and in around the world. At of the time of this printing, 0.5% of Israeli students attend democratic schools, 1% of Israeli university students study in the Democratic Education degree program (including all of the teacher education students), 5% of Israeli schools are undergoing the process of democratization, and four of the ten major cities in Israel are working with the Institute under the "Democratic Education City" program.

Globally, the annual International Democratic Education Conference has been held for thirteen years in countries around the world, and has been attended by thousands of educators, parents, students, and others who are committed to the ideas of freedom and democracy in education. IDE has helped to spawn fellow Institutes for Democratic Education in areas such as Australasia, South America, and North America.

With inspiration and support from IDE, and a dose of their courage, it just may be possible to bring respectful, democratic education from the periphery to the mainstream of education throughout the world. As Yaacov famously says, "Sure, it is easy!"

Notes

1. Most Israeli schools are approved and funded through the government and are therefore tuition-free. Democratic schools, due to their non-conventional approach, often start without this funding and frequently go to court to gain approval and at least partial support. As a result of charging tuition, Israeli democratic schools have gained the perhaps undeserved reputation of catering to the wealthy. The city of Hadera's agreement to start the Givat Olga democratic school with full funding is noteworthy.

Claiming our Humanity through Alternative Education in the Belly of the Beast

René Antrop-González

René is an assistant professor of curriculum and instruction/second language education at the University of Wisconsin-Milwaukee. His research interests include urban small school reform, ethnocentric alternative high schools, Latino/Puerto Rican sociology of education, and qualitative inquiry.

A Personal Journey of Dehumanization and Resurrection

I am of two distinct sociopolitical worlds. I am of the colonizer and the colonized. I am a bilingual and bicultural border crosser. I am Puerto Rican and North American. I am a colonized subject who was once dehumanized. Although I am now able to write these words, there was definitely a point in my young life when they would have only caused much anger and shame. To dare reclaim my Puerto Rican-ness was to only accept the reality that I was part of a minority group that had faced and will continue to face the ravages of United States economic, linguistic, and psychological imperialism.

However, there comes a time when one must face her/his social reality. As a result, in my attempt to understand the roots of my previous anger and shame, I began a journey of reading, reflection, conversing, and writing. Along the path to my own self-transformation and liberation, I discovered how my own (mis)education had indeed been of an insidious, rather than liberating, nature.

Schools have the potential to be powerful instruments of a status quo infatuated with undertaking a campaign of deculturalization and absolute truths. Of course, these so-called ways of looking at the world only work to perpetuate a vicious cycle of social orders that benefit only a privileged few while simultaneously undermining the socio-historical realities of countless many. I vividly remember being exposed to school curricula that exalted the worldview of a dominant White, male, and middle-class way of being. In turn, these curricula also had their hidden agenda and conveyed to me that my Puerto Rican heritage and language were not valid for our "melting pot" society. Where were my people reflected within the classroom? Bluntly put, we were nowhere to be found. In fact, it would not be until I became a doctoral student that I would question and challenge this curricular absence in my own life.

As I began to study and analyze the educational plight of Puerto Ricans residing in the United States, I found myself lamenting the apparent lack of curricular democracy that I had experienced in the Orange County Public School System (Orlando, Florida). Almost magically, however, I came across a journal article published in the summer 1998 issue of the *Harvard Educational Review* written by Ana Yolanda Ramos Zayas. In her article, Ramos Zayas specifically mentioned the work of the Dr. Pedro Albizu Campos Alternative High School located in Chicago. I found out that there was a vibrant Puerto Rican community in Chicago that had already decided that our lack of presence within a school setting had been too much to bear.

Consequently, this community decided to take this matter into their own hands. Hence, the idea for a new project of struggle and resistance was born and manifested through a Puerto Ricancentric alternative education. The ensuing excitement that followed upon discovering a school that gave its students the cultural knowledge that I had not been given compelled me to want to contact the school to learn more. After speaking with the school's director via telephone and stating my interest in this unique pedagogical project, I was encouraged to pay a visit. As a result of this first of many subsequent contacts with the school, my passion for alternative education only became more intense, as I learned much from students and teachers and their complex urban lives involving oppressive conditions like poverty, gang warfare, and police brutality.

This chapter, then, is my effort to share with you the kind of work that this school undertakes. Therefore, the first purpose of this brief chapter is to give you insight into the history and curriculum of this unique alternative high school and present its culturally specific curricular model. The second purpose of this chapter is to share the personal experiences regarding two of the school's students.

The Dr. Pedro Albizu Campos High School (PACHS): Historical Roots

The PACHS was founded in 1972 as a response to the Eurocentric-based curricula and high dropout/pushout rates that Puerto Rican students had/have been experiencing in Chicago's public high schools. According to an article published on April 8, 1973 in the *Chicago Tribune* titled, "Puerto Ricans Here Set Up Free School to Aid Dropouts," the high school was originally named, "La Escuela Puertorriqueña" (the Puerto Rican School) and originated in the basement of a Chicago church. As the article states:

> The school, which opened in February [1972], is geared to aid Puerto Ricans who have dropped out of Tuley, Wells, and Lake View High Schools. It also serves as an alternative for Puerto Rican students who are considering leaving school because of academic or personal problems... Puerto Rican students, parents, and community leaders have long complained that the Chicago public school system is counterproductive and generally apathetic to the real needs of Puerto Rican students.

Although the high school was originally established for the educational needs of its mostly Puerto Rican student body, the school also currently enrolls Mexican and African-American students from grades nine through twelve. Although I perceived the school to have an overtly Puerto Ricancentric curriculum, I also noted that the teachers and staff at the PACHS worked diligently to accommodate and address the cultural needs of its non-Puerto Rican students. This cultural and pedagogical solidarity was evidenced in a number of ways, such as encouraging students to integrate alternative reading materials into their classes and to reflect, write, and speak about their own people's struggles and experiences. Currently, the high school enrolls eighty students and has an average class size of twelve students.

Since the early 1970s, the school has been located two miles northeast of the heart of the Puerto Rican community known as Paseo Boricua. The high school itself is on the second floor of a two-story building that once housed a former Walgreens photo-developing factory that was purchased by the Puerto Rican Cultural Center. This cultural center is also the umbrella organization under which are operated various community-based Puerto Rican agencies including the high school. As recently as five years ago, this building was nestled in a predominantly Puerto Rican neighborhood comprised of modest homes and small factories. However, these residents have been forced to find cheaper housing in other areas, as the forces of gentrification and the capital of their White, upper-class "developers" have purchased the surrounding factories and converted them into expensive loft apartments. Additionally, the school's exterior is now considered by many of these new residents to be an "eyesore."

Surrounding the exterior of the school building are a series of painted murals depicting the faces of former and current Puerto Rican political prisoners. Also painted on the outside walls of the school are Puerto Rican nationalist slogans, like "Down with capitalism!", "Long live a free Puerto Rico!", and "No to colonialism!" Certainly, for me, these murals left no doubt that the school implicitly supported a political mission/objective—the independence of Puerto Rico from the United States. This particular political mission/objective is also one that I personally support. However, I feel it is important for the reader to know that I had not always supported independence for Puerto Rico. In fact, I had previously detested it.

In my previous life, I was actually a staunch supporter of the colonial status quo. I had been convinced that Puerto Rico could not possibly survive or prosper without the financial or military aid of the United States colonizer. In fact, I had shown committed support to the Popular Democratic Party (the political party that represents the interests of the present colonial status) through my political involvement, such as working in various PDP candidates' campaigns, working at the polls and completing an undergraduate honors thesis on the poetry and socialist life of Luis Muñoz Marín. Muñoz Marín was the author of Puerto Rico's present colonial status and the first popularly elected governor (with much US backed support) of the Island from 1948–1964. However, there was no doubt that my previous political sentiments had been shaped by the public fears of an Island society (including the media's manufactured consent) that was convinced of Puerto Rico's eventual ruin without United States aid.

Again, it was not until I became a doctoral student at Pennsylvania State University that I was encouraged and steered to investigate the alternative history of my people. More specifically, I became very interested in discovering how schooling actually works to serve the interests of a political power structure that thrives on the colonization of its subjects. As I began to read and reflect on this topic, I began to discover how the Puerto Rican educational system was/is used in the attempt to Americanize and strip us of our culture and language. This same colonizing phenomenon,

I found out, was/is also extended to the 3.5 million Puerto Ricans that are schooled in the United States. This linguistic/cultural imperialism has been carried out through the banning of bilingual education in many urban areas and through the lack of a Puerto Rican presence in social studies/history textbooks in classrooms.

This enraged me and helped me realize that I, and many of my Puerto Rican sisters and brothers, have been victims of what Frantz Fanon would have called the "colonized mentality." Finally, I found myself breaking my mental chains of slavery. Therefore, what I saw at the PACHS was a very important project—the decolonization of the mind through alternative education. Rather than view the school as an "eyesore," I viewed the school as a cultural and political space where students had the potential to free their own minds from the interests of a select power hungry status quo.

The educational goal of cultural/historical pride is also facilitated through the housing of a library where many books, articles, and historical artifacts centering on Puerto Rican, Mexican, and African-American history are archived. The high school students and community members at large have access to these resources. The walls of the school's classrooms and surrounding spaces are also covered with artistic representations of Puerto Rican, Mexican, and African-American historical figures created by students and there is a row of student lockers that is painted in the likeness of the Puerto Rican flag. This artwork contributes to the school's sense of Puerto Ricancentricity, while also encouraging the non-Puerto Rican students to pay homage to their historical heroes.

The Curriculum

Although the PACHS has a traditional academic curriculum similar to that of most Chicago public high schools because of state mandates, the content of the school's curriculum is unique because it stresses the Freirian-based concept of "education as liberation." This concept encourages students to become actively engaged within their Puerto Rican community and to question and analyze their lives in relation to those structural forces, beliefs, and/or "common sense" assumptions that only serve to perpetuate a status quo and maintain colonial control over students and community members. This active curricular social analysis was especially evident as I witnessed much dialogue in classes between facilitators and students. However, perhaps the most potent example of this student power was evident during the school's *batey* sessions.

The word *batey* is the Taíno (the indigenous of Puerto Rico) expression for "meeting area." The *batey* is an open area located in the middle of the second-floor portion of the building in which the school is housed. Sofas and chairs line the outside perimeters of this dialogic space. It is in the *batey* that the students and teachers would meet on Tuesday and Friday afternoons for a one-hour class called "Unity for Social Analysis." During this class, the student voices and life experiences regarding topics such as cultural affirmation, police brutality, the dangers of gang life, and patriarchy/feminism were expressed and celebrated/challenged through song, poetry, happiness, anger, and/or sadness. An actualization component consisting of the planning of activities, such as field trips and protest marches was also integrated during these special class meetings.

Funding and Accreditation at the PACHS

The high school is funded and accredited by several federal, state, local, and alternative agencies. For example, the federally subsidized Title I and Title VII programs are earmarked and applied towards the purchase of computers and other instructional materials like books. The students' lunches are subsidized through the Illinois State Board of Education free and reduced lunch program because, a majority of the student body comes from families that fall beneath the federal poverty level.

State funding is made available through Title XX and the Illinois State Department of Child and Family Services. These particular funds are used for the educational services of those students who may come from foster families. The state then disburses this funding to the Alternative Schools Network of Chicago (ASN), which then provides the school with their share of this program funding. These particular monies are also used for these students' counseling services. The City of Chicago also provides funding the mentoring of low income and "at-risk" students while the Mayor's Office of Workforce Development disburses funding for student job placement and training. Additionally, the school has a five-year program with the City of Chicago Colleges' Dual Enrollment Program so that select students have the opportunity to take college-level courses and earn credit at a city college while they are still enrolled at the school. Finally, the school is a member of the Youth Connections Charter Services (YCCS). The YCCS also secures extra funding to the PACHS and its other thirty schools (campuses) in Chicago.

Finally, the school also charges students yearly tuition. The students who are ninth or tenth graders are charged $1,750. However, once a student has reached the eleventh and/or twelfth grades, she/he becomes eligible for a variety of scholarships that are made available through private donors. Consequently, a majority of the eleventh and twelfth grade students do not have to pay the annual tuition. Although the school has funding from these various sources, the school has to be creative in order to limit their overhead costs. An example of this economic creativity is the fact that the school does not hire a full time janitor. All of the staff members participate, on a rotating daily schedule, in the school's maintenance and cleaning. Finally, the school is registered by the Illinois State Board of Education and accredited by the National association for the Legal Support of Alternative Schools (NALSAS). This accreditation enables the students to receive a regular high school diploma upon graduation.

Overthrowing Dehumanization: Claiming Humanity through Student Voices

During my work at the school as a part-time Spanish teacher, janitor, and tutor I had the wonderful opportunity to speak with countless students, teachers, and community members about the community and the school. However, some of my most intriguing conversations were with Melissa and Damien (not their real names). Both Melissa and Damien were currently enrolled students who had been enrolled at PACHS for several years who privileged me with their time in order to talk to me about their schooling experiences. They also spoke about the power that seems to be inherent within an alternative school curriculum that celebrates cultural affirmation. Although this section is brief, I hope that it will enable the reader to catch a glimpse of these students' experiences.

Perhaps the most exciting theme that was common was that of "cultural resurrection." Damien, in fact, described his previous Chicago public school experience as one of being "brainwashed." For him, a personal brainwashing was carried out through an overemphasis on Eurocentric history. He commented:

> In the Chicago public schools, I was brainwashed. There was always a side of me that always wanted to learn more about my culture. I wanted to learn more than what my parents or

schools were telling me. In my previous schools, they never taught me what I wanted to know. They would only teach me to pledge allegiance to the United States flag and sing the Star Spangled Banner. They [previous teachers] never told me about the colonization of Puerto Rico, Cuba, Guam, and the Philippines. Here, I learn about my history and culture.

Melissa also expressed the same sentiments concerning being exposed to the her/histories of Puerto Rican nationalist figures, such as Luisa Capetillo, Dr. Pedro Albizu Campos, and Hostos. She also told me that she had not been politically conscious or encouraged to explore Puerto Rican issues in her public school experiences

> At my old Chicago public high school I had no idea who Pedro Albizu Campos [former leader of the Puerto Rican Nationalist Party] was or who Lolita Lebrón was [in the mid 1950s Lebrón led three other Puerto Rican males into the U.S. Capitol building, opened fire, and declared, "Long live a free Puerto Rico!" Upon their arrest and convictions, they would serve federal prison sentences. President Jimmy Carter pardoned them in 1979]. I had no idea who these people were. Somebody came up to me and asked me if I knew what the "*Grito de Lares*" was [an important historical event where the "Republic of Puerto Rico" was declared by Puerto Rican nationalist leaders against the Spanish in the town of Lares in 1868]. I was like, "What is that?" My Puerto Ricaness was challenged when they then asked me if I was really Puerto Rican. I was then told that I should know this stuff. None of this was ever taught to me. I think public schools should have different kinds of history classes like African history, South American history, and stuff that isn't normally taught.

There were additional informal conversations that I had with other PACHS students contained similar types of statements from a "cultural resurrection" perspective. For me, it was clear that a school curriculum that embraced and sponsored a cultural space was a determining factor for its students' high retention rates, which are currently about 95%. This, indeed, is in sharp contrast to recent research findings that highlight the average 55–85% pushout rates that plague Puerto Rican high school students in most urban school districts.

The Continuing Journey: The Second "Transformation" of the School

The PACHS is entering a second transformation of various forms. Recently, the school's director of nineteen years was awarded a prestigious fellowship that would allow him to visit other alternative schools around the world. As a result, a new administration was chosen to lead the school. This new administration is unique because it is co-directed under the leadership of two Puerto Rican women who also hold teaching responsibilities at the school. While the administration has been transformed, five veteran teachers have also left the school to seek alternative horizons. In their place, new teachers have been hired.

Another transformation concerns the physical space and location of the PACHS. The strong forces of gentrification have determined that the school no longer has a place among its high priced loft apartment buildings. Therefore, the school took advantage of their location by accepting a substantial purchase amount for their building. Consequently, the money is being allocated for the major renovation of a building, which will house the school and be located in the very heart of the Puerto Rican community of Chicago. There are also new teachers who are contributing new energy and pedagogical practices to the students and community. Indeed, after more than thirty years of struggle and resistance, the school remains strong as it enters the new millennium.

In conclusion, colonialism relies on the physical, psychological, cultural, and pedagogical dehumanization of its subjects for its strength and maintenance. Many colonial subjects from within the belly of the beast, however, have found their own strength and empowerment through organized campaigns/agencies of resistance, such as alternative schools that are actively engaged with oppressed communities. The PACHS has managed to survive serious confrontations with the CIA, the FBI, and local police who have consistently attempted to undermine the community's battle with those who are content maintaining a complacent status quo. Examples of this state-sponsored repression include the FBI's 1983 break-in of the Puerto Rican Cultural Center where student documents were stolen and physical damage to the building was incurred.

A more recent example of this continued harassment includes the issuance of federal subpoenas to teachers and students to appear before a grand jury to testify about the school's so-called involvement with "terrorist activities." The powerful connection between alternative education and communities serves a very important mission of giving power to those who traditionally have none. This powerful connection continues to be evidenced through the school's work with VIDA/SIDA, which is a Puerto Rican Cultural Center project that serves to educate the community about issues related to HIV/AIDS prevention and treatment. Another connection is visible with the school and its work with Paseo Boricua, which continues to be the site of an exciting economic development plan that is attracting Puerto Rican business owners to this area of Chicago. It is also here that an annual Puerto Rican parade and festival are held and where the office housing the Puerto Rican political prisoners' campaign for freedom operates. Thus, because the school is involved with these projects, we still see hope in claiming our humanity.

A School for Today

Mimsy Sadofsky

Mimsy was born in 1940 in Houston, Texas and has three grown chil-
dren, all of whom attended Sudbury Valley School for virtually their entire
schooling. She was one of the group that founded Sudbury Valley School in
Framingham, Massachusetts, in 1968, and has been deeply involved in the
establishment of over a dozen other schools throughout the world based on a
similar educational philosophy. She has served in a wide variety of capacities
at the school—teaching French, cooking, algebra, bookkeeping, management,
writing, English literature; helping produce plays; occupying administrative
positions in admissions and overseeing the school's public relations program.
Mimsy has spoken extensively in public forums about education, has written
several articles, and is co-author of the books Legacy of Trust, Kingdom of
Childhood, Starting a Sudbury School, *and* The Pursuit of Happiness.

In 1968, the group of people who started Sudbury Valley School in
Framingham, Massachusetts, began by examining the values common
in American society in order to determine what values should guide our
schools.

How, we asked, can a school best foster creativity? The answer was
amazingly simple—and amazingly complex. People are learners. They are
born already working on their education! They are born curious—and
striving. How else can you explain the unbelievable development in the
first few years of life from a pretty much helpless infant, with only the most
fundamental communication skill, into a walking, talking toddler whose
universe expands exponentially from month to month. They are born creative.

No one at all has to explain learning processes to an infant. You can't
stop them, and each one learns differently: how to roll over, or to sit up,
how to explore with their fingers, to stand, to walk, to say a few words and
then a few sentences, and then express an infinite number of thoughts, many
complex and abstract. Infants begin life learning in the ways we all use when
we are learning for our own pleasure. They explore. They imitate. They ex-

perience. They build more complex world views from trial and error. It is simple to understand, but terribly difficult to accept, that the individual is best served at every age by allowing that native curiosity and creativity to be undeflected and uninterrupted; that the best schooling may be the schooling that least impedes the mind's free exploration of the environment.

Why don't we have schools today that allow a tremendous amount of individual freedom to follow curiosity? Why do we have schools today that have not incorporated the basic notion that an individual has, from earliest childhood, a world view, and that each individual hungers constantly to expand that world view, to expand the size of their bubble, to bring what is outside their bubble in, to refine their perception of the world? To learn.

What is the school like? How do these principles get put into practice? First, let me set the stage. The school enrolls students from the age of four up. No one is too old, although most of our students are nineteen or younger. The people in the school, no matter what age they are, are each doing what they want to do. Usually that means that some people are doing things with others, who can be of the most various of ages, and some people are doing things alone. Usually it means that most people are doing things not done in most other schools, and some are doing things that are done in other schools with a very unusual intensity and concentration. It more often means that children are teaching adults than that adults are teaching children, but most often people are learning while unconscious that "learning" is taking place. Doing what they choose to do is the common theme; learning is the byproduct. It is first and foremost a place where students are free to follow their inner dictates. They are free to do what we all do when we have the time to, and what we all find to be most satisfactory: they play.

Play is the most serious pursuit at Sudbury Valley. This is not an accident. Psychologists pretty much agree these days that allowing the mind to roam freely has the most potential for mind-expansion. In fact, when we talk about our most creative moments, we describe them as "playing with new ideas." This is a process that cannot be forced. Creativity can grow only in such freedom. Some people play at games, and some play at things which we who have more traditional educations are more comfortable with—writing or art or mathematics or music. But we are quite clear at Sudbury Valley that it is doing what you want to that counts! We have no curriculum and place no value on one pursuit over another. The reason that we are secure in feeling this way is that we constantly see that people play more and more sophisticated "games," explore more and more deeply, that they constantly expand their knowledge of the world, and their ability to handle themselves in it.

Children who play constantly do not draw an artificial line between work and play. In fact, you could say that they are working constantly if you did not see the joy in the place, a joy most usually identified with the pursuit of avocations.

The school has about twenty-five rooms, in two separate buildings. On an average rainy day it is teeming with activity. The rooms are small and large, many are special purpose rooms, like shops and labs, but most are furnished like rather shabby living or dining rooms in homes: lots of sofas, easy chairs, and tables. Lots of people sitting around talking, reading, and playing games. On an average rainy day—quite different from a beautiful, suddenly snowy day, or a warm spring or fall day—most people are inside. But there will also be more than a few who are outside in the rain, and later will come in dripping and trying the patience of the few people inside who think the school should perhaps be a "dry zone."

There may be people in the photo lab developing or printing pictures they have taken. There may be a karate class, or just some people playing on mats in the dance room. Someone may be building a bookshelf in the woodworking shop in the barn—or fashioning chain mail armor and discussing medieval history. There are almost certainly a few people, either together or separate, making music of one kind or another, and others listening to music of one kind or another. You might find a French class, or Latin, or algebra. You will find adults in groups that include kids, or maybe just talking with one student. It would be most unusual if there were not people playing a computer game somewhere, or chess; a few people doing some of the school's administrative work in the office—while others hang around just enjoying the atmosphere of an office where interesting people are always making things happen; there will be people engaged in role-playing games; other people may be rehearsing a play—it might be original, it might be a classic. They may intend production or momentary amusement. People will be trading stickers and trading lunches. There will probably be people selling things. If you are lucky, someone will be selling cookies they baked at home and brought in to earn money.

Sometimes groups of kids have cooked something to sell in order to raise money for an activity—perhaps they need to buy a new kiln, or want to go on a trip. An intense conversation will probably be in progress in the smoking room, and others in other places. A group in the kitchen may be cooking—maybe pizza or apple pie. Always, either in the art room or in any one of many other places, people will be drawing. In the art room, they might also be sewing, or painting, and some are quite likely to be working with clay, either on the wheel or by hand. Always there are groups talking, and always there are people quietly reading here and there.

One of the things most adults notice first about Sudbury Valley is the ease of communication. People, no matter what their age, look right at each other, and treat each other with tremendous consideration and easy respect. Fear is absent. There is a comfortable air of self-confidence, the confidence normal to people pursuing the goals they set themselves. Things are almost never quiet, and there is (to an outsider) an exhausting intensity, but the activity is not chaotic or frenetic. Visitors speak of a feeling of a certain order, even though it is clearly a place full of enthusiasm.

The students at Sudbury Valley are "doin' what comes natur'ly." But they are not necessarily choosing what comes easily. A close look discovers that everyone is challenging her or himself; that every kid is acutely aware of her or his own weaknesses and strengths, and is extremely likely to be working hardest on her or his weaknesses. If the weaknesses are social, the child is very unlikely to be stuck away in a quiet room with a book. And if athletics are hard, the child is likely to be outdoors playing basketball.

Along with the ebullient good spirits, there is an underlying serious-ness—even the six-year-olds know that they, and only they, are responsible for their education. They have been given the gift of tremendous trust, and they understand that this gift is as big a responsibility as it is a delight. They are acutely aware that very young people are not given this much freedom or this much responsibility almost anywhere in the world. But growing up shouldering this responsibility makes for a very early confidence in your own abilities—you get, as one graduate says, a "track record." Self-motivation is never even a question. That's all there is. An ex-student has described some of these effects:

> There are a lot of things about Sudbury Valley that I think are on a personal level, that build your character, things that perhaps enable you to learn better, that public school students never have a chance to achieve. When you're responsible for your own time, and spend it the way that you want to, you tend to put a lot more enthusiasm into what you do, instead of being a lethargic lump

that's molded and prodded into a certain direction. And when
you end up the way you want to end up, you know you've been
responsible for it. It's a lot more rewarding, I think, than when
you end up the way somebody else wants you to end up."

Who are the kids in this school? Are they chosen for creativity, intelligence, or perhaps some other standard? It is a private school—does that
mean it appeals to only the well-to-do? Admission is on a first-come, first-
served basis, and we have never been full. That means that the students in
this school consist of everyone who wants to come whose parents will allow them to. It includes the cerebral and the super-active, the "regular" and
the "zeroed-in"—the full gamut of possibilities. Most of the families who
choose to send their children to SVS are looking for something they wish
they could find in public schools, but cannot: simple freedom for their children to develop according to their own timetables and their own desires.
Is it perfection? Hardly. But it is tremendously stimulating and exciting.

Sudbury Valley is a functioning democracy. There is a School Meeting
which meets once a week to take care of all the management work, either
by directly accomplishing it or by delegating it. Each student and each staff
member has one vote, and the meetings are run in an extremely orderly fashion. The School Meeting makes a budget each year, ever so carefully, because
the tuition is low and it is important to be thrifty and not to spend money
needlessly. Yes, kids know this, and are much harsher judges of what is—or
is not—a necessary expense. The School Meeting passes every rule, often
after weeks of soul-searching debate. This includes the rule about "no litter-
ing," the rules about not ever setting a foot in the pond, the rules that govern
which rooms eating is okay in, and which ones you can play the radio in, as
well as the rules protecting individual rights. It is up to the School Meeting
to approve groups organizing to pursue special interests that want budgets
or space. Anyone who thinks that young children are not wise about these
matters need only attend a few such school meetings.

The School Meeting delegates some tasks to subgroups or to people
elected by them to carry out certain responsibilities. A subgroup called
the Public Relations Committee is composed of people interested in the
school's public relations work; others serve on the school's Bookkeeping Committee. Someone is elected to see to the Grounds' Maintenance.
Another person is elected to keep computer records of all of the judicial
activities. All of us are totally accountable and totally aware of our account-

ability every minute. The School Meeting also debates candidates for staff, votes on them in an all day, school-wide, secret balloting, and awards contracts according to needs determined by this balloting. There is no tenure.

There is also a subgroup of the School Meeting set up to deal with rule infractions. It is called the Judicial Committee, and its function is to investigate written complaints about possible rule violations, and to see that justice is served, being constantly careful about due process. Does it work? You bet it does. Peer justice is amazingly effective. Rules are often broken, but the culprits are usually good natured about both admitting what has happened and accepting their punishment.

We have no curriculum. If you send your children to this school, however, there are some certainties about what they learn. They learn how to debate, and how to ask for what they want, and see to it that they get it. They learn to ponder ethical questions. They learn how to concentrate: they can focus on things the way few adults that I know can, and this gives results. The same focus that a five-year-old puts into sand castles, a seven-year-old puts into drawing, an eleven-year-old into making a gingerbread house, a nine-year-old into chess, a twelve-year-old into Dungeons and Dragons, an eight-year-old into climbing forty feet up in the beech tree, a fifteen-year-old into writing a story, a seventeen-year-old into making armor, or an eighteen-year-old into preparing for graduation. That kind of preparation will serve them well in each and every pursuit they choose as adults.

Windsor House

Meghan Hughes and Jim Carrico

Jim was introduced to Windsor House 1994, after his then eleven-year-old daughter informed him that she was quitting school, which made her so sad and angry that she refused to participate. Jim, Anarose and her little sister Ruby soon became full-fledged community members. They noticed at first glance the freedom that the children were given, and very definitely taking, but it was only later that they began to appreciate the inward reality in which this was anchored: a deep and honest respect for children, parents, and everyone else. They also noticed Meghan, a Windsor House teacher for whom the school was founded in 1971, by her mother, Helen, when she too refused to go to school. Jim and Meghan Carrico were married in 1996 and have since produced two future Windsor House alumni, Miles and Iris.

Situated on a low ridge overlooking the port of North Vancouver in British Columbia, Windsor House School seems at first glance like any other in the district. Constructed to house the Cloverly Elementary School, the building is a paragon of 1960s' institutional architecture. About a dozen classrooms lie astride a single two-story axis, with a gymnasium complex forming the bottom of an L, and a broad, flat field behind. Walking down the hallway on a weekend or an evening when the school is empty, one might glimpse a ghost of the way it was: classes filled with desks in rows, all eyes facing the teacher at the blackboard, every notebook open to the same page until a bell announces it's time to open another. But there's something very different going on around here these days.

A group of visitors were recently somewhat astounded to stumble into the midst of the Saxon invasion of Britain (circa AD 900)—children dressed in flowing robes and cardboard armor furiously defending the castle Camelot against newspaper-sword-toting attackers advancing and retreating in waves up and down the hall. On another day the same group may have seen a group of children hotly debating a new clean-up policy; or a plan to rename and re-purpose one of the classrooms; or whether or not there should be a new voting category, in addition to "in favor," "opposed," and "abstain," called "really don't care."

Or, perhaps, they may arrive on a warm spring day to find nearly every student and staff member outside enjoying the sunshine. It's even possible that they may find a group of students in a classroom, attentive to a teacher at a blackboard, although the "teacher" may be a parent or one of the students. First-time visitors may be inclined to think that Windsor House is disorganized, but there are very strong underlying principles at work, and it is a form of organization that becomes apparent as soon as the usual preconceptions are put aside about what a school is and should be.

The philosophical bedrock on which Windsor House rests is non-coercive education, the belief that human beings will eagerly learn what they are interested in learning, and resent being forced to do, say, think, or learn anything that does not interest them. Complementing this is a strong sense that healthy development must take place in the context of a healthy community, and much effort has been made to create and maintain a micro-society in which parents, staff, and children participate equally. The vitality of the school depends heavily on the day-to-day involvement of parents and other adult members of the community (including former students), who provide a diversity of skills, interests, and enthusiasms, and a strong network of physical and emotional support.

Among the few schools in British Columbia that have attempted to realize this philosophy, Windsor House is unique in that it lies entirely within the administrative bosom of the School Board and the Ministry of Education, and receives the same funding and pupil/staff ratio as any other public school.

The student population of Windsor House has been rising steadily for some time, with current enrollment hovering around ninety, from five to sixteen years old. Some parents bring their infant children to school with them, which further extends the continuum of age and developmental level. Because the students are free to move about the school as they please, the stratification by age that is a fixture of conventional education is entirely absent, and they naturally group around common interests and activities. Learning at Windsor House is sought out and initiated by the children.

Structured classes are provided for those who ask for them, and although "unsolicited" classes may be offered by staff members or parents, no student is compelled to attend.

The community is particularly careful about subtle forms of coercion, typically of the form, "If you don't learn to __, then you'll never be able to ___," which some parents may tend to apply if their child doesn't seem to be "choosing" to learn the basic academic skills at the same rate as kids their age in other schools. This is understandable given the depth of ingrown assumptions about education that most of us have been brought up with.

By painful experience, however, this attitude has been seen to lead directly back to a formal curriculum, or at the very least the creation of hidden agendas that undermine the child's ability and desire to seek out his or her own path. The one thing that cannot be taught is self-knowledge: "What do I enjoy?" "What animates and interests and motivates me?" Ultimately no one can answer these questions but the individuals themselves and, in the absence of this knowledge, all the learning in the world is of little use. Non-coercive education is based on trust, and the conviction that people of all ages have a right to self-determination.

In harmony with this basic premise, the general forms and structures of the school are in a continual state of evolution. Aside from basic safety rules which are insisted upon by the School Board (and to a large extent by common sense), every aspect of the operation of Windsor House is up for discussion and democratic vote by the whole community on a one-person, one-vote basis. Even the basic philosophy and direction of the school is the subject of ongoing debate; thus, Windsor House has no constitution of "entrenched" principles, but always reflects the views and concerns of current community members, and has in fact undergone major shifts over the years. At one time, all decisions at Windsor House were made by unanimous consensus, but this was seen to provide a loophole for a sort of tyranny of the most stubborn, and was eventually abandoned in favor of a two-thirds majority vote.

It is ironic that in a society that sees itself as democratic, it would be taken for granted that children should be raised under conditions of virtual dictatorship. Giving children an equal right to participate in setting the standards and guidelines by which they will live seems necessary if they are to mature into adults that are capable of participating in a genuine democracy. Windsor House is hardly without rules: there are plenty. The important thing is that anyone who dislikes a rule is free to gather support to change it.

Nor is Windsor House without conflicts: they happen literally every day. Every effort is made to resolve them in as creative and constructive a manner as possible. The current judicial system is based on a rotating committee of student volunteers, with one staff member, which meets two or three times a week to deal with complaints and infractions of standing resolutions. The accused are always given the opportunity to defend themselves, and consequences, if necessary, are set appropriately (e.g., mandatory separation for the rest of the day or week for fighting). The ultimate consequence is temporary or permanent exile from the community: there are probably very few schools at which the most dreaded punishment is not to be allowed to attend. But even this can't really be called punishment, it being ultimately a matter of freely choosing to participate in a community, or not, according to rules openly created and enforced by everyone.

In all of this, the structures that are created deal mainly with what children and adults cannot do; what they can do tends to be left open. Over a period of time, different uses have evolved for certain rooms; a library, of course, and an art room, a computer room, and so on; but also a room for just lounging around in, and another specifically dedicated to horseplay. Occasionally, the whole school is involved in a single activity, most notably during the simulation games that have been held on a regular basis for many years. These are conceived of as on-going theater pieces using the entire building and grounds as a stage, for which there is no audience but the actors themselves.

Participants are responsible for developing their own characters, and writing their own parts, and much time and preparation goes into sets, costumes, and collectively drafting scenarios for the plot. In some ways it replaces a traditional social studies class, but develops a much broader range of skills, and happens to be a lot more fun. This past year the game covered the Celtic culture from 200 BC up to the time of King Arthur. Previous games have dealt with ancient Greece and Egypt, West Coast natives, and even the Paleolithic Era.

Students frequently plan and carry out role-playing games on a smaller scale, or other self-organized activities. Recently a group of seven- to ten-year-olds passed a resolution to sell hot dogs and floats at lunch time. With the help of a staff member and a parent, the "Pig-Out Stand" has made an average profit of $50 per week, split evenly between the school and the student entrepreneurs. Some of the younger boys gained approval to begin digging a "mine" in an overgrown slope behind the school, and have been bagging for sale "natural soil," with half the proceeds to be donated to help the Pygmies save their rainforest homes. After about a week, one of the parents took a resolution to a school meeting that children refrain from digging in the roots of the nearby trees, drawing attention to the way our activities can affect our surroundings in unintended ways, and incidentally contributing to the hands-on democracy of Windsor House.

The spontaneous atmosphere belies the years of conscious effort and experimentation that have gone into the development of the culture of Windsor House. The school was founded in 1971 by Helen Hughes (who remains at the center of community) at her house on Windsor Street (hence the name) in North Vancouver. The school evolved out of a parent-participation preschool at which Helen had taught, but was specifically necessitated by the degree to which her daughter Meghan, then age eight, despised public school. The school began with an enrollment of twenty-five children aged five to eight, and was paid for largely by the day care that Helen provided before and after school. After four years of shoestring budgets and overcrowding, a group of parents successfully lobbied the School Board to finance the school as a special program within an existing elementary school.

The next fifteen years saw a slow process by which the school began to resemble more and more the rest of the school system, as one after another piece was introduced: twenty minutes per day of mandatory instruction led to folders of basic work to be completed each day, which led to using the mornings for schoolwork and afternoons for "fun" activities, which eventually led to structured classes and activities all day long. In 1989, a group of community members visited Sudbury Valley School, and our experiences led to an attempt to reverse this trend and return the school to its non-coercive roots. This initiative resulted in a near-fatal conflict that literally split the school in two. But by rediscovering its original philosophy, and recommitting itself to a non-coercive pedagogy, Windsor House has recovered and emerged much stronger.

Sometimes referred to as a "school for the severely unique," Windsor House is definitely not resting on its laurels. Simply maintaining its existence within an occasionally hostile system requires constant vigilance and effort. Part of its longevity is attributable to the political activism of many parents, attending school board meetings *en masse* when necessary to counter any threat to the program. One year, a complaint filed by an unhappy parent led to the formation of an external review committee to assess the situation. The team toured the school, attended meetings and interviewed community members, and delivered a positive report, describing the school as "vibrant" and fulfilling a "critical need." The team went on to recommend that additional space and staff be made available to the school, that it be allowed a permanent home in its current facilities, and that the program be expanded to grade twelve. Some of these requests have been partially met, others are pending, but there have been no guarantees, and nothing is being taken for granted. The only constant is change: children grow, and the community continues to evolve.

Building an Alternative Education Movement in Turkey

Bülent Akdağ and Eylem Korkmaz

Eylem, who is one of the founding members and the director of the management board of Alternative Education Association, has an MA from the Educational Administration and Supervision Program. She is currently studying for her PhD in the department of Curriculum and Instruction at Ylidiz Technical University in Istanbul. She has published a book on the Montessori method and articles on alternative education in various journals.

Bülent is one of the founding members and the deputy director of Alternative Education Association in Turkey and graduated from Hacettepe University Philosophy Department. He received his MA on Education Policies and PhD in Education Philosophy. He submitted papers on Education and Philosophy at various congresses. He was co-author of two books, on human rights in school books and on the profession of teaching. His articles have been published in education and philosophy journals. Currently, he's working as a lecturer in İstanbul at Marmara University, teaching education philosophy.

Any evaluation of the current state of alternative education in Turkey is only possible through understanding the strict centralist structure of its education system. The mentality of creating mono-type individuals in the Republican Era has been maintained for almost eighty years.

In Turkey's path to a secular society, many particular social attitudes have become entrenched: an individual and social submission to power; a conservative social milieu; a lack of awareness among families of the authoritarian state structure, which doesn't allow establishment of independent schools free from state control. These attitudes have undermined debates about alternative education and, consequently, the practice of alternative education. The slow progress of democratization and interruptions to this process caused by military coups has prevented the formation of different voices in education, as well as in many other fields. During periods in other parts of the world when criticisms of mainstream education intensified and alternative schools gained acceleration, the same developments have been unable to take place in Turkey.

In particular, "Though the winds of 1968 created a strong movement in Turkey; this era was closed before any questioning of institutions was initiated"[1] Through the "Code on Reunification of Education" from 1924, all educational institutions were gathered under the umbrella of the Ministry of National Education. The reasoning of this law says that the individuals of a nation can only be educated in one single form; otherwise there cannot be any union of feelings, ideas, and solidarity. Thus, an understanding of state-centred education was legally and conceptually formulated in the foundation of the Republic of Turkey.

The philosophical foundations of this educational concept that emerged were based on pragmatist / instrumentalist philosophical thought and approaches[2]. In 1940, a new model of education was launched in Turkey named "Village Institutes" which survived for about thirteen years and educated thousands of teachers. The Village Institutes are very significant in the education history of Turkey and for training teachers for the enlightenment age of Turkey, and are described as an alternative education model by many researchers and intellectuals. Therefore, it would be appropriate to clarify why we don't deem Village Institutes as "alternative."

The Village Institutes were based on the concept that the education should start in the rural areas and they maintained a work-centred formation. They blatantly pursued the aim of spreading the principles of the revolution of Republican Turkey via missionary teachers and became part of mainstream education project of Turkey during 1940s. It was an attempt an institutionalization which introduced a methodological difference, a new model of education.

The state of Turkey pursued two main goals through Village Institutes; one ideological and one economic. The regime intended a political socialization which would be based on Western values ideologically and regarded education as an important instrument for this. As a matter of fact, the concept of development via education was prevailing during World War II. This approach was a substantial aspect of the modernization theories of the time, and it was influential all around the globe. The economic goal was to boost the agricultural production in the cheapest way using the rural proletariat by means of Village Institutes. The method for that was the policy of mass arts and crafts training which was used to train qualified labour forces for when capitalism made a leap forward via industrialization.[3]

Thus, we do not feel it is appropriate to consider Village Institutes within the panorama of the history of alternative education. The teacher candidates attending the Institutes were raised in line with Atatürk's principles and revolutionary goals. The students can't be said to have the right to identify their needs and make a choice. The Institutes remained a part of our education system and were inscribed in Turkey's education history as a model of a producer work-education school. The Village Institutes were a model of the compulsory education system. Therefore, it cannot be considered within the general framework of alternative education. Rather than being human-centred, it was state and nation-centred.

In the Basic Code on National Education (1973), the attributes of the "person" to be achieved through national education were clarified and described in law. The three goals to be achieved are: "good people," "productive people" and "good citizens." In accordance with these targets, a statist and nationalist education system has emerged. Today, the "positivist" education system of Turkey is trying to integrate with neo-liberal education policies and European Union education models by basing its philosophical foundations on "pragmatism."

In this context, any attempt towards alternative education in Turkey faces many challenges. Unsurprisingly, the strict political and legal structure of the education system has prevented alternative education models from emerging. In Turkey, instigating a debate on "raising a monotype person," which was set by the Ministry of National Education in the course of the Republican Era, and placing alternative education models on the agenda seems to be a long path which is only achievable by changing conventional perspectives.

In general, "seeing the human" in education, thinking about ideal forms of education, considering basic aspects of human nature, and raising concerns about the problems in the traditional structure of our education system are very limited in Turkey.[4] Up until very recently there was very little discussion about alternative forms of education in Turkey, and this was limited to a few books, article translations, and attempts to apply Montessori methods in pre-school education.

It can be said that books and articles published on alternative education gained a slow acceleration only after 1990s. For example, *A Primer of Libertarian Education* by Joel Spring; *The Secret of Childhood* by Maria

Montessori, and some books of Paulo Freire, A.S. Neill, Ivan Illich, John Holt were available in Turkey years after the originals had been published, but unfortunately there wasn't much of interest from the public. We can say that the books translated into Turkish on alternative education are limited to the above mentioned.

Though these are very important reference books, each of them deals with a different aspect of alternative education. Thus, the major task in front of us is publishing books that explain different applications of alternative education all together to provide a holistic perspective to the reader on "alternative education movement." In 2005, a meeting of scholars and individual practitioners was gathered, which has speeded up the alternative education process in our country. Consequently, the goal was set to learn about alternative education models from around the world in an organized manner, and discussions and initiatives were launched for applications in Turkey.

In 2005, Prof. Dr. Muhsin Hesapçıoğlu with Marmara University MA students Burçak Morhayım, Selma Çakmaklı and Eylem Korkmaz decided to organize the 1st International Symposium on Alternative Education, considering the theoretical and practical gaps in Turkey in the field of alternative education. The tools to be used in order to intensify alternative education studies in Turkey were assessed, and a symposium was identified to be the most efficient instrument as it would ensure that we would all benefit from international experts who have worked for years in this field. The symposium also gathered together various people interested in alternative education from around Turkey. In the symposium, many examples of methods and schools from various models of alternative education were presented as far as the budget and conditions of the symposium allowed.

The aim was to provide a general idea on all models without bringing a specific model to the forefront, so that the participants would be able to take initiative on theory and practice of the models and methods that they feel close to. The presentations conducted in the course of the symposium—"Compulsory Education" by Matt Hern, "Alternative Education Philosophies" by Ron Miller, "Waldorf Education" by Jill Sayre Wolcott, "Montessori Education" by Cheryl Ferreira, "Democratic Education" by Yaacov Hecht, "Free Schools, Summerhill Example" by Jason Preater. "Critical Pedagogy and the MST Example" by Metin Yeğin, and "From Authoritarian Education to Free Education" by Tayfun Özkaya—were the presentations which dealt with the critical pedagogy. Besides these names, distinguished researchers from Turkey conducted effective presentations by combining their experiences from Turkey with alternative education. About three hundred people from different cities attended this symposium, which was the first ever gathering of this sort in Turkey. It may be said that this number demonstrates quite a good participation level and high interest in alternative education.

It was planned to set up study groups to sustain the process begun at the symposium. Therefore, at the end of the symposium, two calls for meetings were made; one for the organizations and one for individuals. The meeting for individuals was attended by about twenty people, thus planting the first seeds of the Alternative Education Association. In the first meeting, the symposium process was explained and ideas were put forward for the work to be conducted in the future. A mail list was created and, one month later, the group came together for a second meeting. Now, there is a group of people called the "Alternative Education Working Group," which organizes regular meetings.

This group of ten to fifteen activist members has started to examine alternative education examples from around the world by means of their web-based communication network. They have been intensively discussing "education," "alternative education," and "projects for application" in their meetings. Each of the group members comes from a different background; they have different areas of expertise and different expectations. Furthermore, there is another communication network for participants who have a general interest in the subject apart from the activist members of the Alternative Education Group.

Shortly after the group was constructed, it was decided to establish an association as it would facilitate fundraising for the activities of the group, and the Alternative Education Association was established about one year after the symposium. The main goal of the association was described as creating an alternative education agenda for Turkey, developing methods and practices, as well as supporting initiatives for practical examples. A web site was built on the subject to provide reference material. However, there are still many deficiencies of the association stemming from the lack of human resources and budget. The Alternative Education Association has now found office space for its files and other official documentation at the premises of Buğday Association, while still endeavoring to create a site for itself. The Alternative Education Association has conducted many activities in its year and a half existence, despite limited opportunities.

Currently, the activities of the association are developed in accordance with the people who wish to share their knowledge, the demands of the individuals, and the needs of the association members. Though the founders of the association are familiar with different methods of alternative education, activities are organized with the help of people from outside the association, in particular those who have experience with these methods abroad, as most of the members do not have a practical knowledge of specific methods. Although each member of the association has a special interest or affinity with a specific alternative education method or alternative school, these personal interests are set aside, and all alternative education methods are included as far as possible while organizing activities, because many alternative education methods and alternative schools are unknown to the public in Turkey.

The Montessori method, which is the most commonly known, has attracted the interest of those educators who work in the pre-school education. The other model that is known in Turkey is critical pedagogy, as an area of particular interest for the socialists. Though Alternative Education Association hasn't yet organized activities on all of the methods, it has taken steps forward on the way to become an umbrella organization for all alternative education methods.

At the symposium, the presentation of a wide variety of activities and projects provided people with ample motivation to start new initiatives. Hearing about alternative education in various parts of the world resulted in many people contacting the association. It can be seen as unimportant to mention the activities of the association for the readers, but it is vital to show the low level of knowledge and applications of alternative education in Turkey. Therefore the activities and level of projects in Turkey will be briefly explained.

* * *

Three Waldorf seminars and workshops have been organized since the symposium was held. According to a message received by the Association just before the last Waldorf session, the Turkish-speaking Waldorf preschool teachers in Germany have discussed whether to open a center in Turkey for training Waldorf teachers. Meanwhile, Pinar Hacaoglu, one of the founding members of the Association, decided to set up a Waldorf school in Izmir, and visited Germany to examine such schools. This is one of the strongest attempts at establishing Waldorf education in Turkey. Previous attempts that had been made by Turkish expatriates living in Germany did not yield any positive results. The Association has been substantially successful in bringing like-minded people together and creating links between them.

Participants from the Diyarbakır-based KAMER Foundation (Women's Centre Foundation) also attended the Alternative Education Symposium. KAMER, established in 1997, is conducting women and children's projects in twenty-three cities in Eastern and South Eastern Turkey. KAMER has built twelve children houses and carries out significant projects organizing against honor killings and violence against women. According to the foundation, women and children issues are deeply interconnected, so after the Istanbul Symposium, it sought the Alternative Education Association's help to organize a symposium named " Preschool Alternative Education Models" as a part of their "Give Life to Children Project." Nearly all of the hundred participants at this second symposium, which was held in Diyarbakir, were either KAMER's volunteers or professional workers from different cities. After the symposium, it targeted choosing alternative education methods suitable to the local environment and implementing these to the children houses

Matt Hern, who spoke at both symposiums, also shared his thoughts and experiences in a "Deschooling and Democratic Education" panel discussion organized in Istanbul. This was the first serious discussion of deschooling in Turkey. Deschooling, which is a reaction against the institutionalization of education, against certification, against the monopolization of "knowledge" by governmental institutions, and supporting families' choice to educate their children by themselves will be difficult to realize in Turkey. However, it is worth mentioning that two significant models have been implemented in Turkey along similar lines. Although they do not completely qualify as alternative education projects, "BILAR" and the "Free University" may be considered as examples of alternatives to government-run educational institutions.

The first one, BILAR, was founded by socialist author Aziz Nesin, as an alternative where academics expelled from government universities could give lectures. Nesin describes BILAR thus :

> We conceive BILAR as a "people's university" ... It is a university which low-educated laborers, a housewife, or a university student could attend. We tried to create this opportunity, but couldn't succeed. The laborers didn't show much interest; neither were they desirous enough.

Unfortunately, BILAR did not survive long. The Free University was founded in 1992 and merged with the Forum of Turkey and Middle East Association in 1998. Fikret Başkaya, Director of the Free University describes the Free University in these words:

> We don't aim to replace present universities—because we don't issue diplomas, we don't give exams. We don't have a profession-oriented education. Our studies aim to criticize and abolish these things. We criticize the official history and ideology that infects the educational system. We are trying to create a consciousness against global capitalism. We organize lectures, conferences, seminars; we publish books and periodicals to achieve this.

The Free University, which offers education at two centers, doesn't have any financial support from any institution and collects only a symbolic fee from the students. The Association is trying to survive with Fikret Baskaya's book revenues. The Free University is an important example and has reached thousands of students since 1992.

In terms of home education, only one name stands out in Turkey: Rock singer Erkin Koray who didn't send his daughter to school because of what he calls a "ridiculous" education system. In the entire Modern Turkish history, he is the only person who has openly renounced the Turkish education system. In recent years, Islamic circles have started discussing home education. In Turkey, the headscarf is forbidden at all schools as well as universities. Consequently, many students have left Turkish universities and have continued their education abroad. Islamic circles accept home education as an alternative to this problem, however, since the secular government and the army perceives "religious reactionism" as a serious threat, it is clear that all moves toward home education will, at least in the near future, face a very strong opposition.

Unfortunately, socialist groups and anarchists in Turkey have yet to be much interested in alternative education. Due to their pro-state attitudes and their opinion regarding private financing of education, socialists do not seem to be in favor of alternatives except for reforming government schools. The anarchists in Turkey whom we interviewed declared that they totally reject current educational institutions, but they were not at all interested in creating new alternatives. However, they seem to be more interested in critical pedagogy, which mostly stems from the book *The Pedagogy of the Oppressed* by Paolo Freire, published in 1969, which was translated in Turkey in the early 1990s. Recognizing that interest, Alternative Education Association organized a "critical pedagogy panel meeting." In this panel, the examples of Brazilian Landless Workers Movement and Porto Alegre Citizenship School were discussed in terms of critical pedagogy. In the same year, 2007, though not completely active, a "critical pedagogy working group" was created under the organization of the Comparative Education Association.

In Turkey Montessori education is by far the most commonly known and studied method of alternative education. It was first tried in the 1970s. Under Güler Yücel's leadership, a Montessori education center was created at the Capa Department of Children Psychotherapy at the Istanbul University. Many Montessori preschools were founded in the 1990s but most have closed down. Although many preschools claim to have adapted to the Montessori model, only three to four of them have actually done so. Brain drain and the lack of Montessori teacher training schools are among the most significant reasons for the low success rate.

After the Istanbul Alternative Education Symposium, a series of seminars with Cheryl Ferreira took place to support pro-Montessori teachers, academics, and educators in Turkey. The Alternative Education Association organized a course to train Montessori assistant teachers in collaboration with the International Montessori Association, and issued certificates to twenty-five people. It also plans to open a Montessori teacher training center. After the symposium, independent Montessori activities began taking place and yielding substantial results. A comprehensive Montessori education website with limited material in Turkish language was launched. About a thousand people joined the website within the first year and half. Two Montessori classes opened at two separate universities and there has been a sharp rise in Montessori education research. A state university is considering a project for training teachers for state-run high schools.

As previously mentioned, there is a serious lack of material in Turkey about alternative education. The lack of material in the Turkish language hinders the popularity of alternative education. In order to tackle this problem, the Alternative Education Association is publishing articles about alternative education in the critical pedagogy magazine *Bell and Break*. As well, the Alternative Education Association makes presentations to all kinds of institutions and responds positively to all kinds of assistance requests. Also, at all various workshops, book stands are set up to display books, and documentaries are shown.

To this point, we have tried to explain the activities in Turkey in terms of alternative education. On the other hand, we strongly believe that it is important to get in touch with trainee teachers at the universities to spread alternative education ideas within the existing system. We believe an "academic summit" should be organized as soon as possible to increase awareness of alternative education at the universities, making the alternative education methods part of existing courses and ensuring coordination among interested academics.

Cooperation activities and research between all kinds of alternative education activities is critical. Although individual studies are valuable, they are not enough for a change. In this regard, there is a strong need to organize another international symposium. Our current goals are to establish an alternative education library and translating new books into Turkish. Currently the Alternative Education Association is not planning to open up a school, however, it is trying to give consultancy assistance to people who plan to do so.

To conclude, we may state that Turkey has a long way to go in terms of alternative education. We understand that this process will become much easier if there is cooperation among our friends both inside and outside of Turkey. We do believe that any individual or institution that wants to come to Turkey in order to share their experiences and organize coordinated activities will contribute immensely to this process.

Notes

1. Kürşat Bumin. (1998). *Okulumuz, Resmi İdeolojimiz ve Politikaya Övgü* [*Our School, Our Official Ideology and Praise for Politics*], İstanbul: Yol Publications, p.33.
2. İsmail H. Demirdöven. (2003). "Çağdaş Açılımlarıyla Eğitim Kavramı" [Concept of Education with Contemporary Openings], *Felsefe Söyleşileri I-II* [*Essays on Philosopy I-II*], (Compiled by: Betül Çotuksöken), İstanbul: Maltepe University Marmara Education Foundation Publications, p.94–100.
3. Kemal İnal. (2001). "Köy Enstitüleri Neden ve Nasıl Eleştirilmeli?" [Why and How Should the Village Institutes Be Criticized?] , İstanbul: *Evrensel Kültür Dergisi* [*Journal of Universal Culture*], Issue: 11, p.12–13.
4. Bülent Akdağ. (2006). "Eğitim Felsefesinde İnsanı Görme Tarzı" [Way to See the Human in Education Philosophy] , İstanbul: *Yaşadıkça Eğitim Dergisi,*[*Yaşadıkça Journal of Education*] Issue: 90, p.2–5.

SECTION IV

The Purple Thistle Centre

Devon McKellar

Devon was born and raised in Chilliwack, a drained floodplain on sto-len Sto:lo land. Her parents are educators—she felt like she was at school all the time as a kid. Her favourite childhood memory is her grandparent's giant garden full of dahlias and vegetables in the shadow of a huge stained-glass church with a congregation that liked to sing. She works at the Purple Thistle Centre and has been painting a lot lately.

There's a door to a beige staircase under fluorescent lights, squished be-tween a video store and a sushi restaurant on a busy street. Up the stairs is a tiny landing with many doors. One door is covered in stickers and a shaggy bulletin board. Sometimes there are weird smells coming from it—always weird sounds.

Inside is a 700-square-foot space divided into four awkward rooms. It is literally covered from floor to ceiling in colour and paper and fauna. There is a darkroom in a tiny closet and a library in a back entranceway and a computer lab in a kitchen. There's a tiny rooftop garden and giant ashtray—the perfect place for a radio tower that broadcasts at least as far as the punk house six blocks northwest.

The first time I came into the Purple Thistle Centre, we painted a mural of jungle animals in elevators with lattes and business suits. There's a poster on the wall—an angry Mayan man, immigration papers in his hand, pointing a finger at me, captioned: "Who's the illegal alien, PILGRIM?"

Starting another art class is this huge biker-looking dude in his early thirties wearing ratty and meticulously patched jeans covered in paint. He's surrounded by about a dozen punk ladies and a few dudes in their late teens and early twenties picking at each other and the walls (covered in graffiti and plaster casts of arms, legs, breasts, etc. from a previous art class). Dan picks at an eraser, carving it into a salmon over the course of his "lecture"—a string of tangents about art history, anarchism, and his personal life, punctuated by the comments of the rest of us.

We have a discussion about public space and what it means in a post-industrial setting with a city planning department seemingly inspired by fascist-rationalism. Dan basically just gives us footnotes while we bring up vague theory. We end up talking about *detournement* and surrealist interventions. He gives each one of us a piece of wire and tells us to go make some art in the neighbourhood in a half hour. We'll meet back here and do a walking tour.

The Purple Thistle is a big interventionist piece for some kids. A hooligan clubhouse that encourages kids to quit school and hang out on the streets? A learning centre where the only rules are "no asshole-ism" (a blanket term for bigots and bullies), "don't come fucked up on drugs," and "don't sleep over, cause we don't have insurance"? We're youth run and youth led—most of us dropped out of high school or college. Our token adult writes a lot of our grants, but only sets foot in the Centre once a month or so.

Sometimes it's been all dumpster smell and the biggest collection of weird art supplies, zines, books, and strange alley flail you've ever seen, heated by the thirty smelly kids screaming gang vocals inside. Other times it's this silent den of computer nerds and cold wood floor and stale coffee and printer noises. And others still, it's a bunch of stuffy-looking kids sitting around with tea talking about books. It's a very hard project to explain to people. But it's the most natural thing in the world—a bunch of people who live near each other making a public space.

✳ ✳ ✳

Learning is like breathing when we care. And there's been a lot of violence between sucking up knowledge in earnest from our elders to being force-fed Canon in cold institutions for pieces of paper. Domesticating our natural curiosities to get said Papers, dressing up our crazy animal brains in mental corsets and foot bindings of Institution. Learn deadline, learn note-taking, learn time management, learn shift work, learn instruction-following, learn semi-arbitrary bureaucracy. You catch my drift.

This is the kind of unhealthy shit we're trying to counteract at the Thistle. Learn self-motivation, learn groupwork, learn trust, learn responsibility, re-learn public space, re-learn community, etc. Perfectionists point out that if squatting were more socially acceptable in Canada, we wouldn't need grants to do any of it. That's true.

The Centre was started by eight kids from alternatives schools and public schools and no school—some kids who knew each other from China Creek Park. This rad guy (Matt Hern) had written some grants and they were turning this tiny office space above a video station on Commercial Drive into a little anarcho-community centre.

There was a group of us, like six or seven of us. Just a few of us hanging out with Matt talking shit: What isn't working at (our schools)? What can teenagers do? A lot of kids are bored and fucking around and doing drugs and getting into trouble; they're not really making anything outta their time. What do they want? What do they need?

So we would just meet once or twice a week and talk about stuff, throw around ideas. Basically the eight of us just wanted a place where we could hang out and do whatever we wanted. We'd try to tell everybody about it and see who'd want to check it out.

Matt found this place. Good location on the drive above a video store. So we moved in and it was a rat hole. Like, it looked pretty shitty, but it was ours. We had the eight of us to do whatever we wanted now. And that's when it became real. *"we can invent whatever this is now."*

We spent three weeks ripping up carpets and sanding shit off the floor and polishing it up. There was no furniture yet, but there was a kitchen. We'd need dishes for that. We wanted a phone, clocks, books, a photocopier, some computers. We were just like "let's ask for everything we want right now." We told all our friends to check it out, see if they had anything they'd wanna donate.

At first, not a whole lot was going on; just occasional events or kids hanging out. Then it spread from our circle of friends. Instead of seven kids, there were fifteen, then more and more people just stopped through. The atmosphere changed depending on who was doing stuff. The mood was always changing.

Its way bigger than I thought it would be. I never really looked that far ahead. It was started for very selfish reasons. I wanted this Centre. I wanted it for me and I know a lot of other people who wanted the same things I wanted. I had no real high expectations.

Where we're at now, we're really starting to shape into
something. It blows me away sometimes. That we have this
place and that I can say it's mine. And the wish for it is that it's
everybody's. —Jesse. May 2005[1]

It's not hard to motivate kids. We spent crazy amounts of energy every day on things we care about. It's easy to sustain excitement and bring
people together when there's real interest and real passion—when things
are relevant and peoples' choices are respected. Traditional schooling
fails us because mandatory curriculum is counterintuitive. It's easier than
adults think to be a resource rather than a tyrant in the classroom, but it
takes heart.

I was getting into creative writing on my own and that's when
I found the Purple Thistle. I ran into Keith while I was skating
around, and he told me about the place. I remember the first
time I went. It was the writing group when Josh was running it
and he was really encouraging and helped me get over a lot of
shyness I had with my writing. I was interested in slam poetry
and rhyming and getting out that internal shit. This guy Shyne
came to writing group one night and his advice was to write
about something you never, ever think about. So I wrote about
my abortion.

It was insane. That night everyone wrote about something
so personal and then the eight or nine of us sat together and
read their pieces out loud, and I just felt totally at home after
that. It was like "yeah, this is it. This is where I want to be."

When I first showed up it was like everyone was really
tight, everyone was really close friends, everyone had this
shared experience which was really easily understood. Coming into it at first it was really kind of intimidating, like "how
am I going to weasel my way into this thing?" right?

As I stayed more and more, people came in and the dy-
namics of people kept changing. The space takes on the form
of whoever is hanging out there the most. —Val

Urban and Suburbanization has radically altered the ways we talk to
our neighbours, how we interact with our space, what we expect from our
"work" (what a loaded word!) and the people around us. Groups of up to

two hundred people working together and sharing a space has traditionally been the way to go—even in old urban centres. The car and the apartment and the McJob have not only revolutionized the global economy—they've transformed our societies of interlocking circles into pyramid grids. The Town Meeting is virtually obsolete, discarded in favour of the online poll. Parents still need support and a place their kids can go that's safe, but we don't trust our neighbours anymore.

> I did the exchange to the Northwest Territories before I actually became part of the collective. The exchange was twelve kids from Vancouver. We went up to this tiny little town in the Northwest Territories, Fort Good Hope. Right on the Mackenzie river, in the Arctic Circle. It was fucking crazy. We went up there in August. The sun never set. It would dip below the horizon and then come right back up again. The sunrise and the sunset were the same thing. We went hunting and gutted Canadian geese with our bare hands. And it was just generally crazy.
>
> Like, we were just a bunch of stupid white kids from the city, and here we are living in these people's homes. And then the Fort Good Hope kids came down to Vancouver and that was even crazier. They were here for about two weeks, and we were up there for about the same. —**Magnolia**

The Thistle is a response to urban alienation. Kids don't need an invitation or a membership or an appointment. We don't have minimum requirements. There are tiers of involvement, but if I drew you a picture of what that looks like it would be a circular spider's web, not a pyramid.

> The cool thing about this place is that you can just do whatever you want. If you want to do something, it's just about you putting it together and doing it. —**Sylvie**

> I liked the place so much because it was a free space run by the people who use it. Its based on anarchistic, egalitarian ideals. It's not exclusive to anarchists though. It's not elitist. Anyone can come and hang out. That really attracted me to it. —**Sean**

The Thistle...well if it could be a show venue, that would be great. My favourite thing about the Thistle is the part that gives people freedom to explore what they want to explore with practically zero bureaucracy. That's awesome. —k-la

I sat down the other night and made a list of all the things that went down at the 1163 space, since I could remember:

Spanish & French classes, food not bombs, queer night, theatre, the Fort Good Hope exchange, songwriting with Kinnie Starr, pirate radio, land in Enderby, fireweed storefront, anarchist picnic, food and nutrition stuff, talking on gentrification, coffee, HRDC zine-making job, prison solidarity with Joint Effort, DIY silkscreening, mental health support group, music night, Britannia mural project, art group, talking with Dan Chodorkoff from the Institute for Social Ecology, the free closet, beat boxing, writing group, circus, reclaim the streets, chain mail workshops, stencil workshops with the Dark, reading group, hip hop night, DIY chopper building, talking on rape/sexual assault with Vancouver rape relief workers, movie nights, photo group/darkroom workshops, DIY comix workshop with Fly.

All in an office space we've grown too big for. We couldn't have asked for a better time to get evicted. —Nathan

Now we've moved to a much, much larger space.

The new centre is up some stairs too. A fourteen- foot glass wall with a door is our entrance. There's room for bikes and a huge notice board area. There's a big table for art and a bunch of couches behind that. The libraries are behind a half wall in the far corner. There's a wall full of art supplies and a drafting table, a moveable wood table. Behind that, a room specifically for silkscreening, a room adjacent specifically for Animation. Our darkroom, computer lab, bike area, and kitchen round off the area. There's so much here to use. We've got 2,500 square feet. The collective is twenty-five people now. We moved northeast—closer to that punk house. Our radio isn't up right now, but we still have it kicking around if someone wants to use it. We do tons of partnerships with other local groups, especially radical or really artsy ones, but also other youth centres. We'd like to be known for our politics more than our demographic, honestly. We're almost at having operations funding—which is huge. But we still wish we were a squat.

The Thistle is a perfect example of people in a community coming together to reinvent their public space and by extension their lives. I say we're about politics, but I don't mean who to vote for or pray to. Beyond the lefty-buzzword "grassroots" straight down to seed activism—questioning the roots that make "Left" and "Right" (it's a sign of the times that there already are "seed" activists in another much more literal sense.) The Thistle is about rethinking the fundamental ontological elements of our daily lives—the basic assumptions that keep us in school, work, and prison. It's crucial right now to turn off the TV (even educational programming) and go outside for a while.

Notes

1.   All these quotes are from Thistle kids and are gathered in a history of the Purple Thistle Centre in: *Shoes* #6 (school issue) get copies from: Nathan po box 1986 Coruna Ontario Canada N0N.1G0

A Face Without a Name: Struggles of Stateless Children Along the Thai-Burmese Border

Saowanee Sangkara and Jim Connor

Saowanee Sangkara (Nao) is a Thai native and has taught art and classes based on Thai culture and awareness of cultural studies. She has dedicated her life to work in grassroots organizations and moved to a rural area of Thailand to lead a self-sufficient and sustainable life. Currently she has found passion in filmmaking, animation, and media work which will inspire and raise awareness of simple living, sustainability, education, and community work. Over the years, she has been writing reflections on Whispering Seed work and illustrating children's picture books, making photo essays of ethnic and minority children along the border and community building work.

Jim has been working with children for most of his life, from infants to high school age children, as well as teaching at The Evergreen State College in Washington State. He has traveled abroad extensively, often by bicycle, visiting intentional communities, alternative schools, and children's orphanages. He co-founded Whispering Seed in 2004 with Saowanee and has been living along the Thai-Burmese border since then. He is working with other groups to start an Resource Center for Alternative Education and Sustainable Living in Southeast Asia to support the development and growth of democratic, holistic approaches of working with children and education.

Winding slowly through the mountain scenery, stark peaks burst through the lush green vegetation carpeting the forest floor. Far from the bustling streets of Bangkok and Kanchanaburi in this Land of Smiles, bamboo huts take the place of concrete store fronts, rivers overflow with thick, chocolaty water in the rainy season and barely trickle in the dry season. Faces change and greetings flow from behind *tanaka* faces (*tanaka* is a bark from a local tree used to color the faces of women and children in intricate patters) in numerous foreign tongues. The borderlands along the Thai-Burmese (Myanmar) border are a land of extremes; in weather, geography, people, and cultures. A land of beautiful, smiling people, rich cultures, and a land steeped in struggles, hardship, and ethnic genocide.

It is here among these mountains and valleys which we now call home, that the dream we once only dared to dream has slowly begun unfolding before our eyes, revealing a shared vision of how we can serve the world. The Whispering Seed is a village-based Sustainable Living and Learning Community Center and a Home for Children who have come from orphaned, abusive and neglected backgrounds. We provide emotional, medical, and nutritional support and care, as well as housing and learning opportunities for Burmese refugee children and displaced and disadvantaged people from Burmese, Karen, Karang, and Mon ethnic minority groups in the region.

Within all of our work, we aim to bridge sustainability and education. Currently, our programs focus on five major areas; Children's Home, Bridging Sustainability and Education, Youth Empowerment, Community Work and Communicating with Society. Some of the programs include: teacher training for teachers from Burma, a support program for families and young mothers, training in sustainable living (Permaculture, Earthen Building, Appropriate Technology, Organic Farming), camps and empowerment training for local youth, photography and film making for local youth, vocational skill workshops for local women (traditional weaving, spinning, natural dye, flower making, and sewing), and conferences supporting sustainable living and alternative education. Our mission is to provide models for sustainable living and learning consistent with the traditions of the varied local cultures.

Struggles Along the Border

The local communities with whom we have chosen to live and work are primarily ethnic minority groups from within Burma. For almost fifty years, the State Peace and Development Council (SPDC), as the ruling Burmese authoritarian-military dictatorship currently refers to itself, has been waging genocide against the ethnic people of their country. Inside Burma, these ethnic minority groups constantly face forced labor, rape, use of child soldiers, and widespread torture and murder. Under the rule of this repressive regime, political, economic, and social conditions have become so intolerable that many individuals and families from these minority groups have fled to Thailand for survival and hopes of a better life.

Refugee camps along the border or illegal work inside Thailand (with the constant threat of abuse, imprisonment, and deportation) are the options Burmese refugees and migrants face living at the edge of Thai society. Within Karen State in Eastern Burma, those who do not make it to Thailand suffer in the jungles. Referred to as IDP's, Internally Displaced People, they face hardships even greater than those who reach the camps. Trapped within their own country and running from the military, the plight of many IDP's is only now truly being realized. Currently the estimated number of IDP's within Burma is estimated to be over 300,000, however numbers are unclear due to their inaccessible locations.

The border town of Sangklaburi, Whispering Seed's current location, is a region where many of these minority groups have sought refuge. More than 80% of residents in Sangklaburi and its surrounding areas are displaced Burmese, or are from the Mon, Karang, and Karen minorities of Burma and Thailand. Here in this border town, Burmese migrants and refugees face new challenges. Although living conditions are far better inside Thailand, life is far from easy. Having fled from Burma or belonging to an ethnic minority group within Thailand, the majority of people lack basic human rights, including citizenship, access to basic healthcare, education, rights to own land, and basic employment opportunities. Health issues such as malaria, dengue fever, malnutrition, and growing rates of HIV/AIDS and tuberculosis compound the issues even more. Impoverishment, which generally includes lack of access to clean drinking water and unhygienic living conditions, results in greater susceptibility to diseases already prevalent in the region. Insufficient Thai language skills, with little source of income and fear of harassment from local Thai officials, contribute to a feeling of hopelessness. This often leads to child neglect, abuse, and even abandonment, with women and children suffering the most.

A Different Approach

When this does happen, we are there, assessing each situation as to how we can best support the children and families. More often than not, families simply need a little support to be able to stay together. In some cases however, the children must be separated from the family because they are in vulnerable situations which jeopardize their lives. In these cases, the children come into our care—sometimes temporarily until they can be reunited with their families—while others will be with us forever. The decision to separate a child from their parent is a very big decision and our ultimate aim is to support families to be together if at all possible. However, standard policy for many large NGO's (non-governmental organization) caring for hundreds of children is to quickly remove the child from the family. It has been our experience that taking the time to get to know families and their specific situation is essential and taking this time often enables families to stay together who might otherwise have been separated. Because the diversity of cultures and languages in our region, it is important to truly understand the needs of each family and the needs they have without imposing external standards and judging their needs based on Western values.

Often removing children from their families is based solely on the level of poverty and their chance for a better opportunity, which often means the opportunity to learn English. Many NGO's providing care for children tend to be overcrowded, understaffed, and the children do not receive the quality care that is necessary to support them during this extremely crucial time in their lives. With issues that these children come with—physical and mental abuse, malnutrition, health conditions, abandonment issues, many suffering from RAD (reattachment disorder)—children need a caring and supportive community around them. It is for these reasons that we have chosen to be here, in a land that so often does not make sense, supporting people as best we can, who simply long for a country they can call their own.

Smiling Eyes Behind Tanaka Faces: Life with the Little Ones

The majority of children who have come to live with us are from inside Burma. They come from very different backgrounds, with each child's story more disheartening than the one before. All of the children have faced horrendous physical and emotional abuse and hardships. Most of the children have been referred to us from other NGO's who work with HIV positive migrants along the border. They range in age from infants to young teenagers. Some of the children have families who cannot take care of them and others come without any knowledge or history of their past. In the case that children do have family, we do our best to facilitate an ongoing relationship with their family, even though it is often difficult.

When children first come to us, there is always a very difficult adjustment period. Not only have they been abused emotionally and physically, but many have been malnourished, causing issues around food, such as excessive eating and stealing food. Our first priority with each of the children is to support them in a re-bonding process. Healthy vegetarian food, caring adults and a warm family environment with no strict schedule of schooling allows them a feeling of safety and security from which they can begin their healing process. If the children are young, holding and massage are used to further support the bonding process. Supporting them to know that they now have stable, caring adults in their lives becomes a top priority.

Faces Without a Name: Citizenship

The other enormous obstacle that we face with most of the children besides their physical and emotional state is with citizenship. Most of the children we care for are referred to as stateless or undocumented children. These children have no identity, no ID cards, no nationality, no passports, and sometimes—as was the case with one of our first boys—no name. Legally, these kids are not allowed to leave the town of Sangklaburi to go into mainland Thailand. There are thousands of children and adults along the Thai-Burmese border in a similar situation. They have no possibility of returning to their country which is under military dictatorship, and the Thai government does not want or support them in Thailand.

Besides citizenship, loss of cultural identity is another huge factor facing all of the ethnic minority groups living along the border. Pressures to assimilate into mainstream Thai culture come from all directions. The way they speak, dress, look, and their local traditions often leave them feeling inadequate. Having to learn Thai language and culture to fit in forces them to deny and often be ashamed of their own cultural traditions. Thai is often a second or third language for the children and they therefore do not speak clearly. Without language, children so often lose connection with who they are and where they came from, quickly trying to blend in to mainstream Thai society. One of the ways that we can best support the children is by supporting their native language. Immediately, it became clear that we needed to not only learn Thai, but also to learn to read, write, and speak in Burmese and Karen so that we could support the children in feeling proud and maintaining their mother tongue.

Cho Lwin Nyunt: Born into a Brothel

Our first little one came to us when she was nine years old, having been raised in a brothel along the Burmese border. Never having been to school and the primary caregiver for her mother, a sex worker with HIV/ AIDS and tuberculosis, she hardly had a chance to experience childhood. Collecting garbage in the slums on the Burmese side of the border by day and purchasing alcohol for the women in the brothel by night, she was then sold for twelve US dollars to a Thai plantation to raise cattle to support her sick and dying mother. Like most of the children that have come to us, she came speaking only Burmese language with no documentation or citizenship, and her age unknown.

When she first came, she was given a great deal of freedom and support to just live in the world without all the burdens she had carried for most of her life. There was no emphasis on academic learning, but many opportunities to learn were offered to her. After the passing away of her mother, she has been able to move into a new place in her development. Time to laugh, play, and swim, and having caring adults and siblings around her has supported her development. Within just three years of being with us—part of that time still caring for her mother—she is now fluent in both Burmese and Thai, and able to speak in English as well. She is learning to read and write in all three languages. Having had the opportunity to feel safe and let out her past pains, and to be able to share that pain with others has allowed her to now be ready to learn, grow, and approach her academic studies.

Nyein Myaing: Endless Tears

One of our little boys came to us when he was around two-and-a-half to three years old. We did not know his name, age, or much about his background. It was clear, however, that he had been extremely abused physically and mentally. Diagnosed with thalassemia, a form of sickle cell anemia affecting mostly people from Asia and Mediterranean, we were informed when we took him in that he would only live three or four months.

After almost two-and-a-half months of crying twenty-four hours a day, he finally could sit by himself and eat without screaming. He was also severely malnourished and could barely sit up after eating. Holding him close for what often seemed intolerable amounts of time, he continued screaming, crying, kicking, and one occasion urinating and defecating on us and our belongings. Although it was difficult at times to hold him, that was the medicine that he seemed to so desperately need. After several months of healthy food, holding, and clear boundaries, he began to walk normally and sit up by himself. One day we saw him run across the floor, something we had not imagined would happen. Slowly, laughter, play, and smiles followed. Even today, three years later, he still struggles playing alone, but the improvements in his attitude and demeanor are incredible. It has truly been a miracle to watch and go through this process with him.

Win Ye Tun: Sensory Touch

Some of the other struggles that we face not only with the children but also local villagers are around health care. Because most the children and adults in the community are not Thai citizens, they do not have access basic needs such as health care. A three-year old boy came to us not long ago, also from a brothel along the border. After just two weeks of living with us, he came down with a high fever. After a negative test of malaria, he went into shock and had to be raced to the hospital, using CPR to keep him alive. Unable to help him, stating that he had contracted malaria in his brain from the region he was living in inside Burma, they rushed us three hours away to the next closest hospital. The Thai hospital staff was not supportive upon arrival because of this foreigner man with a young Burmese child. The nurses were not caring for him properly, but after several days of treatment he had recovered enough so we could care for him ourselves at home. Even with a sick and dying child, the prejudice and lack of support these children receive is unimaginable. Having recovered fully, we are finding that he is showing characteristics that make us believe he is somewhere on the autistic spectrum. Again, he will face an uphill battle, as services are completely unavailable to him.

Sanda Kyi: The Wild Girl

She is another young Karen girl who has lived off and on with us for the last three years. Her father is in prison for shooting her mother, and the mother now lives and works in a factory in the nearby city. With four sisters and another on the way, they all have been left behind in the village to be cared for by incapable grandparents. She learns through all of her senses, diving in and engaging fully with the world. For this, she struggles greatly in school and frequently received beatings both at home and school. Often speaking half Karen and half Thai, she embraces each day as a gift and learns her lessons from the world around her. It is a crime for her to be forced to sit in a classroom all day, often when the teachers don't even come to school. Allowing her the opportunity to learn with us at home, she has chosen to be with us where her own unique rhythm of learning can unfold and develop in its own time.

Life Long Learning

All of the children have responded incredibly well to simply having a healthy and safe environment and loving and supportive adults around them. We put very little pressure on the children, but work with them very closely to support them through what is often a very challenging healing process. Freedom to just be is crucial. These children, like many other refugee and orphaned children need to learn how to laugh, to dance, to sing, and to simply play which all supports their healing process. Having this support and freedom allows them to get down to often deep levels of pain and suffering from which they can then begin to find who they truly are and begin the foundations of a healthy human being.

As for the children's "education," we feel that working through these issues is the most import work they have at this time in their lives. In regards to academics, much of that is left up to them, but with a strong support system around them. This is not to say that we leave the children alone without stimulus or opportunities to work on traditional academics. We are always there with the children, supporting, helping, and offering them opportunities; it is their choice at which level they engage.

However, it is rarely the case that they do not engage, for all children are naturally curious and have an innate desire to learn. More often than not, it is schools that destroy this inner curiosity to learn. We are confident that the academics will easily come once some of their pain and suffering has been addressed. Feeling comfortable with us, and knowing what it is to be loved and cared for, is the foundation they need for a healthy and happy life.

A Gift of Land

It all began three years ago when a small piece of land was purchased for us by a group of three very spirited young Thai friends and family.

They started the Rainbow Caravan, with the intention of traveling around Thailand and the USA to promote cultural exchanges and raise money for us to purchase land to be the home of Whispering Seed. After just a few months of traveling between Bangkok and Chiang Mai, playing music on the streets, passing the hat, and holding a donation ceremony through a famous Thai temple, the group had raised enough money to purchase the land which we now call home.

Beginning with principles of Permaculture (a system of sustainable design) and using all earthen, mud brick buildings and bamboo, we began designing and building our first houses on our twelve-acre tropical farm. Soon the establishment of organic fruit orchards, veggie gardens, and rice paddies followed. Located just a few kilometers from the Burmese border, we have chosen to live in a small Karen village among the people with whom we work. With no electricity or running water, we are in the process of designing a hybrid electrical system using solar and water power. Bathing, washing clothes and playing in the local river which rolls through our land from the mountains of Burma, using composting toilets and cooking with wood, we aim to be as sustainable as we can, leaving as small a footprint behind as possible. With six months of monsoon flooding and six months of extreme dry weather and no rain, the environment makes it even more challenging.

Inspiration

Drawing inspiration from the work Janusz Korchak with orphans in the ghettos of Warsaw, Poland during WWII, Vinoba Bhave and Gandhiji's work in India, A.S. Neill's radical work at Summerhill, and countless others who found joy in serving others and committed their lives to service keep us moving forward in often troubling times. Whispering Seed is a place where traditional, sustainable models of living on the Earth are united with holistic ways of learning. We provide children who have been left with nothing in the world a loving family and community where they will forever feel loved and have a place that is their home.

The idea of the Whispering Seed emerged in 2003, co-created by Saowanee Sangkara from Thailand and Jim Connor from the United States. The name for the project was a joint effort, a combined dream of the founders. Saowanee has always seen those that inspired her as giant trees providing the shade and nutrients needed to help her dreams sprout and grow into reality. Now, she sees Whispering Seed as a place where young and old can find the support and nourishment needed to make the seed of their dreams come true. Jim has always wanted to support and care for children coming from disadvantaged backgrounds. Children are small, but powerful. They are the hope for the future and it is their voices that will help to change this Earth. To Jim, children represent the image of the strength and power in the quiet voice, the potency of prayer, the strength in a whisper. Combined, the images are perfect for the work we are trying to create on this little piece of land in the region along the Thai-Burmese.

Sustainable Funding

Before starting the project, we traveled all over the world to other intentional communities, alternative schools, and children's homes to learn of their success and struggles. Funding was always an issue. Not wanting to rely solely on outside funding from grants, we have taken a multi-faceted approach to fundraising. We draw our sources of funds from several sources; internship and volunteer programs, courses and conferences, donations in the form of money and necessary supplies, sale of traditional crafts through fair trade, a sponsorship program, and finally from grants. Volunteers play an enormous role in our organization. For instance, we have built all of our buildings ourselves, with the help of volunteers. Our playhouse, has had well over five-hundred hands and feet mixing and plastering mud for its completion. This way, others learn how to build earthen houses and we get our houses built, all while having fun and building community! To learn, including ways to volunteer and donate, visit us at www. whisperingseed.org.

Final Thoughts

Each day we arise with the uncertainty of what the day will bring. Although it has and continues to be a challenging path, when times get hard all we have to do is look into the eyes of the children and see their suffering and the weight they hold upon their tiny shoulders, and immediately we know why we are here. It is these little hands that are to be the ones to hold up this great Earth of ours, and it is our duty to support them with all we have to make it a healthier place for all.

[For privacy and safety of the children, all names have been changed.]

Shikshantar: An Organic Learning Community

Shilpa Jain

Shilpa is a learning activist with Shikshantar: The Peoples' Institute for Rethinking Education and Development, based in Udaipur, Rajasthan, India. She has researched, written books and articles, and facilitated workshops on topics ranging from globalization, creative expressions, ecology, democratic living, gender, innovative learning, walkouts, and unlearning. She herself is unlearning many things from her many years of living in the US, and especially trying to find more ways to free herself from the readymade world. She loves learning with/from children and youth, and has extensive experience doing so around self-esteem, creativity, collaboration, identity, and conflict resolution. She also enjoys being in an intergenerational household, with her grandparents (who are in their eighties), brother and sister-in-law (in their thirties) and her four year old niece, Avanika.

Over the past seven years, Shikshantar Andolan has developed an organic learning community to nurture fellow co-creators. It is a space for doing, for discovering one's own path—not an individualistic path (which breeds selfishness), but one that is deeply connected with all beings in a web of life. (Some friends have even affectionately called it a space for misfits.) From the very beginning, we have focused on creating spaces in which people can start to reclaim control of their own *shiksha*. This is done in two ways: 1) by exposing and dismantling the culture of schooling; and 2) by exploring and regenerating spaces for learning-sharing outside of the culture of schooling.

It is difficult to describe what Shikshantar is, as it does not fit neatly into one category. It has purposely been set-up as (and evolved into) a hybrid organization—research institute, library, community meeting space, place for retreat, publishing house, filmmaking studio, zero waste upcycling center, site for experimentation—to allow it to cater to varying needs of the larger movement. People from ages three to eighty-five years informally volunteer (real or virtually) with Shikshantar. This group includes those who go to schools and colleges, those who have dropped out of school, working people, housewives, retired people, people from different parts of India and other communities in the world.

At any point in time, Shikshantar also formally hosts eight to twelve full-time learning activists on our core team. As learning activists, we are actively involved in exploring ourselves and our local surroundings vis-a-vis the big questions/debates of our times. We are also involved in actively nurturing the learning and unlearning of others. The learning activists are responsible for supporting and adding to the larger Shikshantar movement. For this, it is critical that the learning activists develop themselves into co-creators.

There is no formal selection process for learning activists. Nor are any degrees or formal qualifications required. Learning activists emerge out of their own declared interests and intent. Whenever any new volunteer comes, we ask them to share what is special or unique about them and about their community or village. We also ask them to share meaningful questions that they are exploring and concerns they have about what's happening around them in the world. They are invited to get involved in some specific aspect of the work of Shikshantar and to understand the vision and activities of the movement as a whole. If and when they feel that they would like to make a full-time commitment to Shikshantar, they can apply to be a learning activist by sharing their ideas about what they would like to do to contribute to the movement. A learning activist is taken on for any period between four months to five years, depending on their discovery process.

There is no pre-set curriculum for the learning activists. Rather, the learning agenda (learning goals, environments, styles and pace, resources, evaluations) emerges from mutual dialogue among all of the co-learners. We have learned that there are, however, some processes that can assist in their deeper exploration:

* engaging in intense interaction with dissonant and paradoxical people, contexts, ideas, and groups;
* revisiting and (re-)valuing their own life experiences and intuitions and expressing these through various media;
* critically reflecting on their experiences with school, newspapers, and TV;

* exploring their ideas about concepts related to *swaraj* such as: leadership, *swa-anushashan* (self-discipline), social justice, voluntary simplicity, collaboration, creative self-expression, *ahimsa* (non-violence/love/respect);

* discovering the possibilities of the local—*desh bhakti* (vs. nationalism), local language, local media, local governance, local economy, local history, etc.—and understanding its links to the global;

* re-examining institutionally-declared "problems" (such as, Population, Politicians, and Pakistan) from new perspectives in order to overcome our self-paralysis and finger-pointing;

* re-examining institutionally-declared "solutions" (such as, "You need a lot of money to do anything.");

* learning with multiple generations—from the very young to the very old;

* creating and carrying-out authentic work on local concerns, which is later shared with people around the sub-continent.

We have learned that there is no particular order or time-frame or even specific exercises for these processes to take place. Each of these is explored with the individual learning activists' own needs, capacities and dreams in mind—along with the flow of activities and new opportunities in the Shikshantar movement. We try to identify together what each of us is passionate about and what each of us holds as our strengths and weaknesses.

On a daily level, the learning activists read and share articles, books, videos, art, theatre, songs, etc. that inspire/challenge them; devise their own projects according to their interests and talents; meet and interview diverse local people; create, as well as attend, workshops/conferences; and host study tours with other groups. At the core, it is assumed that responsibility for one's own learning and motivation rests with each and every individual. There is no hierarchy in learning, so every human being (regardless of formal academic qualifications) possesses learning resources (and can foster more). And every kind of work, if done honestly, is a spiritual act.

Much of the day-to-day efforts of learning activists are plugged into our work in Udaipur as a Learning City. This makes work very real, contextualized and tangible. It opens up a lot of space for interesting discussions, new questions, and critical meta-reflection. The entire process is geared towards shaking the lethargy of the mind, expressing oneself and one's vision of life, imagining new futures, and developing the courage to break the chains of the TINA (There Is No Alternative) mindset. Learning activists are also encouraged to weave their own decentralized networks of volunteer co-learners. Current learning activists and some of the projects they are working on include:

* **Pannalal** is working on regenerating the local Mewari language and the tradition of story-telling; he also connects with local farmers to obtain produce for an organic exchange hosted monthly by Shikshantar.

* **Vidhi** is nurturing a local and country-wide network of "families learning together"; she also collaborates with local artists to invite them to share their talents and time with children.

* **Vishal, Guddi** and **Shilpa** are designing and running craft workshops for children and families using waste materials; they are trying to expand the notion and practice of zero-waste in Udaipur's NGOs, tourism district, and in local families.

* **Ramawtar** is delving into traditional knowledge around herbal plants and natural medicines; he is planting herbal gardens with local families and preparing remedies to share with the wider community.

* **Sunny** and **Manoj** are cooking healthy food (no oil, no white sugar, no wheat, no preservatives or chemicals, no milk) and sharing their creations, along with their ideas about food, nutrition and healthy living, in various corners of Udaipur.

* **Nirmal** is working with local families to develop murals on public/private walls, so as to explore both community expression as well as the aesthetics of urban spaces.

* **Manish** is preparing to launch a community video resource center out of Shikshantar, to make more available the wide collection of films we have, as well as opportunities for learning filmmaking and editing.

In all of the activities, learning activists are encouraged to identify new resources (beyond money) in Udaipur to support their work, and to use "waste" in creative new ways—which helps to break the myth that having a lot of money is necessary for doing meaningful work.

Learning activists take a leadership role in designing and running their own projects. But all work is flexible and shared, and we take the time to give feedback and support each other's work as it develops. There are no divisions like "Research," "Administration," "Computer Operations," "Publications," etc., and oftentimes they have core-team wide collaborations which bring together different strengths and interests. A current example is the monthly organic exchange, *Hamo Desi Mela*, which everyone participates in by hosting a booth and/or coordinating additional participants from the city, to share different aspects of organic living in the city.

Learning activists are encouraged to use their skills and knowledge that they develop across domains. They share what they are doing with their own families, friends, neighborhoods, caste and religious communities and other circles they are involved in. For instance, Pannalal, following his experiences with local communities and the Mewari language, is working with his caste community to organize their community events in Mewari. Learning activists have also contributed to new experiments with our different partners in diverse parts of the country and around the world. They also go on team learning visits, with the dual intention of both being provoked and provoking, to places like Narmada Bachao Andolan and Auroville. From time to time, different individuals and groups come to Udaipur to share their efforts, experiences and burning questions with the team.

It is critical that learning activists feel that they have full access to the learning environment and the ability to add to/change it. So, all learning activists have their own key to Shikshantar. Everyone has the power to convene a meeting when they feel it is needed. They can post things they find interesting on the walls. Everyone is encouraged to bring new ideas, new people and new possibilities into our work. Learning activists are also encouraged to share problems they are having with their work or even personal problems. Nearly every day at lunch, there is a Circle Check-in, in which everyone on the team shares what is on his/her mind. Learning activists also visit and spend time with different groups to learn how they manage (or mismanage) their organizations, and to get ideas on how we can further develop Shikshantar.

There are several challenges that we continue to struggle with in our work with learning activists. First, we have found that there is a certain kind of arrogance that initially develops with the newly-gained knowledge. Sometimes, some of the learning activists use their power to dominate other young people; they move from quiet and suppressed to oppressor/teacher/boss. They may acquire a certain smugness or superiority complex which is not only rude, but also leads to laziness, in terms of seeking our new perspectives.

Second, it takes a while for people to get used to the freedom. Each person has to figure out what is really important to them, how to set their priorities, how to manage their time (without somebody constantly watching them), and how to keep the commitments they make to others. It takes time to generate one's own understanding of responsibilities to the larger community and own concept of self-discipline. It is very difficult for people to be honest (with themselves and with others) about their mistakes. There is a very strong culture of blaming others which takes time to unlearn.

Third, learning activists have difficulty initially working together on a team, and in working with others of opposite sex, different age groups (particularly with older people), and across socio-economic boundaries. It takes time to recognize our own biases and to deal with the biases of others. Learning activists have difficulty giving critical, thought-provoking and constructive feedback which connects (rather than divides) others, and in listening to such feedback. Lastly, while most learning activists have the support of their immediate family, other family members and friends subject them to continuous negative pressure to fit back into the mainstream system.

As a community of friends, we work through these challenges together. As much as anything else, Shikshantar is a space for unlearning, a practice ground for living our lives in alignment for the values and relationships we want to see in the world. Open and honest dialogues are part of this; we try to build them into each activity or into the entire ethos of the place. Not always easy to do, yet such integrity of character is what distinguishes Shikshantar's learning community from other environments.

There are no "teachers" or faculty at Shikshantar. Each of the learning activists is a co-learner. The power dynamic between learning activists is always changing. At times, different people (depending on their knowledge, skills and insights) organically emerge to play the role of "guide"—to help facilitate deeper exploration, better communication and new connections. It is important that the guide make his or her role, his commitment to the learner, and his or her expectations, rules, etc., clear. There is no threat of compulsion or use of punishment. Neither are there any financial rewards to look forward to. The guide must also make himself/herself vulnerable to critique from others and to the possibility (and necessity) of his/her own unlearning and new learning.

Learning activists are not awarded grades. They do not graduate. They do not even have attendance records. We make no attempt to quantify or rank the learning or growth that occurs among the learning activists. We simply observe each other as we grow and try to encourage ourselves to engage in continual self- and peer-assessment. As John Holt describes, "The student, the do-er, can only learn a difficult action insofar as he can put the teacher inside of him. He must be a student and teacher at the same time. He must, more and more, grade his own tasks, get his own feedback, make his own corrections, and develop his own criteria, standards, for doing these things."

Udaipur as a Learning City

> "...cities in developing countries are expected to grow by 140,000 people a day for the foreseeable future." —Janice E. Perlman

> "Cities take up 2% of the earth's physical land space, they consume 75% of the resources and produce 75% of the waste. 27% of India's population live in cities and produce 64% of India's GDP." —Kirtee Shah

Cities are growing, it is quite clear. However, this growth is marked by its quantity, not quality. Within cities around the world, many are facing an astonishing decline of humanness. Trends such as consumerism, corruption, violence, prostitution, pollution, environmental degradation, and drug abuse are increasing alongside economic growth. We feel the fracturing impacts of city life reflected in our selves, in our relationships, in our families and in our communities, as we become more alienated from one another and more dependent on the ready-made world provided by the Market and State. Further, the city as driven by mainstream urban planning cannot grow without feeding off the natural resources, people and wisdom of the hinterland, often to their detriment. Unfortunately, most development efforts are still symptomatic and focused on rural areas with very little attention being given to cities as holistic and healthy systems.

While the city harbors systems destructive to the human spirit, it is also a precise reason why positive re-generation from within is so important. As the nucleus of educational and developmental decision- and policy-making, the city provides opportunities for closer work on related critique, positive regeneration and other direct, meaningful action. This is the impetus behind Udaipur as a Learning City.

The Sanskrit term, *Swaraj* can be translated as "radiance of the self" and "rule over the self." It was re-invoked during India's freedom struggle by MK Gandhi and Rabindranath Tagore in the early twentieth century, as a spirit, sensibility, and form of organization that would value the uniqueness of each individual as well as the diversity of community. *Swaraj* means that we personally and collectively co-create what terms such as "freedom," "progress" and "justice" mean, and try to manifest a way of life where one is neither controlled nor controlling. After the British left India, the larger agenda of Swaraj was forgotten amidst the agenda of nation-building. (See *Hind Swaraj* by MK Gandhi).

Launched seven years ago by the Shikshantar Institute, Udaipur as a Learning City (ULC) is an innovative process to explore what the practice of *Swaraj* means in the context of urban India today. At the core of *Swaraj* is a deep commitment for people in all spheres of society to reclaim ownership and responsibility for their own learning. ULC aims to support this by re-valuing and re-connecting the diverse spaces for deep learning within the city of Udaipur, based in the northwest state of Rajasthan, India. It is an open invitation to people of all ages and all backgrounds in Udaipur, to explore ways of living and learning that are more balanced, more meaningful, more just and honest for them.

All of ULC's processes are geared towards regenerating the local learning ecology. By this is meant that the city is a living organism and people are active co-creators of meaning, relationships, and knowledge. The learning ecology approach recognizes that an infinite knowledge exists within people and contexts far beyond what can be documented and stored.

Principles

The four major principles or process-goals behind ULC are:

 * Developing our own visions and practices of *Swaraj* in Udaipur.
 * Appreciating the unique strengths, capacities, potential, talents, skills of each person.

 * Building feelings of caring and connected communities.
 * Challenging unjust, dehumanizing institutions, attitudes, structures, plans, etc., particularly those related to urbanization and globalization.

These principles came out of a few years of dialogue with local people, and were articulated by Shikshantar during the process of conceptualizing ULC in the year 2000. They have been, and continue to be, integrated into each activity that emerges under ULC. Given the openness and the spirit of the principles, they have not led to debate, but rather have inspired the community's imaginations to make them manifest in practice.

Processes and Practices

The four process goals are present in each of the activities that organically emerge in Udaipur around the practice of Swaraj. Such activities include:

Festivals are seen as potent opportunities for deep reflection and social engagement. For example, ULC has hosted interactive dialogues on both local and international festivals. Here posters, games, discussions, and hands-on activities are combined to deepen understandings of the core meanings and purposes of such celebrations and to open up diverse narratives to define and co-create them. They have also supported dialogues on prominent issues, like water or pedestrian-friendly roads; or by screening thought-provoking films, like *Baraka* and *Modern Times*.

Despite a strong national and international trend toward Hindi and English, strong efforts have been particularly made to regenerate reflections and conversations in Mewari (the local language). Such an approach offers a means by which to more dynamically share peoples' stories, songs, proverbs, etc., and to break down professional hierarchies in order to critically and creatively look at present problems and possibilities with new perspectives.

Unlearning and Uplearning Workshops

These are particularly related to critical media awareness and creative expressions—people making their own music, dance, dramas, films, puppets, masks, sculptures, especially out of so-called "waste" materials. Such workshops predominantly occur within local neighborhoods.

Natural Living in a City

ULC is currently exploring ways that city-dwellers can reconnect to their hands/bodies and to nature, through organic farming on their rooftops, rainwater harvesting, solar cooking, medicinal plants, spinning cloth, and other such efforts at home. These processes enable city folks to link local culture with ecology; for example, the wisdom in Mewari is intimately connected with nature and has to be re-defined for city life. Natural living efforts also give city people a chance to "get their hands dirty," thereby reintroducing them to the beauty and power of labor and physical work, and to new forms of dialogue, knowledge and wisdom.

Learning Exchanges

ULC seeks to move beyond NGO/Government institutional boundaries and agendas and directly involve local artists, organic farmers, artisans, businesses, healers, etc. in questions and experiments related to regenerating urban life. It also plays a role in regenerating the local learning ecology by encouraging youth who are not interested in school or college (or those who want to change their career) and who would rather create their own meaningful paths of living, livelihood, and learning with exciting apprenticeship opportunities. We encourage people to reclaim their own learning processes by building their own learning webs.

The activities of ULC are entirely off-line, as internet use and access is quite limited in Udaipur. People meet face-to-face as needed, depending on the activity (whether a publication in Mewari, a rooftop garden, a theater workshop, etc.). No separate building has been especially constructed for ULC; rather, they have chosen to creatively utilize what already exists in Udaipur: peoples' homes, local neighborhoods, public gardens and parks, art galleries, temples, ashrams, businesses, or local organizations' offices.

Members

There are various levels of engagement in ULC. Shikshantar: the Peoples' Institute for Rethinking Education and Development, an independent not-for-profit applied research institute and open learning community, has been the primary impetus behind ULC. Its local team has supported the emergence of various parts of ULC, either directly by initiating activities, or indirectly by engaging with local people to encourage/involve them in sharing their hearts, heads, and hands in a process. Families, friends, and neighbors are well involved in different aspects of ULC (depending on their interests).

They have also been able to generate many new relationships with individuals from a variety of local organizations in Udaipur, including artists, craftsmen, healers, activists, farmers, story-tellers, academicians, scientists, etc. They make an effort to partner with individuals, rather than institutions, to stay true to the spirit of ULC. In this way, there are no formal mechanisms for getting involved in ULC, no compulsion and no bureaucracy. People co-create what is of interest to them, thereby ensuring fairly strong commitments to the action at hand.

For this engagement to happen, it has been important to invite each person to be a co-creator in ULC. This means seeing leadership in an entirely different way—a leadership that every person innately possesses, that builds upon their own strengths, and that is not about having followers. The core team of Shikshantar and the core volunteers in ULC have had to be ready to listen and to ask engaging questions, in order to discover where they might connect with new people. They have had to maintain a high level of energy, as this becomes contagious and excites others to open up and get involved. And they have to keep a creative mind and open heart, in order to support the emergence of multiple processes—farming, Mewari language, music, festivals, etc.—which often crisscross in fantastic ways.

In this way, people join ULC either through an existing activity, which has been initiated by the interests and questions of others, or by sharing their own curiosities to start something new. It is self-organizing, and the core team of Shikshantar plays a role in fleshing out, supporting, and deepening the emergent activities. This is why the work of ULC is so broad and deep, spanning everything from vermicomposting to antiglobalization campaigns to learning with local artists.

This is a fundamentally different orientation from many other learning city projects in the West, where the focus is on expanding technology (computers and internet usually). In those cases, the definition, purpose, means, and ends of "learning" are often rooted in the military-industrial paradigm of development and rarely ask questions about the direction of this paradigm. ULC is also very different from the popular notion of public-private partnerships, where "public" only refers to government bodies, and "private" only to corporations. ULC is trying to transcend these categories of public and private and to appreciate and integrate the authentic concerns and strengths of local people.

The principles behind ULC lie in paradigms of abundance as opposed to deficit and scarcity-driven frameworks. In practice, this means beginning with an appreciation of what people have and an openness to any and all to join in co-creating. These activities evolve naturally from "ordinary" peoples' own unique gifts, questions, and dreams, to connect to larger systemic issues and concerns. This approach actively nurtures peoples' capacities to say "no" to the institutions/ attitudes/ structures that do not serve them, and to instead organically construct spaces and relationships that do serve them. Much of the approach is built on exploring how to do things with as little money as possible. This not only ensures sustainability and honesty of efforts but also encourages innovation and imagination.

Over the last seven years, the team at Shikshantar have been astonished and inspired by the directions ULC has taken. They have realized that they work more closely with individuals and families in neighborhoods rather than with formal institutions, and that motivation which comes from within is far more invigorating and self-sustaining than forced action. They have found that interactive dialogues in public spaces such as parks have been very effective. It allows them to work at a different scale and increases interaction with a much larger network of children and families (beyond normal NGO circles). They have also been excited by how such resourcefulness of space and materials reminds people that you do not need a lot of money to do wonderful things to start to transform your life and community.

Lastly, ULC is continuously re-energized by a strong team of youth volunteers. Their involvement in many different workshops and activities has helped to shape where ULC goes and how it sustains itself. They have realized that work with youth needs to be more focused on "practical activities" that gives them more self-confidence and encourages their creative powers. ULC offers them a space to create their own concrete projects in specific contexts. It is also important to support them with adult and elder mentors/practitioners from their diverse communities.

Overall, Udaipur as a Learning City has been (and continues to be) an exciting journey. Shikshantar invites you to share your reflections on new possibilities for urban living.

Rebuilding Learning Communities in Mali: The Experience of the Institute for Popular Education[1]

Coumba Toure

Coumba is an African woman trained in a French system. At an early age, her sense of empathy got her involved in community work, starting with charity, then at political level in the Pan-African Youth Movement and the African Women's Movement. Her life has been impacted by contact with very rich people doing charity work; strong women in very sexist societies; young people volunteering beyond what their means and safety allow them, and a community of intellectuals and thinkers, who have given her a space to reflect on her actions. Coumba is also a lover of music, dance, and writing. She is a core member of IEP, working for women's rights in West Africa and building an international exchange program for young people of African descent.

The Oppression of Formal Education

Formal education in West Africa started out as an instrument of oppression. Today, schooling is a way of keeping the status quo. The goal of schooling during the colonial period was to train leadership who would function in the colonial system. The French administration needed translators and local administrators that would represent them to the population. People trained in the primary schools were automatically employed. (They became the most powerful people after the French departed in 1960s.)

But during the colonial period, schooling faced resistance as well. Many people refused to send their children to schools. There are stories of nobility hiding their own children and sending the children of their servants or of the low class groups. There are stories about how families would react to their child's recruitment to a school. How people from other families would come and sympathize with them, and family members would be crying, because sending a child to the French school was the closest thing to death—not a physical death, but a spiritual and intellectual death.

When introduced by the French, schooling was definitely an instrument of moving students away physically and psychologically from their communities. Then, like now, children were taught in a different language, in a setting that tried to imitate, as closely as possible, the setting in France. Traditional educational spaces, political structures and spirituality were undermined and destroyed. Young Africans started to learn and practice European ways, which not only included eating with forks, but also meant devaluing their traditional knowledge and culture. It affected every level of their lives.

Following the independence of Senegal and Mali, there was a major reform movement for the education system. The vision of the new government was to change the education system from being elitist to making it popular. The slogan *"education pour tous d'ici l'an 2000"* ("education for everyone before the year 2000") generated a lot of hope. There was a move to build schools everywhere, to have teachers and programs that were more in touch with the masses. The new government directly recruited students that graduated out of schools. School became more accepted by the masses and became a way of getting a job and being part of the leadership of the new independent countries. While the percentage of people involved in the school system grew, more teachers were hired, more students enrolled, but the expectations surrounding the policies made in the 1960s were not met.

In fact, throughout the forty years following Independence, the whole school system has been in a deep crisis. The model of education was built for an elite and still remains inaccessible to most people. Students have had regular strikes every year, going from fifteen days to months, asking the government to provide more resources for education, more material for schools and teachers, changes in the curriculum. And even though the system has been reformed many times, it is still very westernized and sexist. The language of education continues to be French. Teachers continue to be treated like gods, who cannot be challenged and they are allowed to use all kinds of punishments, including corporal punishment at the lower levels.

Today, in both Mali and Senegal, students, teachers, government and parents are still struggling to fit the education system to the people. I believe it is a lost cause. It is like having shoes made and then trying to make them fit to different feet. You can pull on the shoes, you can try to adapt them, but the person will never be able to walk in them with comfort.

That is why I feel that by challenging the way we are "educated" and what is means to be "educated," we can challenge the whole way our society works today. By attempting to transform the whole content and process of education, we are able to live a revolution. I mean "education" in a larger sense; it is not just schooling, because the wall of schools are too small to contain what education needs to be.

When learning is relevant and enjoyable, when learners have the space to explore and express themselves, when they are not bound by having to "achieve," when the overall objective is both personal and societal liberation, when discussions challenge the race, class, gender power relationships, then education can become an instrument of transformation. For then, in individuals and for communities, things start moving. Even in the worst of social conditions, people begin to believe in themselves and see new possibilities. They count their gains, instead of their losses, and learn from each other, as well as from their own experiences. They begin to own a process of creation, doing things they were never taught to do, creating open, welcoming spaces of joy, where the seeds of change can grow.

In this article, I seek to share some principles of such Popular Education, through my experiences at the Institute for Popular Education (Institut pour L'Education Populaire - IEP). We are working to create a reference center for Africa around alternative frameworks of learning for social change. Our aim is not to reform, but to transform the education system.

The People of IEP

IEP was created with the goal to create and share alternatives to the elitist French-colonial schooling system in West Africa, and what is called "development" through NGO programs of literacy. It seeks to make visible, known and understood, the practices emerging from peoples' resistance to domination in all sectors: education, food security, economics, etc. To do so, it employs a number of techniques: from creating learning communities through group identity development, to using theater, music, painting, dance, and literacy as curriculum-building methodologies.[2]

IEP grew, because a group of people decided to show that there are other ways of being, and they chose to do it in the education field. In this way, IEP not only has the mission to promote alternatives, but also to be an alternative. Its primary goal is not to "manufacture" activists but to give any potential activist space and support to develop their ideas and actions. IEP offers opportunities for diverse groups of people to participate in concrete social change projects.

I could begin to define IEP by enumerating its activities, but I choose to begin by enumerating the names of people. What is called today "The Institute for Popular Education" was born and grew in the minds of people, like Maria Diarra, Cheick Omar Coulibaly, Marie Samake, Deborah Freddo. These people are at the beginning and at the end of everything; they are the feet on which the Institute stands. They have a commitment to justice and believe in IEP as a way to struggle for it. Around them are many more people that I could describe or name, because each person at the Institute (in the present or from the past) is special by what s/he brings to it.

At IEP are volunteers, amazing trainers, curriculum developers, drivers, dreamers, philosophers, feminists, storytellers, singers, dancers, activists, learners, mentors, cooks, counselors, role models, farmers. And none of these roles exclude the other. There is no age, geographical, or professional boundary. The people of IEP listen, educate, sustain, and inspire each other, and the communities they evolve, through their daily actions. They have very strong ties of friendship, trust and love that come before and after everything. People come and go, and there are times with more people and times with less. But because of the specificity of each person's role and the strength of their ties to each other, no one can ever replace another. IEP people eat, work, pray, laugh, cry, and grow together. They come because of the activities and stay on because they grow to believe in the principles.

Activities of IEP

Through IEP's activities, and through reflections before and after the activities, we learn the lessons that help us to move towards our larger vision. The programs of IEP do not stand in isolation by themselves. Rather, they complement each other. By recording and analyzing together our experiences, by participating in direct actions against the sources of oppression, by using literacy, theater and music, not as an end but as a means, we have a direct attachment to the language of the people. We prioritize creativity, and we have tried to design IEP as an innovative organization. We believe in embedding in our activities what we long to see at the end of them. At the same time, we give space to allow things to happen spontaneously and from people who usually would not have the opportunity.

I could go on and on, for any number of pages, since each day comes with its own activities, as every person comes with her or his interest. Whenever the moment and the people are ready, then the activity is born. Activities grow from peoples' needs and their capacities to meet them, and they can die when people do not sustain them. But most of the time, they evolve into something new.

But in my description of IEP, I should also clarify: When we have to describe the Institute for outsiders or newcomers, we generally find ourselves naming some of the structures, "kindergarten," "primary school," "literacy school," as these are the closest to what everybody knows. Moreover, this is what people expect. If you work in Education, then you must have a formal school, and if not, then it must be a non-formal school. But none of those structures are the essence of the Institute. Rather, IEP sees all of these spaces as tools to mobilize our communities for social change. They are based on action-research of local knowledge and their curricula are all built on African identity, gender, health, etc. In these ways, and more, they are very much unlike their mainstream counterparts.

Moreover, it is important to understand that popular education is not a series of exercises, workshops, different skits or tricks. Once the general principles are accepted or understood, there is no standard teaching method. Every activity should be different. This requires a continuous level of creativity from both facilitators and learners, to continuously renew the learning process. They must create the curriculum by adapting to the particular geography and time they live in, by linking to the composition of the group, to their specific interests in the learning experience, to their social environments. Popular education means constant re-creation.

For example, throughout this year, I have been compiling outlines of workshops I have designed and tested with different groups. I have been very skeptical about making a booklet out of these, because I realize that none of these workshops stands alone—I had to recreate and adapt them every time. And, so would any facilitator that would want to use them. Therefore, I cannot fossilize, package and distribute them, as is done with standard curricula.

Many of IEP's activities utilize the arts. We feel that the arts bring a sense of freedom to express emotion, whether joy or pain, fear or anger. Normal academic classrooms offer no space for those expressions; they are undermined or judged as "irrational." But traditionally, music and the art of storytelling have been used extensively by children and adults in West Africa. To create spaces for peoples' voices to be heard, popular education utilizes these and other modes of expression, especially those that learners are comfortable with and interested in. Often, a different mode of communication makes the content more focused and more real, and opens up dialogue processes. For example, we always use songs in our warm-up exercises, to illustrate the particular theme of the day.

Sometimes an art form, like dance or theater, may be central to the practice of a particular learning group. Like the adolescent girls at IEP, whose first point of interest was dancing and theatre, which later facilitated deeper discussions and eventually their own learning curricula. Thus, theory adapts to the context: one can do popular education through art, or art

---

The Many Faces of the Institute for Popular Education

- A "kindergarten," where parents are parts of the staff and people from the community are welcome. A kindergarten, where children are given the space to develop their identity and are exposed to values of justice, peace and communities.

- A "literacy school" for adults who learn to read and write by developing curricula on identity, on gender, race, and class issues.

- A "theater group" which presents pieces on various topics, such as "how the education system evolved in Mali" or "violence against women." A theater group that sometimes asks its audience to be part of the production.

- A "dance group" of adolescent girls, which offers a physical exercise through modern and traditional dances.

- A "chorus" which creates and reproduces music for social change. A chorus which sings about AIDS and other sexually-transmitted diseases, as well as other topics.

- A "primary school" that promotes girls' involvement by transforming the curriculum, so that it is possible for girls to identify with the classes.

- A "youth leadership program" designed to enable young people to take responsibilities and actions in their communities.

- A "training institute" for teachers, non-governmental organizations and other institutions, on Popular Education and gender, economic issues, etc.

- A "university" without walls and without accreditation, where young people seek learning that is linked to their realities.

through popular education. They are reversible, or mutually exchange-able. Like Augusto Boal's Theater of the Oppressed, there is an intention to engage the arts, but also to challenge the status quo.[3] There is also the intention to guide people to a space to express themselves, a space, which in turn, is created by peoples' expression. This part of popular education essentially asks facilitators to constantly be open to changing their method. Personally, at IEP, I have been practicing storytelling with young children, and learning to use theatre with the Atelier Theatre Burkinabe, an organi-zation based in Burkina Faso.

The central piece in all of the activities is the way they participate in decolonizing the mind. We create a rupture in the ideas and the formats that people are accustomed to. For instance, we use local languages as the language of thinking. This forces people to create new concepts, because many times, colonial concepts do not find translation. We also change the format. People are used to presentations, one person speaking, the others listening. But we start discussions through art and physical activities and other forms of expression, so that people will not be able to conform to the colonial mindset. This means being very creative. Each time, we try to catch people off guard, to get them to speak their true beliefs and feelings. But, at the same time, we try to put them in a comfortable situation, so that they realize where their colonized mind comes from and what the conse-quences of it are for them and their community. For example, we spend time discussing why we continue to maintain a system of schooling, which was created to undermine everything we are or know.

As we unlearn together the ways of thinking and acting that have hurt our communities, we also give value to local knowledge through dif-ferent activities. We ask people to find alternative solutions, by research-ing how people used to face their issues/concerns before colonization. We ask each other how our grandparents learned, or how they sustained and created so much when there was no school? Usually, our answers show that our grandparents' generations had deep knowledge of how to live and survive—sometimes better than we do today. They spoke many more languages, engaged in many different kinds of media and art, which opened up diverse ways to interact and resolve their problems together. We ask ourselves if we too can create new ways of educating our selves and our children, in order to respond to the needs of our time, including the urgent need to fight neo-colonialism. Our research into and discus-sions on local knowledge have led us to further study the actions and answers people have developed, either during the workshops or just on their own. We together consider how to help these ideas cross over into today's contexts.

All of the above examples illustrate why and how creating diverse learning communities is the most important part of our activities. The content of a particular curriculum, and the methodology to implement it, depends on the composition of the learners. Facilitators must learn to listen to learners and to facilitate listening among them. This is the first step in discovering each other's experiences, thoughts about those experiences, reactions to those experiences, and plans to change those experiences. The facilitator helps in the expression of feelings, of dreams and passions, strengths and skills. Group identity is built by sharing stories of life, by supporting each other's struggles. IEP's activity groups slowly move towards cohesion by developing a mutual understanding of what needs to be taught or learned, and how to do it together.

Building a learning community takes time, since facilitators and participants need to share a vision and a commitment to work together. Our basic vision is around social justice. We believe that social justice demands radical social changes, and radical social changes demand transformation of education and other dominant economic and political institutions. Before we start, each new group of learners have to demonstrate an interest in going through a process, whose outcome is not completely defined from the beginning. Therefore, most preliminary questions for new groups seek to open up people to such a process. These questions can refer to the past, but they must be personal, so that people can only speak for themselves. For example, in the education workshop, I ask questions like: "What was your experience with schooling?"; "What was your first experience of injustice?"; "What was your last meal, and how did you get it?" We also use a number of group-building exercises, which we adapt to the specific learning community.

We focus on sharing experiences, because this helps begin a dialogue, in which there is no expert and no "right" answer. It also ensures that we all acknowledge the limitations of what we know. To set an example of this, the facilitator honestly shares his/her experiences. As people listen to each other's experiences and see their similarities and differences, we not only learn about each other, but also begin building a community of committed learners.

222 ... Everywhere All the Time

IEP's Principles of Popular Education

Many of the people of IEP are students of Paulo Freire. They have been experimenting with and expanding on his theory of Popular Education in a West African context. Thus, IEP's principles are Freirian principles, with a twist. We are not copying them. Rather, we think that Freire created very powerful and strong principles to analyze communities' situations, but he is a starting point, not an end. We have used him as an inspiration to create our own tools, which are centered in local indigenous knowledges and ways of making-meaning, and which go beyond schooling and beyond literacy. We also have other sources of inspiration and we have our own set of values.

Important Values of the Institute for Popular Education

- Africa, the home of the birth of humankind, is also the cradle of the values of humanity.
- The real participation of local people is *sine qua non* for nurturing livable communities.
- Empowering education leads to community involvement in social change.
- Equity is a fundamental issue, if societies are to evolve toward democracy.
- Youth are a part of the solution, not part of the problem, for building livable communities.
- Local languages are the languages of learning, of intellectual growth, of innovation, and of information.
- Alternatives to Education (teacher-centered, non-democratic) demand ongoing unlearning processes for educators and professionals.
- Connecting people of African descent from around the world is necessary for building a strong movement for social change in the continent.

We aim to use popular education to build a movement. Although theorizing Popular Education cannot communicate a full picture of its practice, the following serves to give a preliminary idea of the principles we are evolving:

The Principle of Non-Neutrality

Our education needs to address power relationships. Every single day, a vast majority of the population of the world goes through tremendous pain, exploitation and inequality, while a small minority benefits from the privileges of their race, gender, and class. By practicing Popular Education, we recognize a fact: real education cannot be neutral. How can it be, when we have been categorized as "women," "children," "disabled," "poor," "immigrants," "prisoners," "transgender," "student," "workers," "Africans"!?! There are people who are oppressed, and for every class of oppressed people, there are one or many classes of oppressors. These categories—of who is what—may change, depending on context. But even though the lines are not always clear, there are definitely situations of injustice, where responsibilities can be (and have been) defined and where changes need to (and can) happen. We can give personal examples of injustice from our daily life experiences, or we can pull such facts from newspapers, government documents, or academic studies.

However, instead of recognizing these injustices, the modern education system goes to the other extreme. It reinforces the status quo. It sustains current injustices by hiding them, by making them seem minor or by making invisible to the schooled. Worse, it breeds future injustice by teaching students how to exploit other people, how to defend their self-interest, how to seek money above all else. Popular education breaks from this so-called neutrality of modern education by recognizing the existence of circles of oppression. There is no pretense of neutrality; rather, we take an automatic and moral stand in favor of the oppressed.

The Principles of Centrality, Objectivity, and Relevance in Dialogue

The people experiencing injustice must be the initiators and leaders of social justice movements. They have to be at the center, not on the peripheries, not the followers. Their experience must be valued, and their objectivity must be taken in account. They need to have the space to express themselves freely about their issues and challenges, to share their stories, to do their analyses, and to develop their strategies for change. Anything less betrays the learning process. Thus, faith in the ability of people to bring about change in their lives is as important as the belief in the need for change.

As Paulo Freire (1970) said,

Some from the dominant class join the oppressed in their struggle for liberation. This is a fundamental role and has been so throughout the history of this struggle. However, as they move to the side of the exploited, they almost always bring with them the marks of their origins. Their prejudices include a lack of confidence in the people's abilities to think, to want and to know. So they run the risk of failing into a type of generosity as harmful as that of the oppressors. Though they truly desire to transform the unjust order, they believe that they must be the executors of the transformation. They talk about people, but they do not trust them, and trusting people is an indispensable precondition for revolutionary change. A real humanist can be identified more by his trust in people, which engage him or her in their struggle, than by a thousand actions in their favor without that trust. To substitute monologue slogans and communiqués for dialogue is to try to liberate the oppressed with the instruments of domestication.

The above quote makes it clear that people should be in charge of their liberation. This happens through dialogue, in which people not only share different perceptions of their own experiences, but also start formulating how to express them. In dialogue, the learner is central to the learning experience, and their knowledge is valued. The line between teacher and learner is broken through this process. The "teacher" in the formal setting become a facilitator, not to dictate or manipulate, but to catalyze learning processes of which s/he then becomes a part.

Because the learner is at the center of the learning process, popular education demands that the learning content be relevant to the learner. Relevance doesn't mean that the education will be narrow; it just means that it starts from something real. From there, links can be drawn to macro- and more general issues. When the content is relevant to the learner, the learning experience has life; it becomes meaningful and fun. The lines between teachers and learners blur—the student is an authority who brings her/his knowledge to class. Learning becomes an exchange expanded through dialogue. Relevant learning also strengthens the cycle of reflection and action, by generating multiple possibilities of applying our reflections to real life.

The Principle of Reflection and Action in Praxis

Popular Education makes knowledge and information accessible to regular people. By accessible, I refer both to the production of knowledge, as well as to its diffusion. In this way, ideas and understandings about health, economics, politics, etc. are not constructed solely by an elite, but rather are created by us, for us. People themselves reflect on the issues affecting their lives, and these reflection processes lead to pro-actively challenge injustice and inequality. Most importantly, people decide on the strategies by which they will change their lives.

Popular Education addresses racism, sexism, class-ism, age-ism on a personal and practical level, as well as on a theoretical and historical level. But dealing with reality, with parts of themselves, touches deep wounds. It is a challenge. We remind ourselves that it takes time for reflection and action to become a cycle, where one is continuously born out of the other.

The Principle of Critical Analysis and Radical Transformation

The general assumption of education is that students are simply recipients, who come to school to take knowledge from a person who knows more and better (what Freire termed the "banking approach"). Popular education, on the other hand, is about problem posing with students. We present a situation, real or fictitious, to challenge their assumptions. In the workshop on education, I posed the following question to participants: Let's imagine there was no university, no high school, no primary school, no kindergarten. How will people learn? What will people learn? The very act of discussing such questions helps us see the relationships between the ways our schools work and the ways our societies work.

The idea of carrying-out problem-posing education is to open up another level of dialogue, after people have shared their experiences. It allows participants to give their opinions on and their perceptions of different issues. It forces people to think out of their old boxes, and also frees them from making pre-mature judgments, so that they are free to bring new ideas to the learning community for exploration. One of the first meetings organized by IEP was conducted as a problem-posing workshop. Many people, from different areas of Mali and from different walks of life, were gathered together and were asked to describe: What challenges are we facing? What do we think is at the root of our problems? Over the day's discussion, people posed questions to try and find the origins and roots of a variety of problems. We came out with a lot of issues, which are still used as the basis of the Institute's general work. Moreover, we go through a problem-posing process every time we work with a new group of people, as it is important for spotting critical issues.

Challenges in Building IEP as a Learning Community

IEP is an organic organization, born out of a vision of participation for social change and empowerment, an organization that recognizes local and individual knowledge and refuses the hierarchy of the formal institutions against which it was born. Over the last six or seven years, the Institute has been struggling to maintain its identity: How do we survive when we are engaged in so many activities?; When we have such demanding principles?; As we work with so many different people?; In such a difficult economic environment? There is no magic secret, no total success.

It is an everyday fight to have people participate in activities, when their daily lives keep them busy just surviving. It is an everyday fight to make sure that those who have just arrived at IEP identify themselves with its principles. Most of the time, they accept one particular principle—the one that fits their need. It is an everyday fight to make sure that each and every action at IEP adheres to these principles, that our vision is reflected in the actions we take. The value of humanity ought to exist in the processes we use.

It is an everyday fight against the solidification of roles. When people get too accustomed to playing a role, they begin to identify themselves with that single role and to classify their position as such. As we grow in numbers and geographically, it is a struggle to maintain the same level of commitment, information and action. We ask ourselves if it will be possible for the organization to stay "alternative," when it goes beyond a human scale of relationships? What will happen if we grow so large, that we no longer know each other's names?

Moreover, how can an organization which promotes alternatives survive in a mainstream environment? Sometimes, we feel ourselves dying. It is a challenge to position ourselves as deep practitioners. It is an everyday fight to not replicate what we see in the formal sector, to not let our alternative innovations be co-opted, to not fit in a system that we have rejected for survival. We particularly struggle when we come into contact with communities that have been changed by the movement of NGOs. These communities have given up on taking charge of their problems, because the programming / planning / financing structure of NGOs has never included them. NGOs' mechanisms do not integrate community innovations into their activities, and there is no space for community expression, except in a limited way during "pre-project research." The problem we often face is that since we are not a government agency, we are automatically labeled an NGO. It is assumed that we therefore must be coming with a big project and a lot of money. Communities expect us to tell them what they should do and expect us to pay them for their compliance.

Because we do not want to fall into the traps of NGO and government structures, we have also been researching the structure of traditional (local and ancient) organizations to see how they work/ed. In this exploration, IEP's research group on organizations considers: What is the structure of our organization? What are our objectives and mission? What in the structure of our organizations prevents us from reaching our objectives?" Our study has already led us to incorporate traditional organizations' elements of music and storytelling, as described above. We also ask older people about the types of organizations they are members of, to see what principles move these organizations and what their roles are in communities.

IEP is still a relatively young organization. Its structure has not yet been frozen by the harshness of bureaucratization, nor has it been disabled by rules and laws (set up to "protect" organizations from the people who constitute it). While the unstructured, non-controlling environment helps activities to bloom, IEP also has to work to coordinate itself, in the absence of a strong organizational structure. It finds itself losing material resources, because people were not responsible in their spending. Moreover, our existing human and financial resources may be insufficient to sustain our growth. While some programs may grow to be independent of IEP (the theater group, the dance group), others seem to have a clear path (the kindergarten, the university), while still others might disappear. Amidst this, we realize that there is a need to be creative and flexible enough, so that people will initiate new activities, rather than trying to replicate the same activities in different places.

It is an everyday struggle to keep open the space, where our actions can be checked against our values, where we recognize our own privileges and act on empowering others. We realize that one way of fighting the elitism in our institution is to create spaces, where people without money or degree-based education make vital contributions. We know that fighting the power of the diploma means accepting people on the basis of their "know-how," recognizing them in the same way (or even more) that we recognize those who have a diploma. Similarly, the donor-driven planning and funding models we subject ourselves to permanently present a contra-diction to IEP's principles of being innovative and open to communities' new ideas and goals. For example, out of a simple theater exercise on teen pregnancy one morning, the Girls Circle program emerged. It grew into a twice-a-week meeting of adolescent girls for two years. Though not part of our "plan," we felt it was important to pursue this innovative idea from the learning community.

Persistent dialogues about these and other issues bring us back to the core of our values. But we are not just accountable to our principles for ourselves alone. External groups judge us, as there is a profound pressure on people who represent an "alternative" vision to be excellent, before they gain any legitimacy. So we face another contradiction: people are expected to give the best of their capacities, but the criteria used by outsiders to judge us are the opposite of what we promote.

In these ways, we still struggle with impact of the French colonial schooling system. Its elitist content and methodologies produce a lot of people, who are disconnected from and/or useless to the well-being of their communities. In addition, most people educated in that system think that it is impossible to learn or to think in their native languages. Similarly, the global economy poses a great challenge. It is operating by the same principles that it operated by hundreds of years ago, when it traded in en-slaved Africans. This economy does not respect humanity and maintains the power of few at the expense of everybody else. While the names have changed, and the ways have changed, the results are the same: the alien-ation of people and the breaking down of communities.

Slowly but surely, the work of IEP is impacting the lives of thousands of people, by re-activating thinking processes that cannot be stopped. In the last few years, we have been working with the Government of Mali to introduce changes in the content and methods of teaching at the primary school level, especially with regards to the importance of local languages. IEP has also insisted on the necessity of education to build competencies. For us, this means knowing how to do and how to be part of a movement for social change. I must clarify that we are not trying to build alternatives and then mainstream them. Rather, we are trying to create models that can stand by themselves, in their own right, and can continuously be evolved by people themselves. We are seeking to reverse the dominant process by inviting the mainstream to transform itself and become the alternative. We call this "alter-streaming."

We also recognize that many of the problems that affect people in Mali do not originate in Mali. They are connected to global systems and global structures of power. Since 1993, IEP has been in touch with several organizations internationally, facilitating meetings that challenge white supremacy and globalization. With an organization like 21st Century Youth Leadership Movement, based in Selma, Alabama, USA, we are building bridges between Africans around the world, re-writing the past and the present, comparing our lives and our struggles, and searching for inspiration and solutions for our different communities.

What the Future Holds for IEP

Where will the Institute be twenty-five years from now? What will we do to make sure that our programs grow, while staying true to the vision and the principles behind them? The Institute has been going through many stages, from being the Nomads Institutes—a moving institute that went from village to village working on education—to meeting with national and international organizations on many different issues. Today, there are thousands of people touched by the activities, as participants, as facilitators, as learners, as people who live in the communities they reside in. As we step forward in the future, we are still changing and still looking for ways to escape "formalization" (i.e, being put in a box—in order to be accepted by other organizations, to get funding, to be trusted).

Through different popular activities, seminars, trainings, campaigns, art programs, model schools, leadership institutes, and youth camps, IEP is trying to create the spaces to push people to think in different ways. We don't seek to provide ready-made answers. Rather, we put the questions that we are struggling with out in front of everyone so that we can work through them with each other. Together, we seek to understand the issues we are facing and to create new tools and actions to rebuild our communities. In doing so, we believe we are helping to nurture a learning society throughout Mali.

Notes
1. This article was originally published in Shikshantar's Bulletin: *Vimukt Shiksha: Special Issue—Unfolding Learning Societies: Experiencing the Possibilities*, June 2002. p. 119. Reprinted with permission.

2. When I say "literacy," I mean the literacy that comes out of peoples' experiences, a literacy not of the word and alphabet, but to understand the world, starting with our own communities.

3. Augusto Boal's Theater of the Oppressed, or "theater forum"/"invisible theater," principally aims to give people space to express themselves on particular issues concerning their life. As Boal once stated in an interview, "The real beginning [of Theater of the Oppressed] was when I was doing what I called simultaneous play writing, using people's real experiences. In one of these, a woman told us what the protagonist should do. We tried her suggestion over and over again, but she was never satisfied with our interpretation. So I said, 'Come on to the stage to show us what to do, because we cannot interpret your thoughts.' By doing what she did, we understood the enormous difference between our interpreting and her own word and action."

Doing Something Very Different: Growing Without Schooling

Susannah Sheffer

Susannah edited Growing Without Schooling *magazine for many years, and also edited the book* A Life Worth Living: Selected Letters of John Holt. *Her books about homeschooling include* A Sense of Self: Listening to Homeschooled Adolescent Girls *and* Writing Because We Love To: Homeschoolers at Work. *She now works at North Star: Self-Directed Learning for Teens, a resource center for teenagers in Western Massachusetts, and also writes about the death penalty and prison issues. Her most recent book is called* In a Dark Time: A Prisoner's Struggle for Healing and Change.

I'm sitting with three teenagers who have recently left school to begin learning at home and in the wider world. On the table in front of us lie notes about possibilities—ideas, wishes, plans for further investigation. I've scribbled down, "Call homeless shelter; find out about marine biologist," in response to Anna's brainstorm of things she would like to do or learn more about. Adrienne and I have agreed to meet next week to talk about the essay she is working on. Ariel says that she wants to work with someone who can help her see what it means to think mathematically, rather than just how to complete math assignments, and I've recommended someone for her to call.

Though these kids have been homeschooling for a few months, they are still becoming accustomed to the freedom, to the heady realization that education can be about figuring out their own goals, rather than figuring out how to meet demands that don't make sense to them. I am struck again and again by their enthusiasm, their interest in learning, the number of things they come up with when they are asked what they want to know more about.

As we scrape the last crumbs of chocolate cake from our plates, our conversation turns toward their friends who are still in school and who are more often than not unhappy there. They say they want to let these kids know that homeschooling is an option for them.

Speaking for the many skeptics, I offer a common criticism of homeschooling: "Some people might say that you are special kids and that homeschooling can only work for kids who are as self-motivated as you are. After all, think of all the interests you've been telling me about..."

"But I wasn't like this at all last year!" Ariel interjects. "I wasn't the kind of kid you would think would be self-motivated. I didn't do that well in school, and I didn't have all these things I wanted to learn about."

The others agree. "Oh yeah," one says, "if you had to go by how I acted in school..."

"It's not fair to look at kids in school and say, oh, they're not motivated, oh, they're not good at this," someone else adds, "because maybe they would be a lot more motivated under a different system. The thing about homeschooling is that it's so different. I wish people could understand that."

"Why didn't school work for you?" I ask.

"No one was paying attention to what I really needed," Adrienne says. "And it was really hard for me to take myself seriously there. I was always doubting myself."

"It's hard to fit in there, but you have to fit in," Ariel adds. "School pits kids against each other."

"And you're cooped up all day, under those lights," Anna says. "It felt like we were being punished, that's what I always used to feel, like we were in there as a punishment."

Some people would call this adolescent griping. Why do I listen to these kids, this growing crop of new homeschoolers and their companions, the long-time homeschoolers who have learned outside of school for years, and feel that they are some of the most important education critics of our time? Why do I feel that these are the voices the school reform movement needs to hear?

John Holt wrote in 1970, "Every day's headlines show more clearly that the old ways, the tried and true ways, are simply and quite spectacularly not working. No point in arguing about who's to blame. The time has come to do something very different."[1]

Homeschooling is about doing something very different. It's about making things better for kids right now, and at the same time it gives us a vantage point from which to look at the experience of kids in school and at the structure and assumptions of traditional schooling. These home-schoolers are worth listening to because they don't let us rest on old assumptions, because they are exuberant, full of interests, eager to learn—and they weren't like this in school a year ago. Something is different. That difference is what school reformers need to study.

Holt published the first issue of *Growing Without Schooling* (*GWS*) in 1977 as a way of supporting the families scattered across the country who were letting their children learn outside of school. Holt had been a teacher for many years, and his *How Children Fail* and several subsequent books had placed him at the center of the school reform movement of the 1960s and 70s. By the early 1970s he was questioning the idea of schooling itself. In the first issue of *GWS*, he wrote that the newsletter would be:

> about ways in which people, young and old, can learn to do things, acquire skills, and find interesting and useful work without having to go through the process of schooling. In starting this newsletter, we are putting into practice a nickel-and-dime theory about social change, which is that important and lasting change always comes slowly, and only when people change their lives, not just their political beliefs or parties.[2]

Growing Without Schooling, as Holt said elsewhere in that first issue, was "to make people feel less helpless," because it would show them that people could change things for themselves, could create new solutions in their own lives without waiting for an entire revolution to occur. Of course, the changes they did make would then be inspiring to others and would demonstrate that "something very different" was indeed possible.

Now many of the children who were babies when *GWS* was first launched have spent their entire lives reading, thinking, playing, studying, working with adults in the community, learning all manner of things, all without going to school. They have learned to read without traditional reading instruction, made friends even though most people think making friends without attending school is impossible, got into selective colleges (ditto), and found interesting work (ditto). John Holt published a book about homeschooling, called *Teach Your Own*, in 1981, and continued to publish *GWS* and learn from homeschoolers until his death in 1985. Holt Associates carries on with his work running a mail-order book catalogue, writing and speaking to and about homeschoolers.

In continuing John Holt's work, we are focused on the immediate needs of homeschoolers, but we also keep a broader or more long term vision in our minds. By helping people envision certain kinds of possibilities and put certain ideas into practice, we are also working to show what a very different kind of world might look like. In time, this actually helps to make our current world look a little more like that other, different one.

In Holt's *Freedom and Beyond*, which was first published in 1972, he wrote:

> Imagine that I am traveling into the future in a time capsule, and that I come to rest, five hundred years from now, in an intelligent, humane, and life-enhancing civilization. One of the people who lives there comes to meet me, to guide me, and to explain his society. At some point, after he has shown me where people live, work, play, I ask him,
>
> "But where are your schools?"
>
> "Schools? What are schools?" he replies.
>
> "Schools are where people go to learn things."
>
> "I do not understand," he says, "People learn things everywhere, in all places."
>
> "I know that," I say, "But a school is a special place where there are special people who teach you things, help you learn things."
>
> "I am sorry, but I still do not understand. Everyone helps other people to learn things. Anyone who knows something or can do something can help someone else who wants to learn more about it. Why should there be special people to do it?"
>
> And try as I will, I cannot make clear to him why we think education should be, must be, separate from the rest of life.

This was my first vision of a society without schooling. Since then I have come to feel that the deschooled society, a society in which learning is not separated from but joined to, part of the rest of life, is not a luxury for which we can wait hundreds of years, but something toward which we must move and work, as quickly as possible.[3]

This parable of Holt's is developed within the context of a much deeper and more detailed analysis of the function of schooling in society than I can give here. The story is useful, though, because it gives a vivid picture of what we are aiming for. It invites us to think about what stands between our current assumptions and those of that mythical future guide. When I think about Holt's conversation with that tour guide, I think about the guide's bewilderment, his lack of comprehension. Though of course I feel myself to be trying to increase people's understanding, I'm also working toward a time when many of the things we now do to children and many of the ways we now think about children's learning simply won't make any sense.

The tour guide didn't understand what Holt meant when he said that schools are places where we go to learn things, and many of the long-time homeschoolers I know don't understand this either. Well, of course they understand it on some level, because it is an idea that permeates their culture, but they don't really understand it because they do learn everywhere, from everyone—at home, curled up on the couch reading or being read to, building or cooking or drawing or playing music or writing or having a conversation, and in libraries, museums, labs, courthouses, specialty shops, veterinary offices, theatres, newspapers, soup kitchens, historic houses, farms, wildlife sanctuaries—the list goes on, and these are all real examples of places homeschoolers visit and work as volunteers.

Naturally, as homeschoolers grow, they may find that they want to learn about or work on something in particular. They may decide that they want help in doing that. Homeschoolers understand the value of teachers, but they are less likely to understand why it's necessary to learn from people who are only teachers and/or to learn only from those teachers who are assigned to them. Homeschooling kids can ask for help, feedback, suggestions, inspiration, and support, and they and their families can create for themselves, as needed, whatever degree of schedule, planning, outside appointments, and deadlines they find useful. These families demonstrate what it means to create a useful structure rather than to labor under an externally imposed one.

Homeschooling is important because of what it rejects, but it is equally (or perhaps more) important for what it reclaims on its own terms. Teachers, help, schedules, organization—these are not school things in themselves. They are school things when someone assigns the teachers, tells the teachers what to teach, gives the students no say in the matter, makes the help be compulsory, imposes the schedule according to institutional rather than individual needs, and so on. But when the teachers are chosen freely, the help is requested (and can be refused), and the schedules and organization serve real needs or goals, then these concepts mean something quite different.

Holt's tour guide wouldn't understand the need for grades and other external motivators, either. In a world where everyone learns all the time, people are learning on their own steam, for their own reasons, and they don't need the promise or threat of grades to make them learn or to tell them how well they did. *Growing Without Schooling* once asked home-schooling kids and teenagers to describe situations in which they had to do something difficult or frustrating as part of working towards a larger goal: "The pronunciation is difficult," a fifteen-year-old homeschooler wrote about her efforts to learn Spanish, but she kept practicing because she really wanted to learn the language. "Although it would have been easy to quit, I decided not to," a thirteen-year-old wrote about his determination to remain on a challenging swim team because of his ambition to become a lifeguard. And after describing how hard she had to work to learn to sight read music, a sixteen-year-old lifelong homeschooler said, "I do things that are difficult, or that I really don't like, for the same reason I do anything else: because I've decided they're important."[4]

This is what our tour guide would understand, but what so many schools fail to appreciate. Young people are capable of deciding what is important or necessary, and once they have decided, they are capable of working much harder than we imagine. Schools, after failing to give children the chance to decide what is important to them and to understand the relationship between their chosen goal and specific tasks, then conclude that children are lazy, no good, unmotivated.

One of the consequences of thinking that people learn only in schools is that the culture ties up more of its resources in schools than in libraries, museums, public art facilities, community centers, and other places that are accessible but not compulsory and not restricted to one age group. Another part of our work at Holt Associates, though a less obvious part, is to support these existing community resources and to encourage development of new ones.

Holt's tour guide wouldn't judge people on the basis of how much time they've spent in schools. Unfortunately, we do judge people on that basis in our culture, but here again homeschoolers can be an exception and a suggestion of future possibilities. When homeschooling kids get into college, not on the basis of a high-school transcript but on the basis of what they have learned and done during those years, they show that there are other ways to evaluate people's abilities.

When homeschoolers choose not to go to college but instead make their way into the adult world through apprenticeships and other interesting routes towards meaningful work, they show that college isn't essential. John Holt took an unusual approach to this problem of living in a culture that evaluates people according to school credentials. Having already acquired a couple of those credentials (though not as many as most people thought) before he developed his critique of schooling, he refused to include any mention of his schooling in public descriptions (on a book jacket, for instance, or on other occasions where such information is ordinarily given). Instead he said, "I have come to believe that a person's schooling is as much a part of his private business as his politics or religion, and that no one should be required to answer questions about it. May I say instead that most of what I know I did not learn in school, or even in what most people would call 'learning situations.'"[5]

John Holt's approach here is characteristic of his attitude toward social change in general. In a letter he wrote during the late 1970s he said:

> During the 1960s, many young people were talking about revolutionary changes in society. Paul [Goodman] used to say to them, "Suppose you had had the revolution you are talking and dreaming about. Suppose your side had won, and you had the kind of society you wanted. How would you live, you personally, in that society? Start living that way now! Whatever you would do then, do it now. When you run up against obstacles, people or things that won't let you live that way, then begin to think about how to get over or around or under that obstacle, or how to push it out of the way, and your politics will be concrete and practical." Very good advice. The trick is to find ways to put your strongest ideals into practice in daily life. I don't mean talking to other people about it, or saying, "Wouldn't it be wonderful if we all did this or that." I mean doing it right now. It is interesting, absorbing, fascinating, satisfying, and useful. You don't have to wait for a hundred million people to agree with you, you can start right away. And when you find that you are able to do something, the very fact that you can do it means that anyone else who wants to can also do it.[6]

This is what I try to do, and what, in a sense, homeschoolers are doing as they simultaneously try to live in a way that makes sense and in so doing illuminates the possibilities for all of us. It's true that we are not anywhere near the kind of society that Holt's imagined tour guide lives in. But what would it look like? How would people live? What would no longer be true or necessary and what would remain? Homeschooling is about figuring out answers to these questions and then—as Holt suggests—about trying to live as though those changes had already happened. Circuitous? Maybe. But it's the most direct route I know to the world where that tour guide lives.

Notes

1. John Holt, *What Do I Do Monday?* New York: Boynton-Cook/Heinemann, 1995. p. 302.

2. *Growing Without Schooling* #1, Vol. 1, No. 1, August 1977, p. 1.

3. John Holt, *Freedom and Beyond.* New York: Boynton-Cook/Heinemann, 1995. p. 117.

4. "Working Toward a Goal," *Growing Without Schooling* #84, Vol. 14, No. 6, December 1991, pp. 14–17

5. *Growing Without Schooling* #48, p. 1.

6. Celebrating 100 Issues," *Growing Without Schooling* #100, Vol. 17, No. 3, July/August 1994, p. 35

Unschooled Kids' Comments IV:

9. How about your sense of who you are, your confidence, your ability to see yourself as an author of your own life: how has an alternative school path impacted your views of your own capabilities?

Russ Gendron: Alternative school gave me confidence to speak what I believed to be true. That has stayed with me. I know regular school to be a very oppressive place at times, so maybe I would have discovered this confidence and trust in myself years later, when I was out of school. I have seen this happen to some of my friends. As they realize that they are in control of their lives, their trust in their own abilities begins to grow. I feel as if anything is possible for my life, some things just take more work than others. I don't know where I learned that.

Sadie Couture: I think that going to alternative schools has really made me stronger in my ability to try new things and make choices for myself. I think my family really helps in that as they support me, I think that I know how many possibilities life has and how many paths there are.

Daisy Couture: I'm not sure since I have never been to a non-alternative school but I would say that I'm in control of my life. Not completely because I'm only nine but as much control as a nine-year old should have I would say.

Maya Motoi: I think I am capable of a lot and I know that I can do exactly what I want to do. I can't do everything just because I am free, but I can certainly try and dream. I have made every big decision concerning my life ever since I can remember. Just because I chose one thing has never meant that I couldn't change my mind a year or two later. I always just did what seemed right and didn't do what didn't seem right. My parents have always supported me in a big way with all my decisions, but in the end it has always been my choice.

Gen Robertson: I think my identity is very connected to my art practice, and to my love for getting out of the city and camping/climbing/adventuring in general. Definitely many of the people and experiences I've been exposed to as a result of my unconventional schooling and the alternative community at large have inspired and supported me greatly. I think without all of it, I would not be so hell-bent on shaping my life how I want it to be, or I would not know where to begin.

Mari Piggott: I think that my sense of who I am has been so clear especially since I have had alternative schooling. I feel like I don't have to fit into any kind of box, I can just be me. I don't think there's any such thing as shy: I think some people are just afraid to show who they are to some people (which is ok), but I think everybody can open up to somebody if they're encouraged.

Nigel Boeur: I'm definitely the author of my own life, and I'm very confident that I will be so for the rest of my years. I think that the path I took has totally impacted my views of my own capabilities, and having the time to do so many amazing things has really broadened my horizons as to what I can accomplish.

10. What would you say to kids thinking about not going to school, about dropping out of school, of going to an alternative school ... doing something different? What would you say to them and their families?

Mari Piggott: Look inside your self, what triggers you, what makes you feel alive and strong? If it's singing, dancing, joining the circus, doing academics, or not, go for it and, if it's not something you can do right away, then do something that can help you eventually achieve that goal.

Nigel Boeur: It's not for everyone, but if you are considering it, why not give it a try? You can always go back to school if it doesn't work for you. There are so many different ways of alternative schooling out there, I think there's a pretty big chance that you can find something that suits your needs. I know I did.

Russ Gendron: I would encourage the kid to step out and take a chance. There are too many young people complaining about their current school situation so it only makes sense for those people to start acting.

Why not try something new, something different, if the current situation isn't working? Don't let the fear of not succeeding bog you down, for you are succeeding everyday.

Things work best when kids and their families are in communication about what needs to happen for a kid to go for what they want. To the families, try to be supportive and keep an open mind. Your kid is brilliant in ways you don't know.

Sadie Couture: I would say... A) Go for it! B) Try everything until you have a situation you are happy and comfortable with. C) Never stop learning. Whatever interests you, learn about it. Whether it be Math, Geography, Sewing, Music or whatever but keep on learning. D) Go to the library. It's awesome. And don't be afraid to talk to librarians. They can be helpful.

Maizy Thorvaldson: I always tell everyone that non-coercive education is a wonderful option. I've personally convinced some people to try an alternative option.

Gen Robertson: To both kids and their families: Let go of feeling like high school graduation holds any particular importance. If it does in your life, it is probably partly because the people around you are misinformed, or have not thought about positive alternatives.

If you do decide to do something different or alternative for schooling, don't waste time and energy feeling like you have to defend your decision, or prove yourself to those who don't agree.

Daisy Couture: Well it depends if they were happy in a normal school. If they didn't like it, I would say "if you don't like it don't go, do something different go to an alternative school or homeschool; don't stay and be unhappy, quit and be happy." But if they just wanted to try something different I would say, " if you want to try it, go ahead."

Maya Motoi: If it seems right, go for it! But even if you feel a little hesitant, go right ahead. Even if it doesn't end up being the right decision, after you have tried it, you can always go right back to what you used to do. In the end, there will be nothing to lose in trying. But I will clarify that just because not going to regular school has worked perfectly for me and many others, doesn't mean that it is for everybody. But try!

David Gagnon: Go for it. It's scary as hell to be different in this world, but it sure is worth it. The sooner you start living your own life the better off you will be. The public school institution is far too big to serve your needs as an individual. Take care of yourself and explore who you are. And if you do decide to use that institution, make sure you use it consciously: that it is your choice. The worse they can do is not give you a graduation certificate, and that is a very small carrot at the end of a very long stick, hardly worth chasing.

Play, Practice, and the Deschooling of Music

Mark Douglas

Born in the Canadian Arctic, Mark has traveled through most of Canada, wired houses with his dad, picked fruit in the Okanogan, helped build a couple of houses, and hitchhiked across the country by the time he was fourteen. He was a prospector in northern BC and the Yukon for a number of years and spent time as a camp cook and railway surveyor, did time as a school janitor, electronics salesman, saw mill worker, and mushroom barn cleaner. Mark then became a composer, music director, and band leader, worked with dancers, actors, and choreographers, all while playing in rock and funk bands across the country. He taught piano for many years and worked with an independent alternative school, then worked for four years at Windsor House School. He became a public school teacher in 2002: "One of the strangest lines of work I've explored."

How can you deschool music? Stop thinking about music as a thing to learn and start thinking about it as a thing to do.

Despite academies and conservatories, methodologies and method books, pedagogies and pedagogues, and millions of rapped knuckles, the active verb in relation to the word music is "to play." You play music. You can also make music. Playing and making are the essential elements in becoming a musician.

In becoming familiar with an instrument and how you can use it, you should play with it as much as possible. I don't mean practice it, I mean play with it. When you like, as often as you like or don't like, for as long or as little as you feel like it. In this way, you find how playing and making music fits into your life and what kinds of sounds you enjoy producing.

Encourage playing and making as opposed to practicing and working on. If you practice you aren't really doing it. You are always in preparation for when you're really going to do it. Well, when are you really going to do it? At a lesson for your teacher? For adjudicators in an exam or judges in a competition? For parents or friends? Once you've really done it and your parent/teacher/judge lets you know whether you've succeeded in making music or not, are you ever going to really do it again?

Practicing and performance go hand in hand with what has become our most common and most powerful concept regarding the purpose of music. This concept places an emphasis on the performance and the performer as the most important aspect of music. Performers (image) and performances (recording) are crucial in this concept because they are so eminently marketable and, increasingly, we are accepting the market as our ultimate judge. Within this frame of reference, the only real music is the stuff that passes this ultimate test.

No wonder practice becomes such a bogey to parents and kids alike. When you "perform" at a lesson or on request for relations and you haven't been practicing and doing the work you know you should have been doing and you fail to perform up to everyone's expectations (real or imagined), including your own, you feel bad. You do not feel like a musician. You may feel like lying. You may dislike yourself and feel guilty. You may resent your teacher and parents for putting you through all this. You may feel all these things and you may feel them even more intensely because you were the one who wanted the lessons! Whatever you feel, I guarantee that you will not feel very musical.

Focus on performance, whether it be for your teacher or anyone else, can initiate a complex of feelings; guilt at being unprepared and anxiety about the coming "performance," frustration at doing poorly, resentment that it takes so much work to be "good," that it doesn't feel like fun at all, that your parents (or other people) are always reminding you to practice.

Ultimately, what's known as "resistance to practice" sets in. To a child, refusing to cooperate may feel like the only option available. It's an effort by the child to regain a sense of control of the experience of music, which by the time she reaches this stage, probably hasn't felt rewarding for some time. Eventually, persistent refusal usually elicits a conditional warning from a parent and/or teacher, "Better get down to work and show some commitment if you want to keep those lessons and that instrument." If things go further, then lessons end and the instrument goes back to the store, is sold, or worse, sits there in the house, a silent but powerful testament to the child's failure and proof of their lack of any real musical ability.

When a youngster first expresses interest and enthusiasm for learning music, what happens in an adult mind? I wonder how differently we hear the request from what is meant by the child? I think it must sound very different to us and mean something very different to us than other requests that we deal with; can I have a chocolate bar? get a video? go camping? visit a friend? and so on. These are things we expect from a child and they are in fact childish requests. But the request to learn music or an instrument? This is a very adult thing. It may feel like the first indication from the child of something "serious" they wish to undertake, a first request that isn't some form of "play." So the request often gets taken seriously and serious results are expected because we know that music automatically means Lessons from a Teacher and a serious adult-sized Purchase of an Instrument, not to mention Scheduling. After all, adults know (even if they aren't musicians themselves) how much hard work, dedication, and commitment is required to become a good musician. They also know how much it might cost.

Music is something that connects the adult world on a long, broad continuum to childhood. An interest in learning to play an instrument may seem like a tentative request to enter the adult world, a world of conditions and demands. "Look, if we're going to pay for these lessons, we want to see some progress." "If you stick to it and work really hard for a year, we'll see about getting you your own instrument." "You've got to practice thirty minutes a day, or there's no birthday party on Saturday." "If you're going to be any good, you've got to work hard. I've got to work hard at my job and practicing is your job, so go do it."

All this pressure flies in the face of the purpose of doing music: to make or be a more well-rounded person, to acquire another form of expression, for enjoyment and fun.

I think it is cruel to hold a six- or eight- or ten-year-old kid to adult terms of commitment, when many adults do not themselves understand the meaning of the word. The many failures and tragedies that we adults have lived through and still carry with us cannot be healed by enforcing default regimens on the young around us. Music is to be enjoyed on its own terms, not because it fills another's agenda.

Currently, I make my living as a music teacher. From the beginning, I've been suspicious of myself and in a state of watchfulness. This has led me to examine my students more from their point of view (boredom, resistance, and anxiety) than from a teacher's point of view (failing to measure up to what I think they must learn).

I try to create a relationship and environment in which students are free to explore a musical side to their creativity without my judgment. I only rely on "teaching" when I am at a complete loss, usually when I am too tired to listen and just be there for the student. At such times, I actually announce, "OK, I'm going to be a teacher now."

I have come to feel that a period of several years is consumed in exploring and experimenting with ways to make music before anything like technical "practice" can take place. The length of this period probably depends on many factors—the age of the child, how long they've been playing, their affinities, their home environment. I suspect that this period of experimentation lasts two to five years and ends approximately with the onset of puberty.

This period should be one of uncompromised and unjudged support. There should be no talk of long commitments, of conditional instrument acquisitions, or of when they will learn some real music. This type of conversation/pressure/expectation/deal puts the endeavor under the control of someone other than the student, usually a parent, and then a new game has begun. The child will surely find ways to regain control of the experience and most of these ways produce anxiety for the parents. The original intent becomes subverted.

A child should never, under any circumstances, be forced to play—even if it seems like a waste of money to the parents. If a child knows he or she can ask to go to another teacher, change instruments, or quit without guilt, then they will surely do so when they feel the arrangement is not giving them anything.

During the period when a child learns language, adults have no end of patience. Indeed, they expect that the child will produce numerous ineffective, idiosyncratic, and original attempts to communicate. Some of these may be memorable, humorous, irritating, or even disturbing, but we let them go because in the end we realize that the child will learn to talk.

I approach each student with the same faith that musical language will result. I also consider that, given an unjudging environment, I have no idea what the nature of a particular person's expression may be. I try to make no assumptions. I do not know whether a child needs to know how to read standard notation. Maybe they will be better served by designing their own system for remembering their ideas. Maybe all their music will exist on tape or computer disk or in their heads. Maybe they need to learn how to play just one song well. Maybe they will be a composer. Most of the world's music is made by people who don't need a notation system and who haven't learned their music from a teacher in the same sense that we have.

The best way to learn music is to play it, play it, and make it with your family and friends.

Homeschooling as a Single Parent

Heather Knox

Heather worked as a childbirth education and labour support person, in addition to working with homelearning families, while she single-parented her daughter Megan. Heather and the now-twenty-year-old Meg live in British Columbia when they are not traveling or volunteering overseas. Heather works with an arts organization, volunteers with refugees, and is currently writing a children's novel. Meg continues learning in traditional and non-traditional ways. She is pursuing her life-long goal of nursing. This article was written for the original collection and is reprinted unchanged, although suffice to say, both Meg and Heather have changed significantly.

I am the single parent to one daughter. Although there are only two of us in our immediate family, our circle stretches far beyond that. When my daughter was still very young, I chose to homeschool her. Homeschooling comes with many challenges at the best of times; as a single parent it has some extras. To me the joys of learning with my daughter are worth the sacrifices, and far outweigh the challenges. When I say I am single, I am referring to my marital status only. I do not believe that we are meant to do this most important of all jobs, solo—and so I don't. We live a life full of meaning and people.

Megan arrived during a time in my life when I was learning for the pure joy of learning. She was conceived while I was traveling and exploring in Europe with her father. It was a time of awakenings and new beginnings. During my pregnancy, I knew that it was important to me that I raise this child in a responsible and thoughtful way. I wanted her to have a strong sense of herself and what she wants out of life. I did not want strangers raising her, and immediately started thinking about ways that I could be at home with her full time. I knew that I did not want someone else caring for my child in a daycare and that I wanted more than the public schools were offering. Five months pregnant and on my own, I came back to Canada to await her birth.

With the birth of my daughter, I became completely and totally immersed in parenting. I read everything I could get my hands on. I devoured alternative parenting magazines and then started reading about education. I was fairly isolated at the time and looking back, I realize that I didn't have many influences—positive or negative—to pressure or sway me, and so had no doubts about following my non-mainstream instincts to have Megan sleep with me, to breastfeed her until she was three years of age, or to raise her as a vegetarian. From her infancy I enjoyed observing and participating in her explorations of the world around her, noting her innate curiosity and unstoppable desire for learning. With more reading, it became so clear to me that homeschooling was the choice that would allow her to remain in this beautiful state of exploration and learning. This decision brought many challenges to my life. At the time I was so determined to do it, I didn't think through how tough things could and would be.

The questions that I am most often asked as a single parent are: "How can you afford it?" "How do you find time for yourself?" and "How do you avoid burnout?" These are all part of one issue—support. Support is a key component of all homeschooling and in fact, a key component of all real education. Creating that support presents many choices and challenges, especially for the single parent.

The greatest challenge for many parents who choose to keep their children home from school seems to be financial. In Megan's early years, one way I found to manage my budget was to share accommodations, childcare, and household chores. Initially I lived with my parents in an extended family situation (an option which may not be available to everyone) and at two separate times, with other single mothers (each had one daughter as well). Besides sharing the rent, the cost of groceries, and the childcare, we shared the cooking, each doing three nights a week—an economic way to give each of us more time to spend with our respective children. This way of living eased our workload substantially and provided myself and the other mom with the support and companionship of another adult when our daughters were young babies and toddlers. It was a wonderful way to create a stable family environment for all, and both Megan and I have very special memories of those times.

In terms of making an income, there are a number of choices for those choosing to homeschool as a single parent. These include going on social assistance, working part-time and arranging childcare, working at home, or working outside of the home in a situation that allows the child to come along. I have experienced each of these. Each, of course, has had its drawbacks as well as its advantages.

On social assistance, I was able to focus all my attention and energy on getting used to being a new mother and getting to know my infant. The down side was the minimum amount of money coming in and the negative feelings associated with receiving welfare.

Working part-time gave me a chance to get out into the world beyond motherhood. I continued to do the work that I had done off and on for years—working as customer service representative in a bank. It was not my favorite job but it paid the bills. Mornings were tough when I would wake my sleeping daughter to dress and feed her, then leave her crying and screaming with a baby-sitter.

Running my own business and working at home provided me with a real sense of responsibility. Shortly after Megan's birth I became involved with childbirth education and support. I taught prenatal classes in the evening, did labor support for couples, and taught the ancient art of infant massage in my home. The challenge was living with the uncertainty regarding the amount of income each month.

Now I work part-time as a consultant with an independent school where I have the flexibility of working from home or going into an office where Megan comes along. I have the wonderful privilege of working with other homelearning families that have registered their children as homeschoolers. We offer a variety of services—a bimonthly newsletter, workshops, and an annual conference for families. In addition to the opportunity to do challenging and fulfilling work, the assurance of regular pay and the advantage of flexibility are huge benefits. The challenge comes when Megan really wants and needs to stay home when I really need to go into the office.

Finding and creating time for one's self is another of the greatest challenges of being alone at home full time with children. We all know how the best of us can, over time, become overworked, overtaxed, and oversocialized. As many parents have experienced, there are times when one does not even get to go to the toilet alone! Wouldn't it be easier for me to use the free baby-sitting service the public schools have provided for me? At times I think it really would be, believe me! And that is why I believe in finding time to be alone.

For my daughter and I to maintain a healthy relationship, it has been essential to our survival that we help each other out and that we both get times to ourselves every day. I have created this in a number of ways, the primary one being our daily routine. For years Megan has awakened at least an hour before me. She has established her own morning rituals in which she gets breakfast for herself and her three pets, gets dressed, writes in her journal, brushes and braids her hair, and listens to story tapes. (Her passion for a number of years has been audiotapes of books, even more so in the last few months. Some parents teasingly refer to their child as a "bookworm." Poor Meggie gets referred to as a "tapeworm.") In the evening we have a special bedtime routine: Meg goes to bed early while I stay up late. I do my studying and playing then. I often have a friend over for a visit, do my writing, or watch a video, or, if I really need some extra special time, I treat myself to a massage from the massage therapist who lives in the top suite of the house we live in.

Megan has grandparents and an uncle who have been very supportive and involved in her life from the minute she was born. They have always taken their roles with the same seriousness and care that I have as her mother. We are very fortunate that they include her in their lives as a special person. She has regular overnight visits and outings with them.

I love the African proverb, "It takes a whole village to raise a child." For single parents, there is more motivation to find that village. Over the years I have created a wonderful community for Megan and myself. Megan has many people who "parent" and influence her in positive and meaningful ways. Our lives are full of people who go to school, people who don't, straight and gay neighbors and friends, elderly people and babies. I get involved with many community events—I volunteer and manage events and I bring Megan along with me. Often people do not quite understand why my child is with me.

Given time, they see that she is a capable and willing worker and an interesting person to talk with as well. Because of this, she has had many opportunities that otherwise may not have presented themselves to her.

In addition, I have always made a conscious effort to know and befriend my neighbors. I make myself available to do childcare, to cook meals and even to walk their children to school. As a result Megan is invited and encouraged to be involved in others' lives. She is easy to have around and people comment on her willingness to help out. I have learned to swallow my independent pride and accept help when I need it. As a result, I am able more easily to take breaks—to take time for myself when it is really needed.

Sometimes things don't go all that smoothly: often I feel that I am doing the job of more than one person; at times I feel lonely and discouraged. But when Megan and I go for walks and I hold her hand in mine, everything feels at it should be. I am incredibly grateful for my family and friends who have always been available and loving to both of us; I know that things would look much different without their support and companionship. I am very content with the life I have created for my daughter and myself. I value the special times we have had together and look forward to many more.

The Root of Education

Patrick Farenga

Pat worked closely with the author and teacher John Holt, until Holt's death in 1985. He is the President of Holt Associates Inc. and was the Publisher of Growing Without Schooling *magazine (GWS) from 1985 until it stopped publishing in November, 2001.* GWS *was the nation's first periodical about homeschooling, started by Holt in 1977. Farenga and his wife have homeschooled their three girls, ages twenty, sixteen, and thirteen. In addition to writing for GWS for twenty years, he has written many articles and book chapters about homeschooling including his own book,* The Beginner's Guide To Homeschooling. *His latest book is* Teach Your Own: The John Holt Book of Homeschooling. *Farenga now works as a writer, speaker, and education consultant.*

One can view the history of education as an ongoing struggle between those who feel education is something to be done for someone and those who feel it is something people do for themselves. Educationists love to point out that their job is draw forth the latent talents of their students, to push and expose them to ideas and experiences they feel are necessary for children to know. Educationists find the origin of the English word "educate" in the Latin word, *educere*, meaning "to draw forth." Our English word, educe, has the meaning "to make something latent develop or appear" (according to Word's on-line dictionary) so it is not surprising that educationists find their justification for pulling out students' potential in that word. Indeed the political idea of "universal compulsory schooling" and the pedagogical concept of "making students learn what we think they ought to learn" are rooted in the educational concept of "drawing out," even by force of law. This model of education is all about doing something to someone—whether they want it or not.

Though the United States is a democratic republic where "the pursuit of life, liberty, and happiness" are paramount, we school our children in a most undemocratic manner. Just over 150 years ago, America created compulsory school laws "for people's own good" and these laws and educational customs have become so rooted in US culture that most citizens think they were ordained in the US Constitution. However I think the political, spiritual, and ethical histories and reasons against universal compulsory schooling deserve a fresh look by us in the twenty-first century.

Politically, John Adams, Benjamin Franklin, and Thomas Jefferson did their best to argue the need for government-supported public schooling, but it is an argument they lost. Education was considered, in those days, to be a personal, local and state issue, not a Federal issue. Spiritually and ethically, theologians and philosophers contend that it is wrong to compel someone to do something against their wishes, which is why God can't make us always choose the right thing to do. It is also why in a free, democratic society we tolerate weird ideas, alternative lifestyles, and odd religious practices. Today these issues get ignored or are dismissed with the arguments that compulsory schooling is, at best, the only way to ensure children become good citizens, or, at worst, a necessary evil because we have no place better to put children while their parents work. I hope we can create many more places and reasons for children to grow and learn in our society than the narrow options these arguments allow, which is also why I see homeschooling as a hopeful path for education.

What complicates my position is that I'm not calling for the defunding or abolition of schools. I find it disheartening to continually have conversations about schooling revolve around issues of funding and curricula, which, to me, are conversations about the tickets and deck chairs for the boat we call Education. Instead, I want to at least talk about coming up with a completely redesigned boat! John Holt wrote that we shouldn't even be thinking about boats—perhaps the entire concept is just wrong and we should be thinking about cars, or trains, or planes.

I challenge the need for compulsory school laws, not the need for places where people can learn. Compulsory school laws prohibit innovation in schooling, cause constant increases in the costs associated with more hours and credentials required to pay for more years of schooling. These laws infantilize our youth by keeping them in school well into adulthood and, though we are led to believe compulsory schools are a tap root for democracy, we must also remember that they are also a relic of slavery from Ancient Greece. "Skole," in ancient Greece, was where only privileged men could discuss in leisurely fashion how best to lead and use the lower classes of people for the good of their country (as defined by the privileged): The lower classes of people included women, slaves, foreigners, and freed slaves. These people were considered natural resources that are processed in schools, and the government could lay claim to and manipulate those resources however it needs to in the name of the security of the national economy.

There were schools in early America, of course, but they were ad hoc, short-term arrangements, not the womb-to-tomb credentialing bureaucracies we have today. Further there will probably always will be schools, in one form or another, because it makes social sense to organize materials, knowledge, and gathering places in central locations for people to share. Indeed, as the homelearning movement continues to grow it is creating its own types of schools, often called learning co-ops, learning centers, or resource centers. I hope these new forms of school will not just be replacements for brick and mortar schools, nor more educational institutions seeking to turn themselves into brand-names for privilege and prestige. I hope the creators of these centers will challenge the status quo of school and curricula, rather than gently seduce families into doing school at home. I want to remind people who feel compelled to build such places, and all adults, to be guided by the true meaning of the word "education," rather than the accepted wisdom of what it means.

"Educere" is not the origin for our words "educate" or "education." Educators who feel I am mistaken need only open the Oxford English Dictionary to see the origins and etymology of "educate." Our word originated from the Latin word "educare," which means to nourish, to rear, to bring up. Education's roots are in the concept and image of breast-feeding, a moment when the child is an active recipient of nourishment. It is a moment of repose and sharing for both adult and child. Ivan Illich, who explained our modern confusion about the root meaning of the word "education" to me, noted that in early European Catholic monasteries one can find statues of Abbots that portray them as having breasts to dispense "the milk of knowledge" to the monks. This meaning of "education" is related to the word "educere"—drawing forth—but, in the context of a child drawing forth a mother's milk.

Over time we have forgotten not only our educational roots, but the roles of patience, love, and hope that should be integral parts of any educational environment. Indeed, the educational environment for children, today, is more workplace than home: patience, love, and hope are replaced by time frames, curricula, and expectation. A parent is considered to be educationally neglectful if their children aren't in school (and the younger

they start school, and the longer they are in it, the better) or; if they homeschool, the parent is negligent if they aren't hovering over their child,
making sure lessons are dutifully tended to every day. To allow a child
to roam freely and interact with people of all ages in their home and local community is viewed with suspicion in today's world and borders on
neglect to many authorities. This is why we need to deschool society—not
to do away with places to do things collectively, but to do away with the attitude that children and adults can not be trusted to discover and discipline
their minds and bodies in their own ways. Compulsory schooling, increasingly supervised and operated only by those who are products of compulsory schooling, increases the need for compulsory schooling. As Ivar Berg
noted in Education and Jobs: The Great Training Robbery (Beacon, 1971):
The need for education feeds upon itself.

I see Berg's use of the word "education" as a product produced by
schools for the sake of our national economy and international competi-
tiveness. This conceptual shift moves the primary responsibility for learning away from children and their parents and places it in the hands of
external authorities.

But the conceptual root of education is nourishment from parent
to child. Educationists will readily admit that children who do poorly in
their classes probably come from a poor home environment where the parents are clueless about what their children are doing in schools, or they
will blame communities that don't support education. Yet rather than deal
directly with the root issue of why homes and communities are not nourishing places for children to grow up in, educationists clamor for more
school hours, as if mastery of state education standards can replace a lack
of adequate housing, basic health care, and a living wage so parents can
have time at home with their children rather than having to work more
than forty hours per week just to meet rent and expenses.

If we can keep the original meaning of education foremost in our
minds when we discuss it, instead of focusing on more laws and techniques
to draw forth what we expect from students, we can learn how to work
with young people to create new solutions to the problems of growing up
today.

Lunch at the Westin:
A Father and Son Talk
of Education

Richard Westheimer

*Richard is the father of five, ages fourteen through twenty-seven. He
and Debbie, mother of the five, live on a small farm outside of Cincinnati,
Ohio. He feels pleased and privileged to have spent time and studied with
great poets, philosophers, friends and family. After teaching public school
for sixteen years, he earned his Ph.D. in Educational Policy from the Union
Institute and subsequently abandoned all hope and became an investment
manager. Life is strange that way.*

*In early 1994, my parents' concern about the "mis-education" of their
grandchildren—my five children, then aged one to fourteen—came to a head.
The following is excerpted from a book-length essay about how we learned
from addressing those concerns directly.*

Lunch at the Westin was the backdrop for the first of a series of formal conversations with my dad about educating his grandchildren.
We'd spoken on this topic before, mostly in the context of his worry and
my defense. A typical conversation opened: "Your mother and I are very
concerned. We didn't realize that Hannah (my seven year old daughter)
doesn't recognize all of her letters. I just can't tell you how upset this makes
us. I really don't want to talk about this but we feel you're actually mistreat-
ing her."

The pattern rarely varied:

* My mother or father would express grave misgivings about our
failure to educate our kids.
* We would defend our approach—alternately by citing the obvious strengths of our individual children or by addressing the pedagogical principles underlying our "unschooling" life.

I lament excusing our actions into such neat and inadequate compartments. Our children's virtues are relative and, more to the point, not a standard by which we measure others. To do so, to speak of how kind or well-mannered or confident they might be, trivializes the lives of youth into containable, knowable, and measurable commodities—territory amply plied by schools and their champions. Similarly, reducing our family's *élan vital* to "pedagogical principles," assumes a particular vision of family/ community life that fails to reflect the synoptic aspirations we hold.

I proposed these formalized conversations with my father subsequent to one of our more difficult exchanges. We had recently returned from a week-long visit with my parents at their winter retreat. My oldest three kids had written their farewell greetings in the family guest register: thirteen year old Gabe in his halting script, eleven year old Nathan in his blocky manuscript, and seven year old Hannah by someone else's hand as she dictated her valedictory message to a trusted writer. All revealed a writing skill level that placed them well behind many of their age-mates. The public nature of the guest book forum compounded the impact of that revelation: All visitors to my parents' home could see, if they cared to, that the grandchildren wrote poorly.

The "substandard" attributes of those journal entries brought home to my already concerned parents the reality of the "appropriateness pedagogy" that informs our educational practice. Not only were we not teaching our kids to write, they weren't learning to write—at least not in a manner considered timely in the chronometry of schools. Their grand-daughter really didn't know her letters. Their proto-teen grandson wrote uncomfortably and without luster. In the panlogistic realm of schooled expectations, this seemed an almost abusive state for these presumed intellectual and otherwise privileged children. The syllogistic framework:

> **Major Premise**
> The chronology of common school skills constitutes an unquestioned good
> **Minor Premise**
> Our young friends lacked those skills according to the normative timetable
> **Conclusion**
> Those responsible for that lack (their parents) are guilty of abuse by way of educational neglect.
> —*The Concerned Grandparent Syllogism*

The validity of any syllogism, of course, rests on the validity of both its premises. In the case of The Concerned Grandparent Syllogism, the major premise, though widely accepted, embodies the difference—the issue of contention—between my parents' perspective and my family's practice. This was the impetus for the solemn summons that eventually resulted in Lunch at the Westin.

As I drove from our first visit, unhappy at our predictable failure to come-to-terms, I considered a means for making these confrontations more productive—and controlled. The subjects we discussed interested me a great deal and, actually, I was irresolute regarding the role of academics in young people's lives. It remains a matter of exploration in both my professional and personal work. I mulled over various means of engaging in this exploration with my father. We shared a common concern for the well-being of my children and the "conversation" would go on in any event. I wanted to identify a design for engagement that could leave each of us enriched and might move our conversation from palaver to productive dialogue. When I got home I conceived of a proposal for a series of formal, almost academic discussions.

To begin the conversations, I presented to my father four questions I thought embodied his anxiousness about our homeschooling practice:

1. Is there a "canon" of unassailable, essential knowledge that all "educated" members of our society should know?
2. If such a canon exists, how are its contents conveyed? Does it have a hierarchy of knowledge? Must it be learned in sequence?
3. Should children engage in academic activities? What are the hoped for ends of such activity?
4. If children should pursue academics, at what time in their lives should that happen? By what means and in what form?

Even before our food came to the table at our first Lunch at the Westin, we agreed that my planned format was too impersonal, too academic to take advantage of the generational spirit that brought us together. We needed instead to look at the lives of my children: real kids, real lives, real differences.

"What," I asked my father, "do you want for Hannah? If you close your eyes and imagine her a woman, what would you hope for her?"

Dad replied with his four points. "I hope my young friend is well enough educated for four things to happen." He picked up his fork, as if to continue eating—and then placed it back across the top of his plate and continued. Though the list's enumeration was interrupted by requests for clarification, contended assumptions, Dad made his expectations clear:

1. I want the judgments she makes to come from a mind trained to consider consequences in a serial, logical manner with a process of thinking that leads to rational conclusions.

2. She should be exposed to the fine arts and humanities so she can enjoy what I've enjoyed ... from art and history and literature.

3. I hope she has a sense of morality—of right and wrong—and a desire to leave the world a better place.

4. Perhaps this should be at the top of the list. I hope she can function in the economic market place. I want her to have as many choices as possible for sustaining herself, for securing resources for herself.

The list brimmed with love and a sense of righteousness that would endure no argument. These were not merely positions my father took. They were my father: serial, logical, a lover of the arts, a student of history, moral and committed ... and successful. With these as his being, he had all the desires for perpetuation of his most ancient forbearers: those who walked in skins and those who pored over ancient Talmudic texts; those who hauled stone, those who fled social and economic coercion, and those who flourished in the markets of St. Joseph, Missouri. Each sought to make the world in his own image with his offspring as tool-of-choice.

"I know this seems outrageous," I had interrupted more than once. "But I am not so sure that 'serial and logical' reasoning and 'a trained mind' are exactly what I want for my children. I don't deny their importance but I hope for more." How could I discuss the merits of non-linear thought to a man who couldn't doubt logic's wisdom? The good world, the great world built by linear reasoning, the thread that drew Western Europe from the "dark" ages through the Enlightenment, the wisdom of the Founders, the organizing structure of capitalism, the language of civil liberties: How could one argue with the foundation of these modern miracles?

"Too much serial logic can lead to some pretty horrific ends." I recounted the epilogue of Haim Ginott's Teacher and Child where he reminds readers about the horrors visited on the world by cultured, educated, and learned Nazis—of the perils of worshipping false gods in the guise of "educational excellence." I realized in the telling that the story I told was not a direct challenge to Dad's values. After all, his list and life are infused with a moral sense. But Ginott's words still reminded that logic can serve evil as well as good.

I continued, a bit self-consciously, "I do want Hannah to know the logical world and ways that you and I know. But she has the opportunity now to experience and revel in other ways of knowing. I cannot teach her these 'other ways' because they aren't my own. But I can, we can, grant her the privilege of living them herself. This, perhaps more than any other, is the promise of not sending her to school: She has the freedom, the time and place, to experience and revel in non-linear, fantastic worlds that are not of adult making. This is the time in her life when she can learn of such ways. They require no teaching. And they will inform and enrich her life immeasurably as she grows into the wider world."

I shifted uneasily in my seat. Not only was it hard to eat and talk at the same time, but to plea passionately for an understanding of anti-Modern values amidst the Westin's lovely and material best be-gotten trappings of the Modern era seemed somewhat disingenuous. "I've no doubt," I continued measuredly, "she will ply the logical seas. She's immersed in a world of books and reason, and delights at juggling linear constructs. But, to exalt pure reason over her current experience would cheat her of a certain profound prosperity that will never be available to her so simply again. She can always learn to logic. But once she does so fully, she can't go back and learn to live in its absence.

"And who's to say if the world might not be better off if we relied on spirit and intuition and ancient wisdom and Love to the extent we now trust reason?"

I looked up from my half-eaten sandwich. I felt distinctively graceless and, having revealed what must have seemed a wildly fuzzy side of myself to my distinctly un-fuzzy father, I felt a need to surface for rhetorical air.

An Aside

Just what does a day of unschooling look like? (Psst. Don't tell my father.)

My father and I chose to talk about educating Hannah because we agreed that addressing our assumptions about rearing a seven-year old seemed manageable: neither prohibitively complex nor too emotionally charged. Had we directed our attention to Hannah's older brothers, we would have encountered insurmountable barriers in our perspectives. His wishes for their education differed so broadly from our practice that we'd have too little common ground for a productive conversation.

When asked what our older boys' "school day" looked like, I've often replied that it looks more like summer vacation than school. We engage in little formal instruction; the boys spend much of their day scheming and building, traipsing through the woods behind our house and converting junk filled outbuildings for mysterious ends. Their indoor time is peppered with elaborate culinary exploits and rapid-fire backgammon games, the disassembling of junked electronic devices and rapt attention to a squawking short-wave radio. As often as they work with each other, they can be found babbling and bouncing with baby Daniel, building gauzy forts with four-year-old Eva or reading surreptitiously in some isolated corner of the house. They pour over a most recent (or most aging) National Geographic, rifle through the mail for the latest Time Magazine, or scrutinize one of the numerous maps they've hung on walls and cork-boards about the house.

During spring and summer, our growing season, they, along with Hannah, spend some time cultivating their small market garden, find ways to avoid work, scale trees, pick and sell their organic produce, and scheme and build. They pile creek rock in intricate formations to attempt to dam up a small portion of Little Shayler Run, build "clubs" with kids on the street, and swap lies with an ailing neighbor. One takes off several days a week to assist a local camp for folks with special needs while the other sorts and resorts his baseball card collection, dreaming of his future Cy Young award.

Scattered among these unschooled pursuits, and aside from routine household chores, both boys regularly practice their respective musical instruments, more or less following a course of study set forth by their instructor. Nathan edits a sports page for a homeschooling newsletter. Both take interest-based classes ranging from cartooning to SCUBA diving to soccer refereeing.

Recently, and intermittently over the years, we've included periods of "study time" when each of our older children has worked to refine an "academic skill" of his or her choosing. For a few hours each day throughout our less active seasons, the kids work independently or in consultation with a more skilled household member on a school-like subject employing school-like means. Old math text books and handwriting and manuscript practice cards can be found scattered on work surfaces alongside of plans for cold frames and seed catalogues.

Even so, school skills fill little of their time and constitute far less of their education than my parents would like. I am sure they are not alone in their disapproval (or even dismay) at the clearly non-academic life led by their grandchildren. School is the standard to which we are held. And against that standard we fall short.

After years of conversation about my work in schools and our life as homeschoolers, my father came to accept that an experiential pedagogy for young children had some merits. This approach, which seems as radical now as it was widely presumed in less schooled times, holds that experience with everyday life and immersion in the rituals and means of culture constitute "right-education." Allowing ample time for uniquely childlike processes—such as fantasy play and activities that command a rigorous integration of body and mind—contributes holistically to a child's maturation. Contact with the earth, a full and voluntary association with natural forms, gives profound support for all hearts and minds. Involving children in "real" (but not exploitive) work, work that contributes to their community's material well-being, upholds their sense of belonging and gives concrete meaning to their future studies.

And Back Again—Conversation on the Safer Side:

So, Dad and I decided to speak of Hannah. Her non-academic state was more palatable to my father than that of her older brothers. Perhaps she was not unschooled to the point of no return.

"From your perspective, are we hurting her now?" I wanted to hear my father expound on his vision for "educating Hannah." "What do you think we should do to further her chances for attaining those things that you want for her?" I referred to those four wishes Dad had for his grandchildren.

He responded with a sort of pedagogical manifesto: "The amount of knowledge and information to learn is enormous and starts accreting in the first three years of life. It's so very important that certain things are learned at certain times in a child's life. The information required of adults has to come early and continue throughout a child's education."

Dad echoed the "theory of instruction" propagated by Jerome Bruner in the early 1960s. Bruner's "gift" to our contemporary view of schooling. He said: "We begin with the hypothesis that any subject can be taught effectively in some intellectually honest form to any child at any stage of development." Any activities, he insisted, that do not "introduce [a child] at an early age to the ideas and styles that in later life make an educated man (sic) clutter the curriculum."

The Obvious Questions: Just because one can teach something, does that confirm its Goodness and appropriateness? Just because something is "intellectually honest" does that mean it is wise and prudent? Does the "considerable evidence [that] is being amassed" imagine a child (or an adult) as anything but intellect? Does "any stage of development" to which intellectual honesty applies extend to infancy? To the womb? If it does not, then what qualifiers must replace "any"?

"Nature," Rousseau chided the would-be educationalists of his time, "wants children to be children before they are men. If we deliberately depart from this order we shall get premature fruits which are neither ripe nor well-flavoured and which soon decay. We shall have youthful sages and grown-up children."

Then again, what evidence is there that either Rousseau's romantic vision or Bruner's scientific claims are anything more than assertions? And of course, these questions no more "prove" wrong the theory supporting my father's and Bruner's curriculum than does their assertion make them right.

Dad continued addressing his pedagogical vision: "Early childhood stimulation is absolutely essential to a young person's intellectual development." My father spoke without hesitation. His words issued decisively and purposively. I felt as if I were in the company of a confident lecturer. "Everything I've seen about raising children points to that. The knowledge they accumulate early on builds and contributes to what and how they learn as they mature," he continued assuredly. "If that's true, and I believe it is, then academic foundations must be vital to later learning."

As Dad spoke of accumulating knowledge and early childhood intellectual stimulation I recalled Paulo Freire's comments on what he called the "banking concept" of education. Freire, who championed a liberatory, "problem-posing" pedagogy reprehended the banking model that turns knowledge into a tool of oppression:

> Knowledge is a gift bestowed by those who consider them-
> selves knowledgeable upon those whom they consider to know
> nothing. Projecting an absolute ignorance onto others, a char-
> acteristic of the ideology of oppression, negates education and

knowledge as processes of inquiry. The teacher presents himself to his students as their necessary opposite.

This corresponds closely to John Dewey's disdain for "pouring-in" methods of teaching." In *Schools of Tomorrow* he criticized a pedagogy where:

Knowledge consists of the ready-made material which others have found out ... [and where] to learn is to appropriate something from this ready-made store, not to find out something for one's self.

I asked Dad, with a hint of impatience in my voice, if his means for teaching children to "accumulate" knowledge, resembled that which Dewey decried.

"This has nothing to do with 'pouring in' knowledge." Dad clearly felt I had mischaracterized or misunderstood his design. "But knowledge is cumulative. The foundations laid in early years undoubtedly support a richer and deeper understanding of all there is to learn as a child matures."

✳ ✳ ✳

We called for our check and, after looking about the table for forgotten belongings, we left our tip and headed for the doors. "I hope we can continue this conversation." I ventured. "It seems we've only scratched the surface." I had many more questions I hoped to explore with my father and we had hardly addressed the ones broached in this short meeting. Dad invited me up to his office but I declined because of other work obligations in town. We walked down the three steps to the expansive Westin atrium. The blanched light issuing from the frosted skylights thirty feet above the tile floor muted the conversations, the rustling newspaper pages turning, and the hurried footsteps of those in our company, under the Westin roof.

My father grew up in a time and place prior to the propagation of the post-modern relativism that colors so much of my generation's discourse. As a story-teller, more in the tradition of Appalachia than Hyde Park, Dad succeeded, as I have alluded to before, in conveying the Virtues and values of an earlier time.

Listening to my father meant listening to someone whose spirit was born sixty years closer to that era. But those sixty years, in an age of accelerated proliferation of culture, places my father's youth immeasurably closer to cultural foundations that had changed little (in comparison with what followed) in the preceding many generations.

My task, as a story listener as well as a conversant, was to blend the breath of these older, closer ways, with the phenomena of my current experience, the substance of my studies, and the ongoing discourse with my nuclear family. Debbie and I, along with our older children, considered these same issues: how do we integrate study with experience—often, never quite sure if our experiential, constructivist pedagogy might result in any of us roundly growing toward a responsible maturity. I agree with Wendell Berry when he says: "Education in the true sense, of course, is an enablement to serve."

The act of study is as much a part of their experiential heritage as that of baking bread; the process of organized inquiry as important as exploring the wide woods around our home. Study and method, algebra and political history do not reveal themselves overtly as do the silky feel of ripe dough and the acrid smell of molding leaves. One cannot eat the pages of Galileo's Dialogues, any more than she can quantify the cool ooze of a fresh-plowed furrow under running bare feet. And yet, Galileo's intellectual poetry nourishes. And they inform the steel plowshare's geometry as surely as they describe the motion of the planets.

Then, too, we have obligations. First, we are obliged, as Marge Piercy wrote, to "remember backwards a little and sometimes forward." Thus, as a parent and citizen, I am obliged to include political, community, economic, cultural and intercultural experiences in our family's life. Without an experiential intimacy with concrete, material events, the ideas at their foundation have no meaning. Concrete experiences, in turn, gain meaning when one has a familiarity with their related abstract ideas—the history, the science, the art.

✳ ✳ ✳

If we succeed, our young friends will come to responsible maturity, enabled to serve their "living human community in its natural household or neighborhood and the precious cultural possessions." They will be good "caretakers of what they have been given"—the care of the good earth, the company of its people, and their ideas. They will have the foundational ideas of citizenship and the capacity to exceed by far what they have been given.

And they will visit with and talk of their grandfather often. If we succeed.

Epilogue: It has been fourteen years since my father and I spoke of education. He has since died. Hannah has grown to become an independent confident young woman. She has lived in Mexico, studied international relations in college, raised money for environmental organizations, run a summer day care for Spanish-speaking immigrant kids in Cincinnati. She loves improvisional rock-and-roll, cherishes her college coursework and doesn't care much for grades (she's never even looked at her college transcript).

Oh, and she visits with and talks of her grandmother often.

Valedictory Address

Ben Kelly

Ben lives and works in North Vancouver. He is currently taking a year off after graduating high school, and plans to go on to post-secondary education in the fall. In his spare time, Ben enjoys music, cooking, hockey, reading, and continuing his rapid ascent into the upper echelons of rock stardom.

Ben attended Windsor House up until grade ten, when he decided to go to the local Learning Centre, where he graduated from grade twelve. This is the speech he delivered to the 2007 graduating class.

When Linda asked me to be Valedictorian, I wasn't exactly sure what that was. So I looked it up in the dictionary. The dictionary stated that a valedictorian gives a valedictory speech. Okay, I knew that but I still didn't know what was expected of me. So, I looked up *valedictory*. Now I was getting somewhere. A valedictory speech is a speech of farewell to a graduating class ... a parting address.

I am both honored and flattered to be given this opportunity but at the same time slightly embarrassed. It isn't as if I have any words of wisdom to offer ... but here it goes.

My educational path has not been a typical one. I attended Windsor House School from kindergarten through grade ten. For those of you not familiar with Windsor House, it is a democratically-run, non-coercive school. In the years that I attended the school, the students, staff and parents all had a say in defining the rules and policies by which the school ran. This wasn't a token gesture or mere lip service. We as students, regardless of age, had a voice in these important tasks. Our opinions were listened to and respected.

The biggest difference between Windsor House and mainstream schooling, however, was in its non-coercive nature. Students attended classes not because they were told to or because they were a certain age. Rather, they went to classes because they were motivated to through curiosity and desire. This meant that for most of the younger children and certainly for myself I didn't spend my days sitting in desks or doing things I wasn't interested in. Instead, I spent hours and hours playing.

Mostly I played floor hockey and the drums. The latter caught the interest of some of the teenagers who invited me to join their short lived punk band, "Death By Fluoride." Sadly, our few recordings have been lost.

Eventually, I did become interested in going to classes and when I did I had a great deal of enthusiasm and interest in studying as I was there by choice. My years at Windsor House taught me tolerance for people's differences and an ability to get along with people of all ages.

My teachers were people I respected and enjoyed being with. Most importantly, I was left with a feeling of ownership over my life and that I was in charge of my education. This attitude led me to leave Windsor House and go to the YLC for my final two years of school.

At the YLC I found the teachers had much the same respect for the students as I had experienced at Windsor House. There was also the same philosophy of students being in charge of their educational process. I learned that sometimes one has to do things one does not necessarily like in order to achieve the things one wants. I had come to the YLC for a grade twelve diploma and in order to get that I had to work for it. Some of the work I enjoyed and some like writing poetry and geography were like pulling teeth.

So I have done it, perhaps not the conventional way but I've done it. I have a friend who has never set foot in a regular school or taken any formal academics. He is one of the most interesting people I know. He is bright, curious, kind, active in his community and working in a well-paying job that he loves. I also have friends who have gone through the regular school system. They too are bright, fun, good people who are out in the world making a difference. What it comes down to is that there is no right or wrong way to get an education just as there is no right or wrong way to live life. There are many choices, pathways, and options.

The important thing is to make choices that work for you and that interest you. I don't know what the future holds for me. I have ideas of what I want to do and what I am interested in. Whatever it is I choose to do I know I have the work ethic, skills and intelligence to achieve my goals. I also know that to get what I want I will have to work hard. Education isn't simply about academic learning. It is about creativity, exploration, understanding and getting along with people. Knowledge is an ongoing, invisible process. Opportunities to learn, grow, and expand one's horizons are everywhere as long as one stays open to new possibilities and stays curious to the world around us.

I hope that those of us graduating today will always have a hunger and curiosity for learning and a belief in their own ability to be anything they want to be.

Good luck and thank you.

AK Press is small, in terms of staff and resources, but we also manage to be one of the world's most productive anarchist publishing houses. We publish close to twenty books every year, and distribute thousands of other titles published by like-minded independent presses and projects from around the globe. We're entirely worker-run and democratically managed. We operate without a corporate structure—no boss, no managers, no bullshit.

The Friends of AK program is a way you can directly contribute to the continued existence of AK Press, and ensure that we're able to keep publishing books like this one! Friends pay $25 a month directly into our publishing account ($30 for Canada, $35 for international), and receive a copy of every book AK Press publishes for the duration of their membership! Friends also receive a discount on anything they order from our website or buy at a table: 50% on AK titles, and 20% on everything else. We have a Friends of AK ebook program as well: $15 a month gets you an electronic copy of every book we publish for the duration of your membership. You can even sponsor a very discounted membership for someone in prison.

Email friendsofak@akpress.org for more info, or visit the Friends of AK Press website: https://www.akpress.org/friends.html

There are always great book projects in the works—so sign up now to become a Friend of AK Press, and let the presses roll!